SECRETS
of the
WIDOW'S SON

SECRETS
of the
WIDOW'S SON

The Mysteries Surrounding
the Sequel to *The Da Vinci Code*

David A. Shugarts

INTRODUCTION BY
Dan Burstein

Editor of the *New York Times* Bestseller,
SECRETS OF THE CODE

An Orion paperback

First published in the USA in 2005
by Sterling Publishing Co., Inc.
First published in Great Britain in 2005
by Weidenfeld & Nicolson
This paperback edition published in 2006
by Orion Books Ltd,
Orion House, 5 Upper St Martin's Lane,
London WC2H 9EA

1 3 5 7 9 10 8 6 4 2

A CIP catalogue record for this book is available
from the British Library.

ISBN-13 978-0-7528-8090-7
ISBN-10 0-7528-8090-x

Printed and bound in Great Britain by
Mackays of Chatham plc, Mackays, Kent

The Orion Publishing Group's policy is to use papers that
are natural, renewable and recyclable products and
made from wood grown in sustainable forests. The logging
and manufacturing processes are expected to conform to
the environmental regulations of the country of origin.

www.orionbooks.co.uk

TABLE OF CONTENTS

ILLUSTRATIONS

Photographs reproduced courtesy of:

Courtesy of Architect of the Capitol: 12, 116. Art Resource, NY: 131.
© Alexandria-Washington, Lodge No. 22 A.F. & A.M., Photography by
Arthur W. Pierson: 117. CORBIS: © Bettmann: 62, 100, 122, 126, 170;
© The Corcoran Gallery of Art: 75; © FPG: 23; © Mark E. Gibson: 123;
© Brooks Kraft: 96; © Larry Lee Photography: 114; © Richard T. Nowitz:
138; © Lee Snider / Photo Images: 105; © Sandro Vannini: 25. © The George
Washington Masonic National Memorial (All Rights Reserved),
Photography by Arthur W. Pierson: 87. Courtesy of Arturo de Hoyos, Grand
Archivist, the Supreme Council, 33°, Southern Jurisdiction, USA: 37.
Library of Congress: 90, 113. Courtesy Mason Lodge No. 1 St Johns: 119.
Courtesy National Oceanic and Atmospheric Administration: 152.
Courtesy National Park Service, Washington Monument: 32, 136. Courtesy
Private Collection: 42

❧ Acknowledgments ❧

My grateful thanks go first to my publishing associates, Daniel Burstein and Arne de Keijzer, along with their families (Julie O'Connor, David Burstein, Helen and Hannah de Keijzer). In addition, I would like to thank Arturo de Hoyos, S. Brent Morris, and Mark Tabbert, of the Scottish Rite; Herbert F. W. Stahlke, Steven C. Bullock, Walter S. Arnold, Roy (monas.nl), Nicholas R. DeLuca, Jonathan W. Shugarts, H. David Leslie III, Gary D. Martin, Francis G. Hoenigswald, and Thomas S. R. Topping; and scholars and librarians throughout Washington.

—David A. Shugarts

The "Secrets" team enjoyed the enthusiasm and support of many people at Barnes & Noble and Sterling Publishing. The vision and encouragement of Barnes & Noble's CEO, Steve Riggio, was crucial to this book, as was the relentless dedication and support of Michael Fragnito. A small army of smart and seasoned publishing-industry professionals offered advice and wisdom that enhanced our chances of success at every turn. Special thanks to Alan Kahn, Antoinette Ercolano, Bob Wietrak, Sessalee Hensley, Meredith Peters, Jeff Batzli, Kate Rados, Marilyn Kretzer, Chris Bain, Beth Renaud, Laura Nolan, Danny Baror, and all those who helped to move this book from concept to manuscript to bookstore...and into the hands of our readers.

—Dan Burstein

INTRODUCTION

> King Solomon sent and fetched Hiram out of Tyre
> …He was a widow's son of the tribe of Naphtali and
> he was filled with wisdom…   —I Kings 7:13–14

YOU ARE ABOUT to begin an amazing adventure. It is a voyage of intellectual exploration and discovery. It is a chance to time-travel through secret worlds and discover knowledge that has been hidden (in plain sight) from the time of Egyptian pyramid builders to that of America's Founding Fathers—and through to the present day.

You are about to be initiated into the mystery of the most enthusiastically awaited novel of our time, the sequel to Dan Brown's mega-selling, quantum-block-busting, much-debated, much-discussed 2003 novel, *The Da Vinci Code*.

The sequel—currently believed to be titled *The Solomon Key*—is widely expected to be published

sometime in 2006–7. But you don't have to wait until
The Solomon Key makes its appearance. By reading
Secrets of the Widow's Son, you can get a jump start on
understanding the intellectual substance of this much
anticipated Dan Brown novel. Fear not that this book
will be a plot spoiler—just the opposite. This book will
allow you to enhance your experience, enjoyment, and
engagement with *The Solomon Key* when you finally sit
down to read it.

In the following pages, David A. Shugarts will take
you on a journey into the fertile jungle of myth and
mystery, art and archetype, heretics and hieroglyphics, and legend and lore that is the world of Dan
Brown. As your field guide, Shugarts will point out
some of the more interesting bits of history, religion,
mysticism, science, cosmology, conspiracy theory,
occultism, politics, art, and architecture that Brown is
likely to weave into the plot of *The Solomon Key*.

We believe that *The Solomon Key* will be to early
American history what *The Da Vinci Code* was to early
Christian history, engendering similar kinds of controversy. We anticipate that the public response will bring
angry denunciations from some quarters and widespread
fascination from others. There will be surprising new perspectives, shocking revelations, and energetic searches to
separate fact from fiction. This book, *Secrets of the
Widow's Son*, prepares you for all of this.

Perhaps you are one of the millions of people (like
me) who looked at Leonardo da Vinci's *Last Supper*
hundreds of times before 2003 and never saw a woman
in it. But then you read *The Da Vinci Code* and, under
the influence of Dan Brown's arguments, you

suddenly found the person seated to the right of Jesus looking convincingly female. Maybe you've always believed that Mary Magdalene was a repentant prostitute but had never heard that the Vatican itself rejected this case of identity theft in the 1960s and acknowledged that Pope Gregory the Great may have been mistaken fourteen hundred years earlier when he "conflated" the character of Mary Magdalene in the Gospel account with another woman who was a former prostitute. If this is the case, you may not have previously heard the theory suggesting that Mary was not only *not* a prostitute, but that she was possibly married to Jesus, might have been his partner in all things from theology to the marriage bed, and might have escaped from Jerusalem to France with the child of their "royal bloodline." Then you read *The Du Vinci Code* and you suddenly wanted to know if this version of history was fact or fiction, plausible or impossible.

I expect that when you read *The Solomon Key* you will have a similar kind of experience. You will want to know, for example, if what is said about people like George Washington, Benjamin Franklin, and Paul Revere is true. You will also want to know more about the Masonic involvements of twentieth century political leaders, including the giants of modern history like Franklin Delano Roosevelt and Winston Churchill. You will also be interested to learn about the connections to Freemasonry of many well-known figures from the European Enlightenment that are likely to figure in *The Solomon Key*—people ranging from Mozart to Lafayette and Voltaire.

If you're like me, then despite having a good liberal arts education, you will be surprised to discover that at least eight signers of the Declaration of Independence were Freemasons; that George Washington took his role as a leader of a Masonic lodge very seriously; that Benjamin Franklin and the leading Enlightenment philosopher Voltaire visited the Masonic halls of Paris together; and that a British captain, also a Freemason, released Paul Revere from British custody on the night of his famous ride, after he determined that Revere *himself* was a Mason. You will suddenly wonder why you never realized that the Washington Monument (and a similar monument on Bunker Hill in Boston, and many others elsewhere) was not just coincidentally shaped like an Egyptian obelisk, but was intentionally designed that way to honor Masonic allusions to ancient Egyptian mystical wisdom. You may have heard Mozart's *Magic Flute* many times, but you may never have known that it was written as a Masonic allegory and is filled with Masonic symbolism. You may have read Rudyard Kipling or seen the film version of *The Man Who Would Be King*, but may not have realized that Kipling, too, was a leading Mason and that *The Man Who Would Be King* is also a Masonic allegory.

You may also have seen the 2004 film *National Treasure*. This entertaining and utterly fictional heist film may have stolen a tiny bit of thunder from *The Solomon Key*. It brought into the popular culture a modern-day story that reached back into the time of Benjamin Franklin and depicted some fanciful legends of the Masons and the Knights Templar and their relevance to the Founding Fathers, themes that Dan Brown is likely to explore in *The Solomon Key*. Brown's prior books have been criticized by many for being too unclear in their mix of fact and fiction. *The Solomon Key* will undoubtedly continue Brown's novelistic style of asserting that certain myths, legends, and speculations are "factual." But whatever liberties with history Dan Brown takes in his next book—and he certainly will take many—I expect that once *The Solomon Key* is published, we will find that he has explored these issues in considerably greater depth than the filmmakers of *National Treasure* did.

If at least a significant portion of what you will read in *The Solomon Key* is news to you, you will also want to know why you were never taught these things in school! Or why Brown's version of history isn't recounted in the recent bestselling biographies of the Founding Fathers by leading scholars. Reading *Secrets of the Widow's Son* will fill in many of those blanks and help you develop your own ideas about the wide range of issues Dan Brown's next novel is likely to touch on.

How does David Shugarts know what Dan Brown is going to write about in *The Solomon Key* long before the book is even published?

First, a quick bit of personal history about my involvement with this book. I am the editor of a book called *Secrets of the Code: The Unauthorized Guide to the Mysteries Behind The Da Vinci Code*, which was published in early 2004. That book grew out of my own interest in *The Da Vinci Code*, and my own personal quest to sort out fact from fiction in Dan Brown's work after my fascinating experience reading the novel. A good indicator of the power of *The Da Vinci Code* phenomenon is that *Secrets of the Code* went on to become a blockbusting *New York Times* bestseller in its own right, spending more than twenty weeks on the *Times* bestseller list in 2004, appearing in roughly two dozen international editions and on at least seven global bestseller lists. We have subsequently created a whole series of "Secrets" books, designed to bring the expertise of leading scholars and thinkers to the subjects touched on by the Dan Brown novels, in a way that allows readers to develop their own informed perspective on fact, fiction, speculation, and meaning in these novels.

When my co-editor, Arne de Keijzer, and I were neck deep in producing *Secrets of the Code*, we asked our good friend Dave Shugarts to look into a rumor we'd heard that there was a code buried in the dust jacket flaps of *The Da Vinci Code*. As you will soon discover, Dave is pretty good when it comes to cracking codes. Indeed, he has found hidden codes in almost all of Dan Brown's past books, and, in the chapters to come, shares many of the secrets he has uncovered.

Soon after we asked him to decipher this mystery, Dave came back with the report that there was a series of slightly darker, bolded letters within the text of the jacket flaps, and that by stringing the bolded letters together they spelled out the enigmatic question, "*Is there no help for the widow's son?*"

From that unusual phrase, Dave was able to draw dotted lines to the apocryphal book of Enoch, to Mormonism, to many other esoteric and occult bodies of knowledge. But Dave kept coming back to the most persistent connection—to the history of Freemasonry. According to Masonic lore, a character named Hiram Abiff is the founding father of Masonic societies—at least metaphorically speaking. This Hiram, spelled and translated from different ancient languages in different ways, is, at least conceptually, the same Hiram of Tyre who the Bible tells us was a master builder and the man tapped by King Solomon to build the first temple in Jerusalem. And the first thing the Bible tells us about this Hiram is that he was a "widow's son." There are many other linkages and shades of meaning to the phrase *widow's son* in the rich history of Freemasonry.

For *Secrets of the Widow's Son*, Shugarts worked relentlessly, tracking the footprints of where Dan Brown had been in his prior books and clearing the brush to see where he might be going in the future. *Angels & Demons*, an earlier Brown novel, provided some important clues, as we discovered working on *Secrets of Angels & Demons*. *Angels & Demons* was published in 2000 to almost no notice or acclaim, even though it was the novel in which Dan Brown debuted Robert Langdon, the fictional Harvard professor who would go on to become a "symbologist" as the protagonist of *The Da Vinci Code*. After the success of *The Da Vinci Code*, *Angels & Demons* was republished and became a huge bestseller. In all probability, we will be encountering Professor Langdon again as the protagonist of *The Solomon Key*.

The secret society highlighted in *Angels & Demons* is the Illuminati, but in telling the history of this group, Professor Langdon dwells on the thesis (erroneous, in my view) that the Illuminati took refuge in Freemasonry and evolved into a kind of terrorist wing of the Freemasons. Throughout *Angels & Demons*, Brown tips his hand again and again about his interest in Freemasonry and its connection to the American Revolution. In *Angels & Demons*—and again in *The Da Vinci Code*—Professor Langdon has occasion to tell the story of how certain symbols associated with Illuminati and Masonic history—such as the all-seeing eye and the unfinished pyramid—found their way into the Great Seal of the United States and onto the back of the dollar bill.

As Arne de Keijzer and I were rushing to finalize *Secrets of the Code*, Shugarts kept turning up more and more indications of Dan Brown's interest in the Masonic movement as the great secret society lying at the heart of the American historical experience. Shugarts was equally convinced that the architecture, art, history, and physical layout of Washington, D.C., would provide Langdon with the same kind of mystical, secretive, conspiratorial, heretical, alternative Christian, and occult material as Paris and London had in *The Da Vinci Code* and as Rome had in *Angels & Demons*.

Armed with hundreds of data points to back up his conclusion, Dave Shugarts announced to us one day in early 2004 that "Dan Brown's next novel will probably be about the Freemasons and will probably be set in Washington, D.C." Shugarts incorporated brief highlights of his theory about Brown's next book in a piece he wrote for *Secrets of the Code*, which was published in April 2004. We then put out a press release in May calling attention to this intriguing analysis he had done. Very shortly thereafter, in one of Dan Brown's only public appearances of 2004, the novelist himself announced that his next book would, indeed, be set against the backdrop of Masonic history and Washington, D.C. Months later, sources at Brown's publisher confirmed this and released the upcoming book's title, *The Solomon Key*.

I have shared that bit of publishing history in order to illustrate Dave Shugarts's uncanny track record. Any interested reader should also read Dave's pieces in both *Secrets of the Code* and *Secrets of Angels & Demons*. No would-be Brownologist will want to miss all that Shugarts has deciphered and analyzed in those essays.

Shugarts is not a psychic, nor do we have any "inside information" about Dan Brown. All our work is done at arm's length, independently, unauthorized by Dan Brown or anyone associated with him. Shugarts is a relentless researcher, a dogged investigative reporter, a dedicated code-breaker, and an intellectual detective in the tradition of Sherlock Holmes or Hercule Poirot. After he finished his work for *Secrets of the Code*, he couldn't stop himself. He wanted to get to the bottom of the "widow's son" code he had cracked.

Soon after *Secrets of the Code* was published, Shugarts came to a bagel breakfast with Arne de Keijzer and myself and placed on the table between the cream cheese and the bread basket a stack of thick binders reflecting the research he'd done to connect the themes in Dan Brown's world. Arne and I listened, fascinated, as Dave took us through a blizzard of ideas and names, showing us how Brown moves from one tantalizing concept to the next, jumping like a living Google search from one period of history to another, across intellectual disciplines from art to religion to alchemy, from a conspiracy in modern times to a legend in ancient times, from the Bible to Gnostic texts to the secret documents of Freemasonry. It was a tour de force that left our heads spinning. We urged Dave to flesh out this body of work into something that ordinary readers (like us) could comprehend. When he did, we knew immediately that Dan Brown fans everywhere would want to learn what Dave had uncovered. Thus, this book was born.

For more than a year, Shugarts has been reverse-engineering Dan Brown's research, going back to all the original sources, generating vast notebooks of clippings and relevant linkages, and drawing up complex data maps of the facts, conspiracies, secret histories, symbols, myths, legends, urban legends, artworks, monuments, city maps, etc., that are associated with the themes Dan Brown has already explored. As it turns out, almost every theory Professor Langdon has in *Angels & Demons* and *The Da Vinci Code* that appears original, intellectually compelling, worth talking about, or downright shocking comes from a multitude of prior published sources. For example, the idea that Mary Magdalene may have been married to Jesus Christ is an argument that can be found in dozens of books published long before *The Da Vinci Code*. Brown has the unique ability to weave together ideas that are on the fringe and in the public domain and use his storytelling magic to transform them into novels that then occupy the heart of mainstream culture. He will surely practice this magic again with *The Solomon Key*, because when it comes to the Masons—as Shugarts discovered—there are hundreds and hundreds of books that tell every aspect of this fascinating history, even if many of us have managed to live our well-educated lives without ever coming across any of this material.

Dave Shugarts has mined this vast field of literature to find the items that will be most interesting and accessible to a general audience. In doing so, he has done us a great service on at least two counts and turned *Secrets of the Widow's Son* into a marvelous "dual use" book.

Its first use is as a superb speculative preview of Dan Brown's next book. But I would never be so presumptuous as to expect, with certainty, that what appears here will actually show up in *The Solomon Key*. After all, *The Solomon Key* will be a unique creative work of imaginative fiction, and it's possible that Dan Brown will go in a very different direction than what Shugarts anticipates here. Even the title, *The Solomon Key*, could end up being a red herring. Remember Bishop Aringarosa in *The Da Vinci Code*? His name means "red herring" in Italian. And don't forget that Brown and/or his marketers created very realistic faux Web sites for Robert Langdon, the Depository Bank of Zurich, and other fictional characters and entities that appeared in *The Da Vinci Code*.

It is not only possible but *likely* that, even if Brown writes about the concepts sketched out here, he will layer in numerous other ideas and theories that Shugarts either did not have time to explore or lacked space to include here. This will probably work both ways: Shugarts has revealed theories and historical episodes in this book that, by all logic, Dan Brown *should* use in *The Solomon Key* because they fit perfectly with what we presume to be the content of the book. But perhaps even the magical Dan Brown has not discovered the same material or, for whatever reason, has decided not to use it. Brown has revealed that he usually ends up working in only one-tenth of the interesting details he unearths when he writes a book, so predicting the exact content of *The Solomon Key* is inherently a speculative undertaking. It is also a remote possibility that Brown will change his mind and *not* publish *The Solomon Key* any time soon—or ever. After all, the book is already significantly delayed past initial publishing industry rumors' expectations.

The material Dave Shugarts has highlighted in this book is material you will find eye-opening and thought-provoking even in the absence of Dan Brown's next book. The second way of reading *Secrets of the Widow's Son* is to realize that it is a book about American history discussed in a way you've never heard before. Even if Shugarts is wrong about some of the topics discussed in Dan Brown's next book, I expect readers will still find their time reading *Secrets of the Widow's Son* well spent.

A final context-setting thought about *The Solomon Key* and the larger picture of where the "oeuvre" of Dan Brown may be going in the future. It appears Brown has read and studied a variety of occult theories of Western cultural history and become fascinated with the story line this alternative version of history tells: It starts back in cave-dwelling times with the prominence of the "sacred feminine" and goddess/fertility cults as the inspiration for the earliest religious and artistic ideas. It comes forward in time through ancient Egypt, where pyramid builders and goddess cult followers acquired secret knowledge of monument building and magic. It moves through Greece, Crete, and other eastern Mediterranean cultures, including the earliest forms of Judaism, constantly combining the engineering skills of the day (the ability to construct great pyramids, temples, and cathedrals), with emphasis on goddess worship, religious mysteries, specialized bodies of occult, mathematical, and magical knowledge, and occasional ecstatic sexual rites as forms of religious devotion.

The thread is then picked up by Jesus (whom Dan Brown has called "the original feminist"), Mary Magdalene, and certain Gnostic circles among early Christians. Some Romans conflate aspects of their pagan beliefs with these new Christian beliefs. The Knights Templar come next, combining the secret knowledge and relics they found during their occupation of the Temple of Solomon during the Crusades, with their role as builders and organizers who extend their secret society throughout Europe in what some have termed the "world's first multinational corporation." After the defeat and massacre of the Templars come all the splinter groups and new secret societies, from Freemasons to Illuminati, from Rosicrucians to alchemists, all allegedly carrying forward elements of the ancient traditions. These beliefs are in contra-distinction to the corruption and dogmatic intellectual hegemony of the Church in Europe. Squeezing through this twenty-thousand-year historical tunnel of secrecy, these old ideas become new again when they finally emerge into the light of day during the eighteenth-century Enlightenment, reaching their high tide with the American and French revolutions and the victory of democracy over feudalism; science and free thought over religious dogma.

The Solomon Key will be crafted into this context. Even after *The Solomon Key*, it is a reasonably safe prediction that Dan Brown's next book will be set against some part of this story line as well. And his next book, and his next book after that. Like J. K. Rowling's equally blockbusting Harry Potter series, Dan Brown's Robert Langdon series draws from the deepest wellsprings of Jungian archetypes and Joseph Campbell's collection of universal myths, weaving this material seamlessly into thoroughly modern, easy-to-read action/adventure stories whose pacing is reminiscent of Indiana Jones or the novels of Robert Ludlum. The dark secrets of this version of history—the cover-ups and conspiracies, the buried treasure and relics, the religious beliefs and practices, the signs, symbols, and artworks lying at the very foundations of the human experience—all will provide Professor Langdon more than enough material to keep his symbological decoding practice going through many mysteries and many more books.

To me, the truly interesting question remains not so

much whether Dan Brown is "right" or "wrong" (he is writing *fiction*, after all), but what it is about our contemporary culture, as well as our human psyche, that makes us so interested and drawn to these particular ideas. Moreover, why is it that in our well-educated, sophisticated, information-intensive times, we know so little about some of these historical matters in which Brown either is demonstrably right or at least elicits valid and incredibly thought-provoking speculation?

As I said at the outset of this introduction, this book is not intended to be a plot spoiler. Instead, it is intended to help the ordinary reader participate at a more engaged level in the extraordinary conversation that Dan Brown's books have invited us to have: about American history and our Founding Fathers; about the intellectual origins of Enlightenment philosophy, Christianity, the sacred feminine, the hidden meanings of symbols in our everyday lives; about mystical knowledge, cosmology, the debate between science and religion, and, ultimately, about the meaning and purpose of life itself.

That's a pretty good set of issues for our culture to tackle at this moment in time. Armed with *Secrets of the Widow's Son*, you will be all the more prepared to join that conversation.

—Dan Burstein
June 2005

PROLOGUE: THE RIDDLE OF THE COVER

There were probably four million other readers ahead of me when I picked up a borrowed copy of *The Da Vinci Code* in late January of 2004. I read it quickly, intensely. Like popcorn at a movie, I gobbled it down.

Of course, it gave me reason to do a double-take once in a while. Among other phases in my publishing career, I had spent about fifteen years of my life as a writer and editor in the aviation industry, so I was surprised to see author Dan Brown talk of a "waiting turboprop" for Bishop Aringarosa on one page, and then, a few pages later, specify an airplane that is *not a turboprop*. Later in the book, a Hawker jet does a "customary" about-face under its own engine power inside its hangar. (This is an unsafe maneuver that no jet pilot would ever do. The thrust could blow out the hangar walls.)

I thought it over for a few days and decided to write

the author about the flaws. In my naïve sincerity, I figured he might actually read my letter and fix the next edition. I even suggested cinematic ways to make the plot repairs in time for the *Da Vinci Code* movie that I was sure was coming (and indeed it is, scheduled for May 2006, starring Tom Hanks and Audrey Tautou).

I didn't get a reply. Still haven't. Later I learned that by 2004 Dan Brown had become pretty reclusive, holed up in his Exeter, New Hampshire, home, presumably working feverishly on the sequel to *The Da Vinci Code*.

Over all, I liked the book a lot. The clever way that Brown had compelled me to turn page after page was something I had not encountered in a novel in a long time, and the fundamental themes of history and religion were powerful, provocative, and seductive.

I have been in various forms of publishing for about thirty-six years, and have been fortunate to work with some very fine people. I was lucky enough to get back in touch with an old friend, Arne de Keijzer, and he mentioned a book project he was doing with one of his old friends, Dan Burstein, a seasoned pro at book writing and a remarkably good editor. The project was *Secrets of the Code: The Unauthorized Guide to The Da Vinci Code*, and it was already well under way.

"Funny you should mention that Dan Brown book," I said to Arne. "I just sent a letter to the author about some plot flaws."

Soon, Arne was back to me with a proposition: "Do you think you could find other plot flaws in *The Da Vinci Code?*"

"Based on what I have seen at a glance, I bet I can," I told him.

"How many do you think there are —could there be ten or twenty?"

"Well, I won't know for sure until I get into it, but I will bet there are," I said.

What followed was about nine weeks of intense scrutiny of *The Da Vinci Code*—or the *DVC*, as we came to call it—itself, plus much of the pageant of Western cultural history that the *DVC* makes its focus. At any given moment, I was digging deep into topics like the Renaissance, Leonardo da Vinci, street maps of Paris and London, with each new topic sparking endless Google searches that led in a myriad of interesting directions. I hit a level of sleeplessness that became its own standard.

A large part of my career as a journalist has been in aviation. This is a very absorbing and demanding field. It requires you to quickly, and accurately, learn all kinds of very esoteric things. It goes without saying that you are expected to know every part of every model of every current aircraft and engine. You also need a working knowledge of avionics, navigation, instrument flight procedures, and about forty other subjects that ordinary people don't feel deficient for not knowing. Aircraft accident investigators sometimes wax poetic over a thing like the fracture face indications of metal fatigue. As a journalist, I not only had to keep up with the investigators, but then explain it to my readers.

Today, because of hit television shows like *Crime Scene Investigation*, it has become common for ordinary people to know something about autopsies and causes of death. I actually had to study hundreds of traumatic injuries (with photos) when poring over thousands of aircraft accident records. One of the most important virtues of a journalist, though, is the sense to know when you don't know something, and to call an expert. So there were times when I would talk to medical examiners, psychologists, chemists, aircraft designers, and anyone else in the world who could help to explain the *why* of an aircraft crash.

Having pilots as my audience simply pushed me to a higher standard of accuracy, for a very simple reason. Pilots trust their lives to the information, so they are very selective about what they consider credible. You typically don't get a second chance if you make an error. For example, if you say the wings have a flaw in the "F" model but the "G" model has a beefed-up spar, you had better be right. If you're wrong about that "G" model, you can just assume that its pilot has canceled his subscription (assuming that the wing didn't break before he could learn of the flaw). I managed to excel at aviation journalism, capturing some five awards for my work.

In Dan Brown's *DVC*, the aviation errors hit me like a two-by-four, and I felt a sort of embarrassment on behalf of the author. I knew that thousands of "aviation people" were reading the same passage I had read about the "waiting turboprop," and then found the author naming a Beech Baron 58 as the airplane. The Baron 58 is not a *turboprop*, although some models of it are turbo*charged*, and perhaps that's where Dan Brown got sidetracked.

The other errors I found were sometimes real howlers, too, and they included simple mistakes on fundamental things, like driving north in Paris when the destination was south. This doesn't require any specialized knowledge—just a map of Paris.

In fact, for me, the whole plot-flaw hunt began, literally, with a bang. On the first page of the narrative, Silas the crazed monk shoots the Louvre curator, Saunière. His first shot has gone into Saunière's stomach. He aims and pulls the trigger again, but the chamber is empty. He reaches for a second clip that is in his pocket, but decides his victim will die soon enough anyway. Later on in the book, we find out the murder weapon is a thirteen-shot automatic pistol, and that Silas has killed three other old men that evening before coming to the Louvre.

Pardon me for stopping to do the math, but this means he averaged four shots per man for the previous victims. With that kind of shooting record, don't you think he would put in a fresh clip *before* going into the Louvre to shoot his fourth victim?

For me, *DVC* became an adult treasure hunt, a kind of video role-playing game in which I got to scamper through a book's little netherworld, picking up gold tokens. Each token was one of Dan Brown's bloopers, and all I had to do was to recognize it against the camouflage.

Eventually, I discovered more than one hundred fifty plot flaws, small and large, and documented one hundred of them in *Secrets of the Code*. My plot flaws section of the book earned special mention from a number of reviewers, but there were dozens of other contributors, including many scholars and experts in all kinds of disciplines, and I was honored to be in such fine company.

We were extremely pleased when *Secrets of the Code* burst onto the scene and rather rapidly climbed the *New York Times Best Seller List*, promptly eclipsing about eleven other books about *DVC*.

Along the way, Arne called me one day and said, "Have you heard there is a code on the dust jacket? It gives a hint about the next Dan Brown novel." So I turned my attention to it, and soon noticed that the two blurbs had some characters that were set in slightly bolder type than the rest. My eyes could not reliably pick them out, so I had my wife and eleven-year-old son sit around the kitchen table and copy out the characters:

ISTHERENOHELPFORTHEWIDOWSSON

This turned out to be a question: "Is there no help for the widow's son?"

So I typed the phrase into the Google search engine on the Internet. This became my first clue.

It immediately led me to a speech given in 1974 by Reed C. Durham, who had become a kind of pivotal figure in the Mormon Church because of this single talk. In it, he related various connections between the founder of the church, Joseph Smith, and certain influences from his period of history. Smith lived from 1805 to 1844.

The history of the Mormon Church? How could this be of interest to Dan Brown? Well, once you have read *DVC*, you are willing to sit still at least for a short lesson, so I read on.

History is definitely not dull when you are digging into material like this. Your senses are even more stimulated when you are constantly paying attention to the potential for a novelist like Dan Brown to bring history to life. I learned how the young Joseph Smith cooked up his religious stew with a pinch of Freemasonry and a dash of occult magic. There were a lot of little brain ticklers, too, because Reed Durham was building a picture of a Joseph Smith who "married" several dozen women, created an entire religion without any significant prior religious experience, and was murdered, all by the age of thirty-eight.

It didn't seem to have an obvious connection to the next Dan Brown novel, but it brought up the topic of Freemasonry, which I instinctively began to research. This led to a lot of hits on Google, and became my second clue.

It also hooked me up quite quickly with conspiracy theories and the Illuminati, and I got a strong vibe about Washington, D.C. I decided to pursue the Washington trail.

Now, things started to make a lot of sense! Having analyzed *DVC* page by page and by now having read *Angels & Demons (A&D)*, I could readily see how Washington could provide Dan Brown with a symbolic playground for his hero, Robert Langdon, in which to race around (no doubt going the wrong way down one-way streets, a Dan Brown thing). Brown had already "done" Paris, London, and Rome. The city of Washington also has a history that is a mystery to most of us. These secret histories could be a ripe background for Dan Brown to deploy his patented mix of symbology, conspiracy theory, occult history, and religious themes.

I circulated a modest guess about the next Dan Brown novel, among my publishing buddies, and became known as "the guy making a prediction." This eventually solidified into a long-term assignment, and I was off on the quest. My earliest prediction was a "Mormon-Mason treasure hunt," probably set in Washington but perhaps involving travels elsewhere. We published this guess in *Secrets of the Code* in April 2004.

I have to admit that I am still not sure about the Mormon connection. When I pursued it, I learned an awful lot about the origins of this religion that involved the occult, the formative years of America after the Revolution, and Freemasonry—all potential Dan Brown themes. So, even if it doesn't come up in the next Dan Brown novel, I am glad to have studied these interesting topics.

On May 4, 2004, our publishing group issued a press release highlighting what I had found out about the dust jacket clues. It took only a couple of weeks for the guess to be confirmed by the best possible source, the author himself.

On May 18, Dan Brown himself let slip a clue or two in a rare public appearance, a speech to the New Hampshire Writers Project. According to news accounts of the speech, he said his next novel would be "set in Washington and would focus on the Free and Accepted Masons, a secretive fraternal organization." Brown said the architecture in Washington is "soaked in symbolism and plays a major role in the novel." My publishing associates were pleased at this. It was nearly a perfect confirmation of my prediction and, in earnest, I now sought to figure out what Dan Brown would do next.

Immediately, there was a sea change in my life. If you do not count technical tomes, aircraft flight manuals, and all of the endless software manuals I've had to absorb in a thirty-six-year career as a journalist with heavy emphasis on technical matters, I had gone the last five or ten years reading only perhaps two "books" a year. Those days are gone for good. I soon settled into a routine in which I was reading two or three books a week and had about five open at one time.

This was in addition to endless hours searching the Internet. Each time I found a particularly good article, I would e-mail it to myself, to keep a running record of my research. The initial effort on *DVC* came to about 475 articles. This was followed by about 350 articles on *A&D*. Now, in the effort to anticipate Dan Brown's next novel, I have over 700 articles. Printed out, it comes to more than 5,000 pages.

The research hasn't stopped. The more I discover, the more there is to discover. Dan Brown says he uses only about 10 percent of the research he gathers when it comes to actually writing the novels, so I probably have much more material than he'd ever use. And, of course, there is no guarantee that I have anticipated everything Dan Brown will explore. It also could well be true that Dan Brown will miss some of the nuggets of gold that I have collected.

Consider this an invitation. Come with me on this treasure hunt through history. My pledge is twofold: to tell you what I have discovered, and to expose you to further mysteries yet to be solved.

I am specifically not attempting to spoil the plot of Dan Brown's next book for you. This book is really in homage to the extraordinary mind and research of Dan Brown. Instead, I am seeking to make you a well-informed reader, ready to have an even richer and more enjoyable experience reading Dan Brown's next book—which the publisher has announced will be called *The Solomon Key*.

Chapter One

THE SEARCH BEGINS

MY ASSIGNMENT was to pursue, without any particular limits or blinders, any lead that might arise from the clues of "Widow's Son" and "Solomon Key." How to begin?

I began searching the Internet, of course, which immediately led to books, articles, and videos. And then it led back to the Internet, to thousands of Web pages, all connected in a vast matrix of linkages. I found myself reading many books on the Mormons, the Founding Fathers, the early history of America, plus the Kabbalah, the occult, Tarot (see Appendix A, Symbolic Systems), all the world's major (and some very minor) religions, sixteenth-century Scotland, seventeenth-century England, and everything I could handle on Freemasonry.

Don't do this at home, kids. I admit that only a nut would read Albert Pike's *Morals and Dogma*, 861 pages of wonderful weirdness, a book that seeks to combine all the world's most important philosophies and symbols for the benefit of Freemasonry. It's just one more notch in my reading gun.

Pursuing the Freemasonry trail, I had the happy experience of reading James Flexner's *Washington: The Indispensable Man*. Did this teach me a lesson! Before I had finished the first chapter, I was stunned by the realization that I didn't really know anything about the Father of Our Country, not to mention the most revered figure in American Freemasonry. (Even so, most historians do not play up Washington's Masonic career. This is true of an otherwise excellent new biography, *His Excellency: George Washington*, by Joseph Ellis.)

❧ Beware of Bogus History ❧

Learning the truth about Washington meant I got to discard the total malarkey about the cherry tree. That myth was invented by a lying fool who felt Washington's life story needed embellishment. How wrong he was—the true story of Washington is so much better than any myth! He was braver, wiser, and more human than the myths portray him.

It is one of Dan Brown's themes that history— typically written by the 'victors'—is not always true. Brown is right, although for fictional purposes he tends to paint history as primarily motivated by conspirators who want to disguise and deny the truth. Here is one example of why historical depictions might depart from the truth. It's a story about George Washington.

Just after George Washington's death, a "parson" named Mason Locke Weems decided to write a quick-and-dirty *Life of Washington*. He won the race to get something published first and obtain a commercial advantage while borrowing Washington's aura. Washington died in December of 1799 and Weems's book came out in early 1800.

Weems didn't let the truth foul up a good story—he just invented everything he needed.

In a failed career as a clergyman, Weems claimed he had briefly led the little church where George Washington had worshipped. But at the time of Washington's death Weems was a traveling book salesman who played the fiddle and followed crowds so he could siphon off some attention for his wares. He scored big with the *Life of Washington*, which went to eleven editions and outsold all other biographies of Washington. In a few generations, it became the version of Washington's life that was firmly imprinted into the American psyche. Americans even today "know" Washington through Weems—which means they don't really know Washington at all.

Weems was a Freemason, and he displayed his membership prominently—on the title pages of his books, in speeches and letters—taking advantage of the seeming authority given him by being a "brother" to George Washington.

Weems invented the idea of Washington praying in the snow at Valley Forge, a theme painted in the 1860s by Henry Brueckner, picked up by engravers to illustrate lots of books, redone on the cover of the *Saturday Evening Post* in 1935, and as a U.S. postage stamp in 1977. It is no wonder that we all believe it, but it's historical fiction. Washington was not a particularly devout man, and it is just not very likely that he went out to kneel in the snow and pray. Among the telltale signs, at the time, were his deathbed requests. Some three or four doctors were summoned, but Washington never called for a clergyman (see Appendix C, Death and Resurrection).

Weems also sold America on the idea that Washington rose into heaven, saintlike, making him a national deity. Weems gave a very detailed lurid description, which led to artwork, such as engravings in books, and, eventually, to one of our nation's most important frescoes, on the Rotunda ceiling in the U.S. Capitol.

As you can see, you can get from George Washington to religious fiction rather quickly, and by golly, that's another example of what Dan Brown likes to do. He often starts a paragraph about history, and jumps to religion. In *DVC*, you get tangled up in the questions of the historical Jesus, Mary, and Mary Magdalene, versus their religious portrayals.

In the Langdon novels, particularly in *DVC*, Dan Brown invites us to look beyond the obvious, to delve far deeper than the history books that we read in grade school. He challenges the entire two thousand years of Christian history by bringing up "alternative" views and hints from scholars that there might be conflicting historical facts. Even if you research a topic and find out that Dan Brown is wrong, you still learn from your research, and you learn to doubt the "official" story until you have personally weighed all the facts.

Apotheosis of Washington *graces the Capitol Rotunda dome. Its full significance is both sacred and profane.*

❧ Symbols and Clues ❧

Another theme of Dan Brown's is that there is symbolism wherever you look. The lead character of *DVC*, Robert Langdon, is, after all, a "religious symbology" professor who sees signs of roses and chalices, blades and phalluses. Langdon likes to point out that such secrets are "hidden in plain sight."

Of course, there's a mighty big example of this kind of symbolism, rising 555 feet from the center of Washington. As an obelisk, it satisfies one of the many requirements of Dan Brown's symbolism. In *A&D*, Professor Langdon tells us (erroneously) that obelisks are called "lofty pyramids" by symbologists, as

A CLOSER LOOK

DAN BROWN'S BOOK CODES

WARNING: Don't read this if you want to solve the codes yourself. Here are the codes, as far as we know them, from the first four novels.

In *Digital Fortress* (1998), the coded clue on the back page is:

128–10–93–85–10–128–98–112–6–6–25–126–39–1–68–78

To solve it, you take the first letter of each chapter (there are 128 short, staccato chapters—a stylistic hallmark of Dan Brown). At first, it's gibberish:

W–E–C–G–E–W–H–A–A–I–O–R–T–N–U

But if you observe that there are 16 characters, it may occur to you to place the characters in a 'Caesar's box' for decoding (see box at left).

W	E	C	G
E	W	H	Y
A	A	I	O
R	T	N	U

Read Column 1 down, followed by Column 2, etc., and you get:

"We are watching you"

This is appropriate for a novel about the government using a huge computer to spy on everyone, the main theme of *Digital Fortress*.

In *Deception Point* (2001), the clue is:

1–V–116–44–11–89–44–46–L–51–130–19–118–L–32–118–116–130–28–116–32–44–133–U–130.

Again, obtain the first characters from each numbered chapter (but retain the letters already present). Count the characters (25). This gives you a 5 × 5 grid. Working across, put the characters in each row. Then read down each column (see box at right).

And out comes the clue: "The Da Vinci Code will surface."

In *The Da Vinci Code* (2003), the clue in bolded characters on the dust jacket is:

T	V	C	I	R
H	I	O	L	F
E	N	D	L	A
D	C	E	S	C
A	I	W	U	E

ISTHERENOHELPFORTHEWIDOWSSON.

In addition, codes are part of the games hosted on *The Da Vinci Code Web* site. For instance, faintly showing and mirror-imaged, in the red portion of the back of the jacket at the edge is a pair of latitude-longitude coordinates:

37 degrees 57 minutes 6.5 seconds North

77 degrees 8 minutes 44 seconds West

Add one degree to the latitude. This will lead to the sculpture of Kryptos at the CIA headquarters. The phrase "only WW knows" is found in a brown area of the *DVC* dust jacket. This refers to William Webster, a former CIA director.

Another code is in a darkly printed circular pattern on the back of the *DVC* dust jacket. It has numbers and little icons of the all-seeing eye within a triangle. If you use the same old Dan Brown technique, the numbers will refer to first letters in the chapters, or

* 20 11 11 68 * 1 10 11 61 15 * 5 87 73 11

becomes * F U U N * R S U P I * M L B U

If you just take this string of characters as something meaningful (which is a leap of faith, of course), you can fool around until you solve it. Or you can just put it into an anagram site on the Web. I went to http://www.crosswordtools.com/anagram-solver/ and it took about five seconds to come up with the famous U.S. motto: "E Pluribus Unum" or "Of many, one."

However, if you discover that the total number of characters, including the little icons, adds up to 16, you again should think of a Caesar's Box code, 4 x 4, which will allow you to fiddle with it awhile and get:

E	U	U	N
*	R	S	U
P	I	*	M
L	B	U	*

"skywards extensions of the sacred pyramidal form." Pyramids and obelisks are thoroughly embedded in both *DVC* and *A&D*. An added attraction of the Washington Monument is that it ties into the Freemasons and, if you like, the Illuminati. Dan Brown in *A&D* repeats the assertion that the symbols of the two groups are on the back of the U.S. dollar bill—the all-seeing eye and the unfinished pyramid.

The Washington Monument has ties to religious strife, as I will explain later, and it has strong ties to Freemasonry. Its cornerstone was laid in a grand Masonic ceremony, and inside the monument are more than one hundred ninety commemorative stones, a couple dozen of them from Masonic groups.

Dan Brown also loves codes. In his earlier novels, *Digital Fortress* (1998) and *Deception Point* (2001), his plots toy with hidden, encoded secrets. Interestingly, there are even codes on the back pages of these novels, at times providing a clue as to what Dan Brown will write next. As we have previously discovered, *DVC* has the "Widow's Son" clue on the dust jacket, plus a number of other clues that work into a *DVC* Web site game.

Around the same time I looked at the numeric codes, I also learned of an August 2001 radio talk show that Dan Brown participated in. It was about Freemasonry and included two experts. Dan Brown was brought on board as an author who had done a lot of research on Freemasonry. In the radio piece, he made *A&D* seem like it was focused on the Freemasons, when in fact that novel had contrived the notion of the Illuminati as a seventeenth-century spinoff of the Masons. *A&D* focused on a fictionalized history of the Illuminati, not the Freemasons, and placed the origins of the Illuminati in seventeenth-century Italy instead of late eighteenth-century Bavaria, which is the actual historical origin of the Illuminati.

The book that was actually *delivered* next in the Langdon series was *DVC*, in the spring of 2003. Yes, when you look at the combined content of *A&D* and *DVC*, the Illuminati and the Knights Templar are mentioned, both of which can be linked to Freemasonry. But there is also a decided lack of beefy content from an author who says he has thoroughly studied Freemasonry. Where has all the research gone?

To me, it seems possible that Dan Brown conceived the general nature of the Robert Langdon series in the late 1990s, and has been writing it ever since. Therefore, he might have felt as though his Freemasonry research were completed. However, since there are an estimated fifty thousand books on Freemasonry, not to mention all the peripheral theories of conspiracies and other secret societies, it is hard for anyone to know that they have come to the last Freemasonry book on the library shelf. As far as I can tell, there are about ten authors writing new exposés of Freemasonry at any given moment.

So, the way I see it, there's a lot more that Dan Brown has yet to write about the Freemasons, and he's probably going to unload both barrels on us in his next book.

Dan Brown puts together intricate mystery plots, but, to date, they have all showed a simple principle:

Conspirators are lurking everywhere, but they are just dupes for other conspirators, the ones *really* pulling the strings. According to Brown, one of the techniques of a secret society such as the Illuminati is to spread plenty of half-truths or downright disinformation. Brown calls this "data sowing," and he asserts that the major intelligence agencies do it, such as the CIA and NSA. The net result is essentially a variation on "hiding things in plain sight."

I believe in listening super-carefully to Dan Brown here. I think deception should never be discounted as a Dan Brown technique for talking about his own book plans.

At any given time, he could be telling a partial truth or just hurling chunks of disinformation. In one of Dan Brown's speeches, for instance, he claimed he had left the "most controversial" assertion out of *DVC*. Even though he had credible evidence that Jesus may have survived the Crucifixion, he said, he left it out of the book. Although this is certainly titillating, I don't think it is likely to come up in the next novel. I view it as a sop we have been thrown, to keep us guessing.

However, in late October of 2004, the press was fed one more vital clue. According to Stephen Rubin, president and publisher of Doubleday, the new book will be titled *The Solomon Key*. Rubin met with reporters, divulged this one tidbit, and reiterated the earlier statements by Brown that it would focus on Freemasonry and take place in Washington, with its rich symbolic architecture. The various Dan Brown Web sites, which had been predicting the next book's arrival in "summer 2005," were now amended to say, "No release date is scheduled." In New York publishing circles, there is a belief that this now means the book will be published sometime in 2006.

You won't get many clues that come directly from Dan Brown, but I did get one that was nearly as good. As I scampered down the twisted trails of history, I encountered a larger-than-life American of the nineteenth century named Albert Pike. One day, I got an out-of-the-blue call from an author, Warren Getler, mentioning a book that he had written, *Shadow of the Sentinel*. It's about Civil War-era treasure that may have been buried in Arkansas and farther west, perhaps in Arizona. But it also brings up historical figures such as Jesse James and the very same Albert Pike.

Getler recounted a little vignette. It seems that he and Dan Brown attended a publishing luncheon together in the spring of 2003, since both were in the final stages of releasing their books. The two chatted, and when Dan Brown inquired about Getler's book and heard a little about it, up came the name Albert Pike.

According to Getler, Brown "blanched" and said, "I don't think I should talk about this further with you, because my next book is going to be about Albert Pike!"

Of course, this inspired me to roar through Getler's book and then order more tomes related to Pike— who is not an easy figure to figure out. But knowing about Pike is important in the study of Freemasonry, and gives meaning to some of the side issues as well. Pike's life, as we shall see, could give us meaningful clues as to a possible theme in Dan Brown's next book—or maybe just some red herrings.

⊷ My Roots ⊶

I had better come clean about a couple of personal things here. They have to do with my family roots.

My Dad died recently, and he was, among other things, a very advanced amateur genealogist. He spent some forty years working on our family history, and had amassed some ten thousand pages of genealogical notes by the time of his death. I inherited all these records and began to try to understand them. Believe it or not, the pursuit of Dan Brown's next novel played right into my getting to know my roots.

We think of our family as average Americans, which is to say that our ancestors came from many lands and intermingled, so that we have Welsh, Scottish, English, Irish, Dutch, and German blood, to name just the highlights. But the predominant line of our family descends from the Germans, and not just any Germans, but the waves who immigrated to Pennsylvania in the early eighteenth century and became the Pennsylvania Deutsch, misnamed "Dutch."

They largely came from a region known as the Palatinate, which has historical connections to the origins of the Rosicrucians and also to the Illuminati of Bavaria. (I know of no actual connections between my family and those groups, however.) Rosicrucians and Illuminati are both thoroughly implicated in Dan Brown's Langdon novels.

While my ancestors belonged to many religions, I would say that the most common one among our early American ancestors was the Society of Friends, or Quakers.

I am going to talk a lot about Freemasonry, since Dan Brown's next book will focus on it. I should make it clear that I am not a Freemason. I know that our family includes some Freemasons, including my favorite uncle, but I had never discussed Freemasonry within the family before I began studying Dan Brown's books. (I think a lot of American families might be like that, in that the older generation was involved in fraternal pursuits, but not the younger.)

However, I am not a stranger to things fraternal. I am an Eagle Scout and a member of the Order of the Arrow (Scouting's fraternity), and was a member of Delta Phi fraternity in college. Both of these organizations initiated me with ordeals and trusted me with secret passwords, which I have never revealed.

Since my ancestors were part of Pennsylvania life in 1776, my Dad did the genealogical work and became a member of the Sons of the American Revolution. Although I would immediately qualify for membership, I have not joined.

Before he died, Dad handed me a notebook that he had started about thirty years before, in which he made a serious hobby out of trying to figure out the ciphers and location of the famous Thomas ("Jefferson") Beale treasure, which I will discuss later.

On my wife's side of the family, some connections go back to Palatine Germany, and some go back further in time, to England, to families that came over and founded Stonington, Connecticut, in the early seventeenth century. That's on her father's side.

I will be talking a lot about the Founding Fathers. An Englishman named Colonel John Washington came to America in about 1655. Among his four children were Lawrence Washington and Anne Washington, who married a Virginia planter named Francis Wright. Down through about ten generations of Wrights, my wife is a descendant of Anne Washington. Down from Lawrence, there descended Augustine Washington, father of George Washington.

Since George and Martha Washington never had children, there can be no direct descendants of George, but—like thousands of other Americans—my wife can claim the next-best thing. She can consider George to be a cousin—very distant, of course. So around our house, we not only revere the Father of Our Country, but we call him, quite affectionately, "Cousin George."

If she gets to count various cousin connections, my wife can also link up to some other famous Americans, such as Presidents John Adams and John Quincy Adams. We believe that the connection can be extended to another father/son combo, Presidents George H. W. Bush and George W. Bush (although we have not yet contacted them for confirmation).

So, at times when I have been a little glazed over with too much research, I have been able to perk up a bit to see mention of Bavaria or Quakers or Washington, because to me they have a personal meaning.

But I would say it is really worth it to read a bit when

you're not actually sure how it applies to the subject under investigation. Time after time, I would find myself wondering, "What does all this have to do with Dan Brown's novels?" That's about when the next paragraph I was reading would hit me right between the eyes, with some powerful connection to a Dan Brown theme. So it's up to us to pursue thoroughly all the clues, particularly "Widow's Son" and "Solomon Key."

Chapter Two

HUNTING FOR THE FUNDAMENTAL THEMES

❧ *A Matrix of Conspiracies* ❧

I N T H E M O V I E *The Matrix*, the main character, Neo, is invited to swallow a red pill to enter the all-pervasive Matrix or a blue pill to return to the "safety" of ignorance. Here is my warning for this adventure: If you read further, you are about to swallow the red pill. Once you do, you will begin to see evidence of a grand conspiracy in everything, throughout history, infecting every element of society. You are either a conspirator or a pawn in the conspiracy; there is no middle ground. If you're at all timid, take the blue pill.

Dan Brown has already revealed one modus operandi in weaving conspiracies as the fabric of his novels. Whatever main conspiracy might be at work, there is always a conspiracy within the conspiracy. The conspirators arrive at the end of the novel and discover that they have been victims of a deeper deception. Carried to the extreme, this could lead to a justifiable paranoia, since nobody in any of Dan Brown's conspiracies can be sure that there isn't someone else pulling the strings. But if there were one group that could be pulling all the strings, it would be the Illuminati.

If you start at the Illuminati, you can work backwards in history to get to the Freemasons, the Rosicrucians, the Knights Templar, the "Priory of Sion," the Holy Grail and the conspiracy of the Catholic Church to suppress it, the Apocrypha, the artwork of Leonardo da Vinci and Caravaggio, the sculpture of Bernini, the architecture of Raphael, the science of Galileo, ciphers and codes, and a cryptex, all of which are familiar from *DVC* and *A&D*.

But a lot of people who have read *DVC* and *A&D* might not be aware of a much longer possible trail. You could continue with links to our Founding Fathers, to presidencies throughout American history, to the Mormon Church, to the legend of Thomas Beale's treasure, to the Knights of the Golden Circle, to the Ku Klux Klan, and to Jesse James. Although no list will ever be complete—and how would you know whether it were ever complete?—it also could include Hitler, the Trilateral Commission, the Federal Reserve, the Wiccans and modern Druids, Skull & Bones, the CIA, British Intel and the KGB, the Council on Foreign Relations, and the International Monetary Fund.

Everything is so interconnected that almost any clue by itself could lead you on a frantic scurry through the tunnels and wormholes of history. Just when you think you've found the best piece of pungent cheese, there is the far-off fragrance of another, luring you further underground.

Let's jump down underground and let the red pill take effect.

❦ The Meaning of "Widow's Son" ❧

How do we interpret the clue on the dust jacket of *DVC*? There is a simple way to construe "Is there no help for the widow's son?" It is said to be a plea for help from one brother Freemason to another. You say it with your arms raised "to the square." You say, "Oh, Lord, my God, is there no help for the widow's son?"

The plea is a powerful one. Any brother Freemason is compelled to help you. There are many stories in which com- batants on opposite sides in battle set aside their weapons in order to answer this plea. Paul Revere was said to have been spared by a British captain who detained him on the night of his fateful ride, because each rec- ognized certain coded phrases that revealed a fellow Freemason.

It is when we try to define a *widow's son*

Paul Revere, as a Freemason, was spared by the British on his "Ride."

that things get richer and more intricate.

With plenty of homage paid to other cultures, such as the Egyptians, the central core of Freemasonry arises from the biblical story of the building of the Temple of Solomon.

This story is told in two places in the Bible (I Kings and II Chronicles) and it speaks of a request by Solomon to Hiram, the King of Tyre, for materials and for a very capable individual to serve as the master architect. Hiram, King of Tyre, responds by sending an immensely skilled man, whose name also is Hiram. He is the son of a widow.

Due to a translation mistake, it is said, the architect Hiram becomes known as Hiram Abiff. The Bible says he is remarkably talented, being able to work in gold, silver, bronze, iron, stone, and wood, as well as fabrics.

The Bible says Hiram does his work very well and the finished temple is almost beyond description. As built, it is heavy with gold and riches, but Solomon also brings all of his prodigious treasure of gold and silver to the temple. In the inner chamber, or holiest of places, he installs the Ark of the Covenant, containing the sacred tablets that Moses received from God. At the temple's entrance stand two hollow bronze pillars, which Solomon names Jachin and Boaz. The names of these pillars are actually very famous in Freemasonry.

In the Bible story, Solomon dedicates the temple and the tale moves on, leaving Hiram Abiff to exit the stage quietly.

The Freemasons, however, have a different version, highlighting Hiram Abiff and developing him as the archetypical Master Mason.

Originally, the legend involved Noah and his three sons, but it evolved into the legend of Hiram and his murder, somewhere in the beginnings of modern Freemasonry, probably between 1724 and 1726. If you want a genuine mystery of history, try to find out where the Hiram legend originated.

Long before Solomon's time, it was said that Enoch had dug down and built a series of nine stacked, vaulted chambers, the bottom one hewn in bedrock. Each chamber connected to the one above through an opening in the top, until reaching the uppermost chamber, which was capped by a special stone door with a golden ring. Eons later, the Temple of Solomon was built on top of the whole affair.

According to the Masonic legend, Hiram, King of Tyre; King Solomon; and Hiram Abiff were all considered Master Masons and, together, the three guarded secret knowledge. Hiram Abiff hid secrets in one or both of the hollow pillars of the temple. (The pillars Boaz and Jachin are described in *DVC* at Rosslyn Chapel in Scotland, and the idea of secrets hidden in a hollow pillar comes up also, in the village church in Rennes-le-Château, France.)

As the tale goes, some lower-level "ruffian" workers envied the secrets and they conspired to obtain them. They waylaid Hiram Abiff and tried to beat it out of him. He did not yield, crying out, "Oh, Lord, my God, is there no help for the widow's son?" He died, whereupon they left his body and fled.

Righteous stonemasons went looking for the missing Hiram and found his rotting body. They wanted to look under the body to see if Hiram had left any clue to the secret knowledge. In order to lift the corpse, they had to use a special five-point clasp (since the flesh was falling off the bone).

The Hiramic legend is one of the central themes of Masonic initiation. The candidate must symbolically "die" and be "reborn" or "raised." This is done with a five-point grip, in an echo of the raising of Hiram. (Since we are sensitized by reading *DVC* and *A&D*, we can see religious parallels. There are literal biblical cases of resurrection, as in Jesus or Lazarus. There are also symbolic rebirths or renewals that can be traced back to many earlier religions.)

Another widow's son legend from a different era has Mormon founder Joseph Smith trying to make Hiram's plea just before being murdered by a mob in 1844. Smith, who was a staunch Freemason, got as far as "Oh Lord, my God" when he was shot and fell from an upper-story window.

Jumping whole continents and centuries, the Parsifal legend, which traces back to earlier tales of Gawain and the Holy Grail, makes Parsifal out as a "widow's son."

Jumping again, to Scotland and the famous Rosslyn Chapel (already dealt with in *DVC*), there is an echo of the Hiramic legend. It's impossible to visit Rosslyn Chapel without being told the tale of an apprentice who carves an elegant column, igniting the jealousy of the master mason, who smites and kills him. The apprentice's image, with a gash in his head, is one of the carvings in the chapel. Not far away is—they say— the image of his mother, a widow.

In *DVC*, Robert Langdon explains the legend of the

The apprentice, with a gash in his
head, at Rosslyn Chapel.

apprentice and the master mason's pillars to Sophie
while standing in Rosslyn Chapel, wrapping this tightly
together with the ubiquitous Masonic pillars, Boaz and
Jachin, found in every Freemason lodge in emulation
of the Temple of Solomon. This comes at the very end
of *DVC*, and within a few pages, Dan Brown will also
reveal that Sophie, the lead female character, is related
to the people who built Rosslyn Chapel. The family
name is Saint-Clair, or Sinclair (see Appendix B, The
Sinclair Family).

I find it a bit astonishing that Dan Brown gives a
relatively detailed description of "two pillars" in
Rosslyn Chapel, when a visitor will find there are

actually three pillars—the apprentice's and master's pillars are separated by a third one. Brown also neglects to tell us that the apprentice is a widow's son, even though the Rosslyn legend about it is extremely well known.

Some might stop pursuing allusions and allegories at this point, but this is exactly the kind of stepping-off point for an author like Dan Brown. That's because "widow's son" might go beyond the strict definition of the son of a woman whose husband is dead. It also could be loosely construed as "man without a father" or "man without a natural father."

If you could manipulate the mythology (as Dan Brown often does), you could make a very big jump and say that Jesus was such a person, being born of a virgin mother and having no human father.

But, as scholars in religion and history will quickly point out, there are many myths going back three thousand years before Christ (or more) that center on a son born without a father. Sons of virgins include the Persian god Mithras, the Egyptian Horus, Buddha, and Krishna, not to mention many pharaohs and Alexander the Great. One of the ways to confirm the mystical and godlike properties of a great figure was to make out that his birth was supernatural.

In Greek mythology, a "hero" is born from the coupling of a human and a god. Sometimes gods just spring from other gods. But, extended all the way, the real issue is how gods came into existence, or which came first, the chicken or the egg? Religions going back to Sumeria and Babylon, as well as the Egyptians, the Romans, and the Greeks, all have versions of "self-creating" gods, and many religions specifically have legends about virgin birth.

So if Dan Brown really wants to be inventive about a "widow's son," we may see various tales of virgin birth. Or—this is a long shot—perhaps human cloning. If *The Solomon Key* ends up weaving its plot through modern-day Washington, D.C., Brown may pursue this theme. In vitro fertilization and cloning were themes in *A&D*.

❧ *The Meaning of "Solomon Key"* ❧

Let's assume that the announced title for Dan Brown's next book will remain *The Solomon Key*. If you apply the principle of Occam's razor (the simplest solution is the best), you can just take *Solomon Key* to mean the keys to the Temple of Solomon. Could it be that easy?

No keys were actually necessary to enter the temple, but if you accept the Masonic legend, there was the nine-vaulted treasure safe beneath the actual temple. The description of the stone door guarding the entrance seemed to make it simple but somehow inscrutable. We will arrive at my little theory of how it opens, but we need to develop some other points first.

Also, it is necessary to see both *Solomon* and *Key* from several different perspectives.

Solomon, for instance, does not get a lot of character-development space in the Bible. The famous tale of his wisdom, of the baby he was prepared to cut in half, plus verses giving rich and detailed descriptions of his house and temple are about all we get. (I'm disregarding a bunch of Solomon-related items, such as the sexually charged love poem, *The Song of Solomon*, or the apocryphal book of aphorisms called the Wisdom of Solomon. These do not pertain to his own deeds. The Bible mentions a missing book called the Acts of Solomon, which probably would have told all.)

But there are plenty of other interesting old Solomon stories—they're just not in the Bible. Quite a number of lively tales of Solomon are included in Islamic books such as the Koran.

In Muslim stories, Solomon is a kind of wizard or magus. He has the ability to summon spirits (*djinns* or angels) and also to converse with animals—so he's the original Doctor Doolittle. In addition, he is said to have had many wives and to have had sex with seventy women in a single night. The numbers seventy, seventy-one, or seventy-two have significance in lots of Hebrew and Muslim contexts.

A kind of amalgamated story that drifted down from Arabic writers expands the concept of Solomon the magus. It is said that he was given a special signet ring from heaven, made of iron and brass, on which was engraved "the Most Great Name of God." It is a tradition of the occult that to control a spirit, one needs to name it. Conversely, it is a fundamental tenet of Judaism that certain names of God must never be uttered.

It was also said that Solomon received four jewels from four different angels, and had them set into a ring, so that he could control the four classical elements: earth, air, fire, water. In addition to being the central building blocks of all cosmology from Aristotle to the

alchemists, these four elemental forces are the themes
that Dan Brown uses in the four murders of cardinals
in *A&D*. Mere coincidence?

What was the seal on the signet ring? Most likely, it
was a six-pointed star formed by two equilateral
triangles. This was given the name "Solomon's Seal"
by Arabic writers, but was known as the "Star of
David" or "Shield of David" when observed by
Hebrews.

Sometimes in the occult tradition, this famous six-
pointed star is used to invoke or ward off spirits. It's
also used by Freemasons.

But when Western occult writers began to express
essentially the same idea and
symbology, they turned to
their old familiar five-pointed
star, the pentacle. Western
occult tradition calls this the
"Druid's foot." It's also used
by Freemasons.

The people of the Middle
Ages often equated the
practice of medicine with the
practice of witchcraft, and
there were plenty of ways in
which "white witchcraft"

*Seal of Solomon, or Star of
David, unites the "blade"
and "chalice."*

could be used for good, while "black witchcraft" could
be used for evil. Over the years from about 1200
through 1500, quite a number of books of magic were
written, known as *grimoires*.

One of the most influential was called *Clavicula
Salomonis* or *The Key of Solomon the King.*

*The ancient pentagram is
sometimes called the
"Druid's foot."*

Additionally, there was a grimoire called *Ars Goetia* (The Howling Art, a euphemism for magic), part of a longer book, *Lemegeton Clavicula Salomonis* or *The Lesser Key of Solomon*. If you are a real lover of language, note that in *A&D*, before killing the scientist Leonardo Vetra, the Hassassin demands "*La chiave...* the password." But the correct translation of the Italian *la chiave* is actually "the key."

The Lesser Key describes how Solomon locks up seventy-two demons in a bronze vessel and gets them to work for him. The book even provides a list of the names of the demons, some Semitic, some pre-Christian—i.e., pagan—and some invented. Solomon's vessel is kept locked by a symbol:

You guessed it, the Key of Solomon.

*Jupiter Pentacle from
Clavicula Salomonis,
with symbols also found on
Joseph Smith's amulet.*

❧ Searching for the Perfect Fit ❧

Now, the trouble with trying to outguess Dan Brown is, even though we have found a key with a perfect fit, we have to examine a number of alternative ideas just in case he drags a weird thought out of left field. Because he always does! Freud said that our dreams are "over-determined," meaning they are brought about by numerous contributing factors, and Brown's plots and symbols are over-determined, too, creating an alloy of many different bits and pieces of his research into history—even when real history suggests they don't fit.

So let us take up other meanings of *key* besides a key that operates a lock.

One meaning worth considering is the key like the legend on a map. Part of the Masonic tradition of hiding things in plain sight was a system of giving coded messages in drawings and engravings, then providing a little symbolic "key" that could be used to decode the message.

In work on codes and ciphers, it is common to have a coded message that might be intercepted, but be difficult or impossible to crack unless you have the decoding key. Today's computer security schemes often rely on "public/private key encryption," in which one of the keys to a message is made public, but is useless without the private key provided by the sender.

There is no way we can completely dismiss a meaning like this for *key* since Dan Brown is so enamored of codes in all his novels, and has written specifically about encryption schemes in several of them.

In myths and magic, sometimes a single spoken word is a key, as in "Abracadabra."

Another meaning of *key* is architectural, as in *keystone*, the stone that makes a vaulted arch possible.

Dan Brown included a small discussion of the keystone in *DVC*. The keystone has a long practical tradition and it has deep meanings for Freemasons.

A very special meaning can be extracted from the device known as a Lewis Key. I believe that this could well have been one of the secrets that genuine stonemasons held dear. It's a long shot, but it could give a method for opening that special stone door on that treasure vault under the Temple of Solomon.

Finally, there is a philosophic meaning of *key*. An idea like "Knowledge is the key to enlightenment" would be a prime example. Many philosophies, and many religions, have this as their tacit promise.

A CLOSER LOOK

LEWIS KEY

STONEMASONS for more than two thousand years have lifted very large stones by hoisting them. Humongous stones, such as those used in the Great Pyramids of Egypt, were probably rollered, skidded, or levered into place, but stones weighing up to several tons can be simply picked up on wooden cranes or tripods, using slings and the mechanical advantage of a block and tackle.

When a stone is hoisted on a sling and set in place, the sling gets trapped underneath. So, long ago, clever stonemasons came up with a device that fits into a hole cut in the top of the stone. It allows easy lifting, and the stone can be swung perfectly and dropped into position, with mortar spread and ready, meaning a significant increase in the speed of construction. In ancient times, knowledge of engineering trade secrets like this were what helped turn masons into secret society members, looked on as magicians of a kind.

In more modern times, a device of this type is called a Lewis, Lewisson, or Lewis Key. It has several parts to it, including two wedge-shaped pieces, a parallel-sided spacer, and a clevis with a pin. In today's usage, the device pictured is known as a Box Lewis, probably because the hole that it fits is box-shaped.

When it is installed in the stone, the Lewis doesn't belie its function—it looks as though the stone is merely suspended from a ring. Therefore, it can be used right in front of uninitiated nonmasons. This was a typical practice of Freemasons. For instance, the very famous picture of George Washington publicly laying the cornerstone of the Capitol

Most of the Lewis Key assembly is hidden in the stone, but it easily hoists a heavy block.

Building in 1793 shows a tripod with the stone suspended by a Lewis Key.

If you look carefully at the Lewis, you can also see the shape of a keystone, inverted. This practical symbolism would be evident to stonemasons throughout history.

There is plenty of evidence that Lewis devices were used by stonemasons as early as Roman times, since the holes are found in the tops of the stones from that era. One retired British engineer, as a graduate student in archeology, discovered a fabulous coincidence when he studied the

A 1754 effigy, built of Masonic tools, with Lewis Keys for "hands."

Lewis holes in a bridge built by the Romans near Tyne, in northern England, and a harbor structure not far away, built in 1750, about fifteen hundred years later. It turned out that a model Lewis Key built to fit one of the structures, fit the other perfectly!

At least one authoritative Freemasonry reference book says the Freemasons contributed the term Lewis to the English language. Lewis has another special meaning in Freemasonry: son of a Freemason.

In a Freemason lodge room, a common fixture is a small replica of a tripod, hoisting tackle and stone block, called an ashlar, suspended on a Lewis Key.

Could it be that a Lewis Key is the secret device that allows the stone door to be opened in the vaulted treasure cellar under the Temple of Solomon?

Chapter Three

BUILDING THE VIRTUAL TEMPLE: THE POSSIBLE PHILOSOPHICAL, SPIRITUAL, AND IDEOLOGICAL THEMES

U P TO THIS point, we have been pursuing leads because they seem to give us quick answers about the meaning of *Widow's Son* or *Solomon's Key*. But readers of *A&D* and *DVC* know that Dan Brown weaves a rich philosophical tapestry as the backdrop of his Langdon novels. The "total experience" of *DVC* is not just to decode the cryptex, but also to absorb history, religion, and philosophy from a variety of ages. Dan Brown's technique of suspended action with each chapter break, combined with a plot that takes place in less than twenty-four hours, is a disguise. It keeps you from noticing how many pages are devoted to descriptions of history or art or religion. But it is this backdrop that makes the reading experience so fulfilling.

Right up front, I am going to reveal the "secret" of this part of the book. We are about to build a temple. It is not a real temple, so we are not confined to any particular floor plan, historical setting, or architectural style. It is a temple in the mind, with rooms of religion, philosophy, science, and mathematics, from all ages.

There will be a lot of talk about the Temple of Solomon, which probably was a real temple at one time, but has long since become a symbol, a kind of paradigm for all temples everywhere. There will be many other symbols in the temple, shorthand devices to represent large ideas with a mnemonic like a cross or a rose.

I know that if we were to look for the true foundations of this temple, we would be searching for levels that were laid down before recorded history. So I will look only at the blocks that form the first visible level. This means we can talk about the Hellenic and Roman eras, the Middle Ages, the Renaissance, and the Enlightenment periods.

When the temple is almost completed, I am going to call in a helicopter. (It will be the world's biggest helicopter, of course, since this is only virtual.) It will pick up our temple from an undisclosed, secure location in Europe, and transport it to America, just in time for the outbreak of the Revolution.

As we will see, it will take a lot of different contributions to build this temple. But if you had to pick one group that knows all about building a virtual temple of this kind, it would have to be the Freemasons. At their allegorical heart, they are temple builders. In Freemasonry, by the way, the word *temple* is construed as a "place to get your bearings, to reorient yourself." Using the symbolism of building a temple in his inner life, the Freemason improves himself, and then goes forth, well-oriented, to help build the temples of daily life.

Because Freemasonry borrowed its ideas from a rich blend of sources, it will seem to be a jumble of architectural styles at times, incongruously putting Egyptian motifs alongside Druid ones, or the like. This is also true of the way Freemasonry has borrowed a collection of the world's philosophies.

Long before the United States was a gleam in anyone's eye, there were the principles that it was founded on. Historians can easily see how the Magna Carta of 1215 carried its meaning forward to 1776 in Philadelphia. The centuries-long conflict between the natural rights of man and the divine right of kings and popes, which had been building up steam for hundreds of years in Europe, was essentially declared over in the American Constitution, which boldly began with the words, "We the people..."

What is less known, and thereby a tantalizing subject for Dan Brown, is how Freemasonry has also been one of the many long threads that tie the history of the Old World with the New. The philosophical foundations of the American Revolution—and, in fact, the high ideals of rationalism, science, separation of church and state, the wonders of nature—were reflections of the foundations of Freemasonry.

❧ *The Matrix of Masons* ❧

First and foremost, Freemasonry can connect so many lives, past and present, that it could simply seem to be a conspiracy to anyone who looks at it from the outside. Take any walk of life, and there will be a prominent Mason represented.

Recognize any names on the following list?

Buzz Aldrin, Louis Armstrong, Neil Armstrong, Steven F. Austin, Gene Autry, Count Basie, Ernest Borgnine, Jim Bowie, Omar Bradley, Kit Carson, Winston Churchill, Roy Clark, Buffalo Bill Cody, Davy Crockett, Bob Dole, Arthur Conan Doyle, Duke Ellington, Sam Ervin, W. C. Fields, Benjamin Franklin, Jesse Helms, J. Edgar Hoover, Bob Hope, Harry Houdini, Sam Houston, John Glenn, Barry Goldwater, Gus Grissom, Burl Ives, John Paul Jones, Rudyard Kipling, Charles Lindbergh, Trent Lott, Douglas MacArthur, Thurgood Marshall, Wolfgang Amadeus Mozart, Audie Murphy, Sam Nunn, Arnold Palmer, Norman Vincent Peale, Paul Revere, Will Rogers, Franklin D. Roosevelt, Theodore Roosevelt, Peter Sellers, John Philip Sousa, Potter Stewart, Dave Thomas, Mel Tillis, Harry S. Truman, Earl Warren, George Washington, John Wayne.

That's just a very small selection of famous Masons, mostly from American Freemasonry. There is a myth that membership is secret, but the truth is that Masons in modern America are proud of their membership and never hide it. But they aren't likely to brag about it, either. So, by paying careful attention, you can find out whether someone is a Mason.

Currently, there are about 1.7 million Masons in the United States and about 2.5 million more worldwide. Due to a general downturn in fraternal organization membership in the past few decades, you will mainly find Masons among the "mature" generation. American Freemasonry peaked at about 4 million in 1980.

In grand conspiracy theories, the Freemasons have long plotted to take over the world. But the conspiracy theory immediately breaks down, since Masons are not governed by a single central council, but rather by a number of separate and autonomous units. Some of these cooperate, and some do not even recognize one another. Historically, Masons have splintered and splintered again over the centuries, and some pieces have never rejoined the whole, although the general nature of American Freemasonry is cooperative. (One of the blots on their sometimes enlightened record, for instance, is their failure to universally recognize the Prince Hall Freemasons, who are black.)

There are supposed to be secrets in Freemasonry, but the brotherhood has been "outed" so many times that there is practically nothing one cannot learn about their rituals, passwords, or symbols. Within a few decades of their existence, people were already "exposing" the rituals. One of the most famous, *Masonry Dissected*, published by Samuel Prichard in 1730, was printed and circulated so widely that it became the easiest way for a Freemason to get a copy of his own "secret" rituals!

In my search, it was rather easy to assemble all the major initiation rites, instructional materials prepared

by Masons for Masons, plus many articles by
Freemasons explaining the history of the brotherhood
and its context in general history. All this is available
on the Internet, and you can read books on it. A well-
stocked library will have a whole shelf about
Freemasonry. Unfortunately, some of the books will
be bogus, written by either incompetent historians or
people with a grudge. There is even a special category
of writing by Freemasons who don't know what they
are talking about—well-meaning fellows who are just
not skeptical enough.

I read, and very much admired, Professor David
Stevenson's *The Origins of Freemasonry*. This describes
the period of 1590 to 1710, when Freemasonry was
incubating in Scotland. I also read and admired
Revolutionary Brotherhood, by Steven C. Bullock,
describing Freemasonry as it relates to the American
Revolution.

I also took a trip to the fabled House of the Temple in
Washington, D.C., home of Freemasonry's Supreme
Council 33°, Southern Jurisdiction, of the Scottish
Rite. There I was given a tour and briefing by Arturo de
Hoyos, Grand Archivist and Grand Historian, who
isn't anything like his title. Art is both friendly and
unassuming. But when Art quoted the exact issue of
the *Pennsylvania Gazette* in which Benjamin Franklin
published Masonic rituals in the 1730s, or broke into
Hebrew to quote some Scripture, I just knew I wasn't
looking at an *ordinary* historian! I also met with Art's
associate, S. Brent Morris, an accomplished writer and
historian, and together they brought out some of the
brighter aspects of Freemasonry. However, they were

House of the Temple in Washington, D.C.,
home of the Scottish Rite's Southern
Jurisdiction.

also willing to deal head-on with the anti-Masonic accusations and conspiracy theories. I could sense their strong belief in the facts.

Freemasonry in modern America is fundamentally focused on charitable work. Freemasons give about $2 million *per day* to all kinds of charities, assisting children, the elderly, and many others. Masonic homes often serve the families of Freemasons, but many other institutes (such as the burn centers funded by the fun-loving Masonic group known as the Shriners) are for the benefit of everyone. A Freemason is involved in giving—both of his time and his wealth—to his community, his country, and to the world.

All American Masons join a "Blue Lodge." This allows them to take the first three "degrees," rising from Entered Apprentice to Fellow Craft and then to the title of Master Mason. It is stressed that at the Master level, any Mason is equal to any other Mason. In the United States, Blue Lodges are organized into state-level Grand Lodges—fifty-one in all (including

Washington, D.C.)—each "sovereign" unto itself.

However, one can go on to pursue other "Rites" to
earn further degrees. In the so-called York Rite, there
are ten added degrees (beyond the first three), while in
the Scottish Rite, there are twenty-nine degrees that
one can earn (fourth through thirty-second), and a
final, thirty-third degree that is conferred by the
governing Supreme Council only as an honor. The
York and Scottish Rites represent different systems
that arose circa 1806, but no ill will comes of pursuing
either Rite. Some gung-ho Masons even take all the
York degrees and all the Scottish degrees.

To the utter confusion of outsiders, it is possible to
hyper-jump from the third degree to the thirty-second
in one day. That is because the main "work" of
earning the degree is to watch and learn from an allegorical play. The rituals are typically playlets that the
Mason absorbs as self-improvement instruction.

Also, the Scottish Rite is divided into the
"Northern Masonic Jurisdiction," based in Lexington,
Massachusetts, and the "Southern Jurisdiction," based
in Washington, D.C. For the purposes of our story, the
fact that Washington, D.C., is the headquarters of the
Southern Scottish Rite Masons is not without significance. The York Rite is associated with divisions
such as the Royal Arch Masons, the Cryptic Masons,
and the Knights Templar.

Knights Templar? Yes, in America, there are many
Knights Templar. While some "Templars" happily
assert that they can trace their origins to the first
Knights Templar (so important to the plot of
DVC), the Masonic variety do not. This Masonic

organization specifically requires that its members be Christians. The group claims 1,600 chapters, called Commanderies, in the United States, Mexico, Germany, and Italy, comprising 260,000 members. When they meet, it is called a Grand Encampment. Because you are required to be a Master Mason to join, a member of the Knights Templar will also hold Blue Lodge membership.

Just to provide the ultimate in confusion, there are a number of alternative Knights Templar organizations in America as well as Europe, totally unconnected to Freemasonry. Most commonly, the emblem for these KTs is a traditional double cross of red on a field of white or a red Maltese cross, whereas the Masonic KTs may use a variety of crosses and symbols, including a triple cross.

I like to imagine, then, the delight of an author like Dan Brown, knowing that he could easily call up as characters fully garbed Knights Templar, with swords and regalia, practically anywhere in the United States (or the world, for that matter), and have them interact by conspiracy and infiltration.

❧ Symbols of Masons ❧

Maltese crosses and double or triple crosses may be of significance to Templar Masons, but the symbology of Freemasonry is practically never ending.

Very important shapes to a Mason are the circle, the square, the triangle. Symbolic language is as important to the history of Freemasons as it is to Robert Langdon. Anything from a five-pointed star to a beehive, from a serpent to a double-headed eagle, from the sun to the moon, is a Masonic symbol. Masons don't stop at five-pointed stars; there is equal meaning in six-, seven-, eight-, or nine-pointed stars.

The sun, or a sunlike "glory" of rays, is a fundamental and ubiquitous symbol representing the light of knowledge. (For conspiracy buffs, this of course builds a word-bridge from *enlightenment* to *illumination* and thence to *Illuminati*.)

Masonic tools are supremely important symbols. Always, there is the compass and the square. The compass allows one to scribe a circle. That circle symbolizes the boundaries of one's self, i.e., knowing one's limitations. The square allows the Mason to build his life virtuously, true and square. To this may be added the letter "G," representing both God and geometry. And there may be a trowel, a level, a mallet (gavel), and chisel. Masons say they "meet on the level and part on the square," meaning they always meet as equals and part in true friendship.

Circles and squares are found throughout Masonic symbology, and they relate to themes Dan Brown has frequently addressed. In *DVC*, the Vitruvian Man symbol (somewhat misapplied by Brown) embodies the artistic "squaring the circle." Its aim was to discover fundamental proportions of the human body using a square and a circle that had a known relationship.

Where ordinary people see just numbers, Scottish Rite Freemasons have a deeper meaning for three, five, seven, and nine. It is common to see three sets of three items, such as columns or turreted towers. There are

A CLOSER LOOK

TRADITIONAL SYMBOLS OF FREEMASONRY

List of the most common Freemason symbols:

- ◆ An all-seeing eye *
- ◆ The sun
- ◆ The crescent moon, usually associated with seven stars
- ◆ A drawing compass and small carpenter's square
- ◆ A capital "G"
- ◆ A mason's level
- ◆ Two columns, possibly labeled Jachin and Boaz, or just J and B
- ◆ A stone arch with a prominent keystone, often bridging the two columns
- ◆ An altar with a holy book, such as the Bible, the Torah, or the Koran
- ◆ A rough-hewn block of stone
- ◆ A smoothly finished cube of stone (at times, the cube will have a pyramid-shaped top)
- ◆ A checkerboard floor
- ◆ Three small columns, in a triangular arrangement, of differing heights, with one each as capitals (column tops): a Doric, an Ionic, and a Corinthian
- ◆ A five-pointed star
- ◆ A six-pointed star
- ◆ A ladder, usually with three rungs
- ◆ A beehive
- ◆ A stonemason's mallet and chisel
- ◆ A symbolic representation of the Pythagorean theorem (Euclid's 47th), using a right triangle—often a 3-4-5 triangle—showing squares drawn from each side.

*Despite the numerous allegations about the symbols on the U.S. dollar bill, the all-seeing eye in Freemasonry is not associated with an unfinished pyramid, according to Freemasonry's best scholars.

symbols of duality, also, such as the twin pillars Boaz and Jachin. A lot of symbology hearkens back to the original masons who built the Temple of Solomon, according to sacred geometric principles. But some of the numerology is borrowed from Pythagoreans and from Kabbalists (see Appendix A, Symbolic Systems).

Masons wear richly decorated aprons in their ceremonies. These are symbolic of the cloth or leather aprons of hard-working stonemasons, but the traditional Freemason apron is soft, white lambskin. The apron is worn along with a black suit and white gloves and, at times and for various ranks, medals, swords, sashes, and "jewels," which are often complex clusters of symbology.

A rose can signify Venus, the Christian Virgin, or even "the final illumination at the last stage of a spiritual quest." A rose on a cross, clearly evocative of the Rosicrucians, is also Masonic and signifies a degree called Rose Croix.

References to the rose as a symbol for all these things are reiterated many times throughout DVC. Because I had looked for flaws in Dan Brown's books, I had been skeptical of the many times that he brings talk of the rose symbol into a discussion of the Goddess legends, or Venus or the Virgin Mary, in a kind of loose association. But I have now seen so many examples of it in so many different places, that I believe in it—with a small caveat. I think that whenever you see a rose in art or architecture, you should suspect the meanings of Goddess, Venus, or Virgin. But you should then look deeper, to try to discover the complete meaning.

Any discussion of Freemasonry and symbology in

The all-seeing eye and unfinished pyramid of the U.S. dollar bill.

the United States eventually arrives at the assertion that the Great Seal of the United States, with its all-seeing eye and unfinished pyramid, is a Masonic symbol indicative of the complete infiltration of the Union by early Masons, particularly the Illuminati branch. Patient Masonic scholars have explained to me that it just isn't so, but the explanation is unsexy, compared to the myth.

For the record, Freemasonry does use the all-seeing eye, but not juxtaposed with an unfinished pyramid. The all-seeing eye doesn't belong to the Illuminati, since it is much older that that, by thousands of years. But the myth survives because the "proof" is on every dollar bill, and Dan Brown has already referred to this myth as fact in his works.

☙ *Origins of Freemasonry* ❧

Freemasonry is a philosophy added onto a practical

craft. Both of these took thousands of years to come to fruition, if you look for the true roots.

To focus on the practical craft, it's clear, of course, that there have been masons for perhaps five thousand years, since there are stone structures in Egypt and the Middle East to prove it. Greeks and Romans, with their celebrated architecture, were relative latecomers in this context. All of the famous cathedrals and palaces of Europe, not to mention modern skyscrapers, occupy only the last fifth (or less) of the history of masonry.

Certain crafts tend to attract more respect than others, and masons over the centuries tended to rise to the top of the building crafts. Stonecutting may seem like a simple task, but it takes both knowledge and skill.

To get a sense of the required humility, just imagine you're standing next to a large rock with a hammer and chisel and think about what you would do to make it into a smooth, squared cube of stone. If you're honest with yourself, you will realize you don't have the slightest clue what to do next. With this humility, you might make a good apprentice mason.

Apprentice stonemasons were taught how to cut squared stones, and journeymen stonemasons— eventually called fellow crafts—had more skills. By the time one became a master mason, and particularly in the context of the great cathedrals, it was expected that a man could carve intricate ornamental work in stone, including statuary such as gargoyles and grotesques. In fact, the great stonemasons could carve these *freehand* (and a few are alive today who still can).

The experienced master masons on the very big

A CLOSER LOOK

POINDEXTER AND THE IAO

IN AN interview about A&D on the danbrown.com Web site, Dan Brown made this intriguing observation:

> Fortunately, I recently learned of another U.S. intelligence agency, more covert even than the National Security Agency. This new agency will figure prominently in the next novel. Until then, of course, mum's the word.

For a long time, I was stumped by this clue, and I am not totally sure I have found the answer. However, there is one outfit—and a unique individual running it—that does seem to fill the bill for Brown's covert agency. It is the Information Awareness Office (IAO) within the Defense Advanced Research Projects Agency (DARPA). DARPA is the forward-thinking branch of the Defense Department that can rightfully brag about at least two big accomplishments: creation of the network that evolved into the Internet, and development of the Stealth series of aircraft, not to mention many other new technology developments.

The IAO was a new arm of DARPA created in the months after 9/11.

Picked to head it was an enigmatic "spook," Vice Admiral John M. Poindexter. If there were ever a single modern figure who could pose as a model for an arch Illuminati worthy of a Dan Brown novel, I think it would be John Poindexter.

ABOVE: In the hands of IAO's John Poindexter, the symbols acquire a sinister, "Big Brother" meaning.

Poindexter is extremely bright, extremely computer-savvy, has occupied top government positions, and is an admitted dissembler (a fancy word for "liar"). He is "Mr. Disinformation." He once lied to his own fellow staffers in the White House about the invasion of Grenada. He was Oliver North's boss in the infamous Reagan-era Iran-Contra affair and later admitted that he falsified a cover story so as to provide "plausible deniability" for President Reagan.

Poindexter was working in private industry when the events of 9/11 gave him a shot at rehabilitation with the Pentagon. With a reported budget of $200 million, Poindexter had a plan for about a dozen high-tech programs, the sort that would scan the e-mails and the personal and financial information of huge numbers of people. But perhaps more chilling was the IAO home page that was put onto the Web, with a logo reportedly designed by Poindexter himself.

It is worth looking at the details. It shows the famous dollar bill symbol, the "unfinished pyramid and all-seeing eye," shining its rays upon a globe. Surely by no coincidence, the region of the globe in view is the Middle East. The motto in Latin is *Scientia Est Potentia*, which translates as "Knowledge is power," a quote attributed to Francis Bacon, but having a very ominous Big Brother meaning in the current context.

When the Web site and the IAO programs got national attention in November 2002, there was an immediate uproar, and the logo was promptly expunged from the Web site (only to be preserved by web bloggers and esoterica buffs). However, the IAO itself continued until 2003, when Poindexter was forced to resign after a scandal over a controversial new program, a futures exchange that would have bet on gambles like the possibility of Arab leaders being assassinated.

It should be noted, however, that observers believe most of his programs were not totally killed. Rather, they may have been redistributed to other DARPA offices or even other agencies. (In fact, if you were a deep conspiracy theorist, why would you even believe IAO has been disbanded? Is anyone keeping watch on Poindexter?)

projects (which sometimes took one hundred years or more to build) would learn a lot more than stone-cutting skills. The ones who served as Master of the Works would study architecture, along with geometry, mathematics, and quite a number of other aspects of science and art. They shared their knowledge with fellow masons when possible.

Thus, by the sixteenth century, if not long before, stonemasons claimed a higher status than other craftsmen. Also, it was already common for masons to be organized into lodges and to have a rudimentary form of self-government within the lodge system. Since building a cathedral or palace required many skilled masons, it was accepted that they would travel and stay at the job site. This was different from, say, an ironwright, who might never leave a given village. Consequently, the term *freemason*, as a stonecutter free to travel, was already commonly heard in the sixteenth century when the craft began to change.

The age of building stone cathedrals was in full swing from about 1100 to 1500 and then it tapered off. It is generally believed that the hotbed of change from practical masonry to symbolic masonry was Scotland at the end of the sixteenth century. For a large part of the seventeenth century, the system incubated in Scotland and found fertile soil in England, where signs of the change had been spotted frequently.

Masons' lodges began to attract men who were never going to cut a stone or wield a trowel. They began to accept members who were not actually stonemasons, and this trend rapidly got out of hand when the noncraft members began to outnumber the

BUILDING THE VIRTUAL TEMPLE 59

craft members in some lodges. A working mason
became known as an "operative" member, while the
others were called "speculative" members. Lodges of
the latter type were "symbolic" lodges.

In 1717, a gentlemen's fraternity of Freemasonry
was formally founded by a transformation of four
lodges in London, into symbolic lodges, forming the
Grand Lodge. This was the movement that took hold
and grew, eventually reaching global proportions.

In the context of Dan Brown's novels, the nascent
Freemasons could also be seen in other poses. For
instance, one could view the Freemasons as the
antithesis of the Church, a refuge from its hegemony
over intellectual cosmology and philosophical
thought. In *A&D* particularly, this is what allows Dan
Brown to put the Freemasons (and the Illuminati) on
the side of science, and therefore "against" religion.

As we have seen so far, the brothers who invoked
the "Widow's Son" plea could call on one another
through secrets and symbols, the very fuel that drives
Dan Brown's creative fires. But Freemasons also
derived certain social advantages from their
affiliation.

❧ Social Advantages of Being a Freemason ❧

In the eighteenth century, the social aspects of
Freemasonry offered men some real benefits in the age
when monarchs and prelates could no longer use
feudal schemes to control the population, as the
merchant class rose to prominence.

It was a time of societal strife. People needed a safe

haven for social interaction. Religious wars in England and on the Continent had decimated whole populations. One of the greatest attractions of a Freemasonry lodge was the opportunity for a "boys' night out" for men of very different religions and philosophies to talk politely about any topic under the sun, while sipping wine or beer. (However, today's Freemasons neither drink within their temples nor discuss politics or religion.)

More important, there was a change taking place in the way that men gained and held social standing. The older system of royal birthright had built-in limits. Meanwhile, the spread of literacy, commerce, and some allowance for leisure activities among "commoners" meant that they could create social groups with at least modest pretensions. There were actually lots of men's fraternal organizations, literary societies, and the like, but the Freemasons offered a mixture of symbology, morality, friendship, and fun that satisfied many tastes. There were plenty of lords and earls among the membership in England, and yet there were plenty of merchants, lawyers, and tradesmen. Likewise, when Freemasonry caught on among military men, there were lodges where colonels, sergeants, and privates could all mingle.

For an upcoming member of the merchant class, Freemasonry was a way to demonstrate that he could "improve" himself, attaining the refinement of a gentleman. In the ceremonies—which eventually became grand public processions—the Freemasons could wear regalia such as regal-looking sashes and jewels, and even swords (hitherto the mark of royalty).

Undoubtedly the real royals among them must have been amused, particularly with the rest of a Freemason's costume, which included an apron and white gloves. They sometimes carried a ceremonial trowel and occasionally even a wand. Undoubtedly, this amused the real stonemasons as well, among those few who remained in the lodges.

❧ Foundations of Masonic Philosophy ❧

So far, we have been looking at the overt part of Freemasonry, the surface veneer. What will surely interest Dan Brown are the deeper roots of Masonic philosophy, particularly how it connects to ancient, pagan beliefs.

Behind the scenes, some very powerful themes were being developed in support of Freemasonry. Interestingly, no one has been able to positively identify the authors of the Freemasons' rituals and lore. Some of it, such as the stories tracing their origins back to the Temple of Solomon, might be part of the oldest legends of real stonemasons, although even this could have been merely an attempt to make the legend appear ancient. But other parts of it were definitely brought in fresh, then sorted, sifted, and assembled into a coherent system.

The melting pot of Freemasonry has at least these ingredients:

Greek philosophy, science, and mathematics
Geometry, especially from Euclid and Pythagoras
Terms and themes of stonemasonry

Biblical literature, especially favoring Hebrew
    Scriptures
Kabbalah, an ancient Jewish system of mysticism
Astrology
The symbolism of alchemy
Hermeticism, said to derive from Hermes
    Trismegistus, a mythical figure sometimes said
    to be the Egyptian god Thoth
"Egyptian" culture (as far as was known)
"Druidism" (as far as was known)
Eastern religions and philosophies (as far as they
    were known)

It's certainly not going to be possible now to figure
out who the authors of the rituals and lore were. But
there are a number of "suspects" and some of them were
brilliant and famous men. In the following pages, I will
talk about a number of these suspects, both usual and
unusual.

❧ Enhancing Mental Powers ❧

A central Dan Brown theme in *A&D* and *DVC* is the
antagonism between science and religion. In *A&D*, we
learn that the Catholic Church supposedly persecuted
scientists, resulting in a four-hundred-year-old grudge.
This was supposedly based on the gruesome killings of
four scientists that occurred in the time of Galileo.

Galileo lived from 1564 to 1642. He was brought
before the Inquisition and placed under a long house
arrest, but there isn't any information to support the
tale of the four scientists.

What there is, is the life of Giordano Bruno, who lived from 1548 to 1600 and was, in fact, burned at the stake in Rome, as ordered by the Church. It was Bruno's trial and death that the Inquisition authorities remembered when they confronted Galileo.

Bruno was a Dominican monk gone amok, from the Church point of view. He became a kind of free-thinking, radical intellectual who could not, and would not, be silenced. His inability to just plain shut up got him in trouble with authorities wherever he went, so that eventually he earned the odd distinction of being excommunicated from three faiths—Catholic, Lutheran, and Calvinist.

Bruno is also famous for proposing that "innumerable suns exist; innumerable earths revolve around these suns in a manner similar to the way the seven planets revolve around our sun. Living beings inhabit these worlds." This makes him a kind of martyr figure for lots of scientists, such as those searching for extraterrestrial life.

History has a way of compressing several thoughts into one, so that the fight over whether the earth was the center of the universe or revolved around the sun got tangled into our collective perception about Galileo, Copernicus, and others. One of the figures tangled up in this was Bruno. In fact, Bruno wasn't burned by the Church for this kind of thinking, but for other heretical ideas, perhaps the most important being that "Christ was not God but merely an unusually skillful magician," in the words of one religious scholar.

Before the Church killed him for that kind of talk,

they kept him in a dungeon for six years, in a famous place for readers of *A&D*: the bowels of the Castel Sant'Angelo in Rome, site of the secret Illuminati room and the fight between Langdon and the Hassassin.

But Bruno was famous for other works. He worked with a number of influences as a neo-Platonist, reviving Greek philosophy and science, but he also wove in some mysticism. And he traveled, popping up in Switzerland, France, and England. In 1584, he was certainly notorious in London and Oxford. After having been turned down in a bid to lecture at Oxford, he wrote an attack on the professors there, saying they "knew more about beer than about Greek."

In 1580, Bruno wrote the *Clavis Magna*, or *Great Key*. It was about a mind-altering technique called the Art of Memory.

❦ *Temple of Memory* ❦

The Art of Memory came from the Greeks, and was written about by Cicero, among others. Here's the basic idea. Suppose you have to listen to a great speech or perhaps make a great speech, and you don't have the ability to write it down. You need to memorize it, but it's long and complex.

What you do first is explore a great building such as a temple (or later, perhaps, a cathedral). Go into each room in turn and look at the statues, the decorations, etc. Always take the same path on your tour of the temple. Become so familiar with the temple that you can envision all this, even if you never see the temple again. While you contemplate the temple mentally, populate it with even more symbols, taken from things that may be significant only to you. You might put a cow, a cornstalk, or a flaming cauldron into one of the rooms, for instance.

Now, as you deal with the speech, take the first part of it and mentally assign it to the first room of your temple, attaching each idea to a symbol you have mentally placed in that room. When it's time to regurgitate the speech, just take another mental tour of your temple!

The study of the Art of Memory was emerging when Bruno wrote about it. It had appeared in certain works by 1482, and a scholar named Guillo Camillo was famous in Italy and France for spreading word of the technique. Camillo died in 1544, just a generation before Bruno, so it is likely that Bruno knew his work.

Camillo even built wooden models of memory-temples, using a classical theater concept from the first-century BC Roman architectural scholar Vitruvius, and mixing in biblical influences, such as the Seven Pillars in Solomon's House of Wisdom.

Vitruvius is significant in *DVC*. Leonardo da Vinci's drawing of the "Vitruvian Man" solved the challenge of combining human proportions into a circle and a square, a challenge that had been posed many centuries earlier in a work by Vitruvius. Saunière, the murdered curator of the Louvre, is found posed as the Vitruvian Man at the beginning of *DVC*.

In Bruno's hands, the memory-temple would be populated with symbology, including icons of the occult, and a philosophy stemming from Hermetics, which now could be construed as a way to achieve oneness with God.

Looked at in a longer tradition, the construction of a memory-temple was a modification of another way of remembering things with a symbolic system, the Zodiac, in which the sun travels through the various "houses" of the stars (see Appendix A, Symbolic Systems).

Using the Zodiac as a memory-temple, one can store the names of hundreds of stars, for example. If you knew this trick and studied "medicine" in the Middle Ages, you might associate certain herbs or incantations with one of the *sigils* (the ancient symbols) of the Zodiac. If you were into Tarot cards during the Renaissance, the cards would also contain a system of image associations. There are a lot of ways to look at the memory-temple principle.

A supporter and disciple of Bruno during his stay in England was a Scotsman named Alexander Dickson. Dickson was such a believer that he gave people practical lessons in improving their memories. According to Scottish professor David Stevenson in his book *The Origins of Freemasonry*, there were other Scots besides Dickson who served in the courts of Mary Queen of Scots and later, James VI of Scotland. One, William Fowler, studied the Art of Memory and may have even taught it to the king.

Among members of the same court was the Master of the Works, William Schaw, famous for writing the *Statutes* in 1598 and 1599 that formally governed Freemasonry in Scotland. Schaw's *Statutes* said that Freemasons in a certain Scottish lodge were to be tested in the Art of Memory and were to be fined if they did not pass. So it sure looks as though Bruno talked to Dickson, who talked to Fowler, who talked to Schaw, and the Art of Memory was inserted into early Freemasonry.

I think it is worth a pause of amazement here. An idea reaching back to the Greeks, brought forward into Italy, finds a path all the way to Freemasonry in Scotland, where it gets thrown into the stewpot of ideas and philosophies. (And this stewpot, by the way, will feed the American Revolution.) Dan Brown must have had a feast in trying to figure out what among all this to use.

❧ Sir Francis Bacon ❧

When Dan Brown picks his cast of likely historical suspects, he could find Sir Francis Bacon a worthy candidate.

Bacon was an early philosopher and pioneer of what would eventually be called the scientific method. It is important also to view him in the context of a world full of great discoveries, just over the horizon.

He not only figured in Freemasonry (in all likelihood), but also had direct connections to the New World and to his own concept of New World Order.

According to some (non-Masonic) scholars, Bacon could have been secretly the head of the early Freemasons. He was certainly in the right place at the right time, and was very influential. He was prominent in the court of Queen Elizabeth I, but also developed ties with two courtiers of the Scottish king James VI (who became James I of England). These two were William Schaw and Sir Robert Moray, both very important figures in the beginnings of Freemasonry.

According to many theories, Bacon also was among the earliest of German Rosicrucians, perhaps even serving as president. This secret order hit the public mind with the publication around 1616 of the *Alchemical Marriage*, purportedly by a Christian Rosenkreutz (an obvious pseudonym—the surname is German for "rosy cross").

As a young man, Bacon received instruction in a number of arcane subjects from Dr. John Dee, perhaps the foremost magus in England at the time. From Dee he learned the gematria of the Kabbalah, which led him to master codes and ciphers.

Dee was a mathematician, alchemist, cipher writer, and was adept in various sciences. He was the royal astrologer for Queen Elizabeth, advising her on matters as weighty as the date of her coronation in 1559 and her strategy for dealing with the Spanish Armada in 1588. There are strong connections that make Dee a likely source of the ideas that later emerged as Rosicrucianism in Germany.

While Bacon was a student of Dee's, he also traveled to Europe and was exposed to a wide variety of philosophy and science there. Queen Elizabeth died in 1603. Where Elizabeth had been interested in astrology and the occult, her successor, James I of England, looked on these subjects with disfavor, and Bacon was careful—or downright secretive—during the latter's reign.

The establishment of the colonial empire of Spain

throughout the sixteenth century meant that England had some catching up to do as the seventeenth century approached. The Spanish had conquered South America, Mexico, and parts of the western United States. Even the French had a strong presence in North America. In Bacon's time, English colonies were attempted at Roanoke, Virginia, in 1585 and in Newfoundland in 1610. Bacon, heavily into affairs of Parliament, had direct connections with the organization of these early colonies.

Bacon was deeply impressed by the fundamental significance of Columbus's voyages, and he saw a very strong symbolic message. For sailors who had confined themselves to the Mediterranean Sea, it had been a long-standing custom to call the approaches to the Straits of Gibraltar the Pillars of Hercules, and legend held that there was nothing beyond these "gates." However, by sailing to America, Columbus had demonstrated that there was something more, something beyond that horizon.

As a sign of this and its growing dominance of the seas, the Spanish crown took the motto *Plus Ultra* and the two pillars into its coat of arms. *Plus Ultra* means "more beyond," as in, "There's a lot more out there than we thought, and we Spaniards are going to grab it all!" This began with Ferdinand and Isabella and continued, most notably, under the Holy Roman Emperor Charles V—who, of course, felt a divine purpose.

Spain found gold in the New World and rather promptly started mining it and minting coins, among them the gold doubloon and silver *reale*. From a very early date—about 1537—these coins bore the Pillars of Hercules and *Plus Ultra*. The dominance of the "Spanish dollar" was overwhelming as time went on. In America during Colonial times and all the way through the Revolution, it was still the most available kind of money, and still had the pillars on it.

Bacon adopted the pillars and Plus Ultra into his own symbology. In several books, it appears in various adaptations, often showing a ship sailing out between two columns. But Bacon was also enamored of the pyramidal form, so sometimes the columns had tall pyramidal tops.

Bacon wrote a book called *New Atlantis*, in which he imagined a utopian society on a remote island. In a time of kings, Bacon described the society as being governed by a kind of committee of elders. The book also contains a description of a House of Solomon.

Take Bacon's concept and, if you put a bunch of the ideas of the day together, you could make an interesting legend. First, assume that some Lost Tribes of Israel are still wandering somewhere in the wilderness, looking for a home. Then fashion a new utopian colony—in the New World, of course—and populate it with people who now could be considered the Chosen People, descendants somehow of the Lost Tribes. This could be interpreted to mean that a colony in America, or a new religious faith, is the heir to the Kingdom of God.

Although a direct connection would never have been acknowledged by John Winthrop, the first governor of the Massachusetts Bay Colony, it was an idea of this nature that he put forth in his famous sermon of 1630, the "shining city on a hill" sermon, and in later writings. Many different sects and political movements would assert themselves as the anointed ones—and this practice continues today.

Bacon had a strong influence on other thinkers of his day, including John Locke. According to one scholar, Thomas Jefferson was so profoundly influenced by Bacon that he thought that by founding the United States, he was fulfilling Bacon's dreams in *New Atlantis*.

The experimental method figured in Bacon's death. It seems he stopped his carriage one cold day in 1626 to stuff a dead bird with snow, since he wanted to study the effect of cold on decomposition of animals. He caught bronchitis and died—a martyr of "science." Some years later, he would be revered among scientists in the Royal Society.

Dan Brown's books about Robert Langdon so far have not pointed directly at the Royal Society, but they have alluded to "persecuted scientists" in *A&D*, as well as a long-standing feud between the Catholic Church and Enlightenment thinkers, some of whom were scientists, in *DVC*. If Brown were going to search history for a scientific group that connected to the early Freemasons, he need look no further than the Royal Society.

⤃ Science Club ⤂

Around the mid-seventeenth century, a number of men in England formed a fraternity out of their mutual admiration for knowledge gained through "experimental" methods. They coalesced at Gresham College, starting in 1645, in informal meetings and lectures. They called themselves the "Invisible College" (a phrase that would echo in conspiracy theories for centuries to come).

Sir Thomas Gresham, founder of the college, had once been a General Warden of the Masons. He specifically mentioned geometry as among the areas of concentration for the college. It was a hallmark of Gresham College that its professors discussed practical applications. As such, they were known to work closely with the Royal Navy, helping to make better and more efficient ships, and to plumb the mysteries of global navigation—the very knowledge that would give Britain its dominance of the sea in later centuries.

It is said that, following a lecture by the highly influential Christopher Wren, twelve men met in the chambers of the professor of geometry at Gresham on November 28, 1660, and formed the group that would come to be called the Royal Society. Wren at the time was the Gresham professor of astronomy, but was to become a rebuilder of London after the fire of 1666, and his name is synonymous with great architecture.

The English crown was restored to Charles II in 1660, commencing the Restoration period. Among Freemasons was a famous Scot named Sir Robert Moray, who helped Charles II back into power and thus had the king's ear.

Moray approached the king and got approval for a royal charter for the new society, which was granted in

1662. Charles II not only liked the idea, he asked to be a member—talk about instant prestige!

There were thirty-five original Fellows of the society, including about nineteen scientists, as well as influential men, among them wealthy science buffs who were willing to pay the bills. Charles II was happy about that, since he was strapped for money at the time.

Among the scientists was Robert Boyle, known for the gas law of volume and pressure; William Petty, called the father of modern statistics; Laurence Rooke, who worked on methods of determining longitude (this was not solved for another hundred years, until the accomplishments of John Harrison). There were also students of antiquity, including Elias Ashmole; later, there would be William Stukeley.

Later joiners included the venerated Isaac Newton, who served as president from 1703 to his death in 1727. He was a source of many a spirited debate. The great philosopher John Locke was a member, as was Gottfried Wilhelm von Leibniz. When Benjamin Franklin came to England in 1757, he was welcomed with open arms by the Royal Society.

Moray, Wren, Ashmole, Stukeley, and Franklin were all Freemasons. Although it is disputed, Boyle, Newton, and Locke may have been Freemasons. So were many, many members of the Royal Society during its first two hundred years or so. It is completely fair to say that there was constant cross-fertilization between the two organizations.

Dan Brown cast Newton in *DVC* as a representative of the forces of science and reason, and made use of the inscription on his monument in Westminster Abbey

RELIGIOUS MASONS

THE MOST populous form of Freemasonry does not specifically require any particular religion, but merely requires that the member believe in a supreme being, known in Freemasonry as the Great Architect of the Universe, or GAOTU.

This means that the Holy Book found on the altar of each lodge may, at times, be a Bible, a Torah, or a Koran. Theoretically, any man of any religion can join the Freemasons, although certain churches, such as the Roman Catholic, have historically threatened excommunication to members who join.

But, since there is no central authority for Masonry, there are many separate orders of Freemasons, and some of these may be specifically oriented to one religion. Going back to the times when stonemasons built the great cathedrals, the mason lodges would have been devoutly Catholic.

In fact, some early Christians, specifically those who were persecuted by the Romans, may have actually been martyred masons. As the tale goes, in AD 298 the Emperor Diocletian intended to build a temple to honor Aesculapius, the god of health. Five masons were told to create the statue for the temple, but they refused, since they were secretly Christians and would not craft a statue of a pagan god. They were executed. The emperor found other artisans to do the work. Two years later, in a grand ceremony to honor the finished statue, the army and militia were ordered to march past it and throw incense on the altar as an offering to the pagan god. Four master masons among the militia, again secret Christians, refused to do so and were executed. They became known as the Quatuor Coronati, or the Four Crowned Martyrs.

They were perhaps not the only sanctified masons. Recent scholarly arguments have been put forth to assert that Jesus might actually not have been the son of a carpenter, but a mason!

According to this notion, the Gospel of Matthew (13:55) refers to

Joseph as a *tekton* in Greek. In English-language Bibles, the word has traditionally been taken to mean "carpenter" but it actually can mean any "craftsman," such as a bricklayer, stonemason, or carpenter. Indeed, a worker of this kind often learned all these skills.

Freemasons honor the feast days of both John the Apostle (December 27) and John the Baptist (June 24), but it is the latter saint who has gotten the bigger celebration.

On June 24, Freemasons celebrated St. John the Baptist's birthday with fireworks and salutes, solemn processions, and revelries. The date lies around the summer solstice, midsummer, which in pagan observance was celebrated by wild dancing and revelry. It is said that the Catholic Church positioned the feast day of St. John in order to replace the wild pagan observance with a more somber one.

Besides the Knights Templars, the other great order that arose from the Crusades was known as the Knights Hospitallers, and they inherited certain lands and assets when the Templars were dispersed by the pope and French king after 1307. Their longer name is the Order of Knights of the Hospital of St. John of Jerusalem, and their patron saints were John the Baptist and Mary Magdalene.

Jesus and his cousin John the Baptist may have been members of the Essene sect. In the tradition of some adherents, Jesus actually broke off from the true faith, while John kept it. In an odd twist of history, these adherents carried on through the millennia as the Mandaens, misunderstood by Muslims and Christians alike, and are now found mainly in Iraq.

to lead Langdon and Sophie to the clue that finally opens the cryptex.

✎ Early Eclectic Influences in Scientific Development ✎

Some of the inspiration that made the early scientists brave enough to challenge the Church's domination came from sources that were not strictly scientific. Some of these influences may be fodder for Dan Brown's next book.

One of the wellsprings of philosophy in Restoration times was Hermeticism. It had been known in ancient times. A concise expression was said to have been written on an Emerald Tablet, or large green crystal, which had been lost. It may have been buried secretly on the plains of Giza, Egypt, before AD 400, in the time when the newly "Christian" Roman empire was seeking to obliterate other religious traditions.

The tablet was said to contain a mere thirteen lines, and so it was certainly plausible that it could be hidden and preserved, to emerge centuries later. Copies of these verses were circulated among scholars and alchemists in the sixteenth and seventeenth centuries. Referencing a mythical Hermes Trismegistus (thrice-great Hermes), who was also linked to the Egyptian god Thoth, the philosophy was expressed: "As above, so below."

The meaning of this is that the world below (earth) is patterned after the world above (the cosmos). Further, divine fire (knowledge or enlightenment) flows between the two. It could be taken to mean that man can aspire to be godlike, or "perfectible." It could also be interpreted as alchemical, giving veiled instructions about how to create the Philosopher's Stone.

Very significantly, two adepts (masters of occult knowledge) who were known to have translated the Emerald Tablet were Francis Bacon and Isaac Newton. Although not proved to be Freemasons, they were both part of the swirling currents of thought that flowed through Freemasonry. Here are a few lines from Newton's translation of about 1680:

> Tis true without lying, certain and most true.
> That which is below is like that wch is above and
>   that wch is above is like yet which is below to
>   do ye miracles of one only thing.
> And as all things have been and arose from one by
>   ye mediation of one: so all things have their
>   birth from this one thing by adaptation.

It must also be noted that among these scientists and adepts of the "experimental" method, sometimes *experiment* was a euphemism for *alchemy*.

Alchemy was not laughed at in those days. Many of the brightest minds among scholars and gentlemen were attracted to alchemy, not just because of the fabled lure of learning to turn lead into gold. Rather, they also saw it as a way to learn the secrets of the universe. Scientists as diverse as Newton and Franklin were interested in alchemy. Alchemists were, in essence, the first scientists, predating the Royal Society, as seen in the lives of John Dee and Francis Bacon, among others.

These men and others were eager for all kinds of knowledge. They absorbed such authors as Euclid, Plato, and Vitruvius. It was difficult to offer them a book that they would not read. John Dee, for instance, amassed a library of several thousand volumes at a time when the mighty Cambridge University had less than five hundred. Gentlemen of education began to travel and interact with one another, sharing knowledge.

One seeker of knowledge through books was actually an abbot of the Catholic Church who wrote about—and attempted to practice—black magic. This was Johannes Trithemius, a Benedictine who ran an abbey at Sponheim and later at Würzburg, Germany. He lived from 1462 to 1516. He accumulated a library of more than two thousand volumes. One of his own works, *Polygraphia*, is considered the first printed book on cryptography. In the massive three-volume *Steganographia*, Trithemius gives instructions in a system of communicating secrets through angels and demons. To do this, you conjure the appropriate angel or demon for the task, and you supply a cover message, as well as a secret message. You then send the cover message by courier to the receiver, who conjures the same angel or demon and receives the secret message. It's interesting to note that authorities from the Catholic Church simply omit all of these occult aspects when writing about Trithemius, so I see no evidence that this incredible coincidence was known to Dan Brown when he was writing *Angels & Demons*.

A student of Trithemius was a legendary Hermetic writer, Heinrich Cornelius Agrippa, who inherited

Trithemius's extensive library of books on magic. Agrippa melded the occult, Hermeticism and Kabbalah, medicine (particularly the use of herbs and natural medicine), astrology, and alchemy. He not only wrote major books on the marriage of these subjects, but also traveled and lectured extensively, so that his ideas surely spread throughout Europe, particularly after he gained access to a publishing patron. At one time or another, he was found in Germany, Switzerland, Italy, France, and Belgium, up until his mysterious death sometime after 1533.

In those days, one of the functions of a learned person who had occult and astrological skills was to predict the future. When Agrippa was in Lyon, France, in 1524, he was among astrologers who had overflow business because of a grand conjunction of planets. He ran afoul of his patron, the mother of King Francis, when he failed to give her a horoscope correctly predicting the outcome of a war with Charles V and the Bourbons (Agrippa predicted a loss). Influential people, including most royalty, were in the habit of hiring astrologers for all kinds of predictions, from the trivial to the earthshaking, such as wars, plagues, and other cataclysms.

Around 1640, a Portuguese-Jewish rabbi who had been brought up in Holland, Jacob Judah Leon, later known as Judah Templo, was thinking in terms of a coming millennium—when, according to Scripture, it would be necessary to rebuild the ancient Temple of Solomon, for the Messiah's Second Coming. In order to prepare, Leon consulted the Bible's descriptions. He also read the work of Flavius Josephus, the Jewish

historian who had been present at the destruction of
the Temple in AD 70.

Leon drew up plans and engravings that showed
the Temple, then went a step further and constructed
detailed models of it. He made pamphlets and even
promotional posters of his work, including portraits of
himself, which became famous around Holland. In
1675, Leon went to London, where, among other
audiences, he was able to give a presentation to
Christopher Wren.

Whether on his own or because of this transfer of
knowledge, Isaac Newton—friend and fraternal
brother of Wren's—later spent time making his own
sketches of the floor plan of the Temple.

None of this points to Newton or Wren as the ori-
ginators of the Solomon Temple myths in Freemasonry,

Isaac Newton and Christopher Wren
were among history's many students of
Solomon's Temple.

but it does clearly show a fascination with the Temple
among important English Freemasons of the time.

Likewise, William Stukeley, as a Freemason

interested in Stonehenge, may have contributed what influence there was of so-called Druid lore in the mixture of Masonic rituals. Stukeley, following in the footsteps of an earlier antiquarian named John Aubrey, was considered a good "field man" as an archeologist. But when it came to explaining who the builders of Stonehenge might have been, he went off into spasms of total invention. Stukeley was almost single-handedly responsible for assigning Stonehenge to the Druids (which was not correct), and then he went on to make up a rich Druid cultural history that didn't exist, either. It is said that Stukeley was so obsessed with Stonehenge that he had a replica erected in his backyard and, upon the death of one of his children, conducted a Druid burial ceremony at the altar there.

Stukeley was certifiably weird, but the Freemasons generally had behaviors that helped to spread suspicion and fear among the uninitiated.

For one thing, they had secret signs of recognition. To the public, this was truly eerie, because two Freemasons could approach each other and, before they were in speaking distance, could establish that they both belonged to "the craft." They would embrace and begin talking in coded ways, such as "We meet on the level." They would even whisper the "Word" to each other. (Styled as the password that got an operative mason admitted to a particular lodge at a great cathedral, the "Mason's Word" could be a number of secret passwords, although *Mahabyn* is probably the most common.)

Freemason lodges typically started life at taverns

and inns, so that drinking and carousing were not unfairly part of their early public image. One of the earliest artistic depictions of Freemasons shows a group outside a tavern, trying to navigate the raucous streets of London. It's a satirical treatment called *Night*, by William Hogarth, one of the era's most influential artists. Hogarth was a Freemason but was perhaps caught up in a period when the Freemasons were being mocked in London. All kinds of fraternities of the times were also drinking/debauchery clubs, so the Freemasons were not unique. There were even sex clubs in eighteenth-century England, including a very famous one that Benjamin Franklin is said to have visited.

However, as they developed, the Freemasons learned to distance themselves from this image. They banned drinking in their lodges and, in fact, they did study morality in their lodge "work," something very different from many other fraternities.

Freemasons met at night, and it was fairly common for lodges to select a monthly meeting date by picking the full moon. It was a practical way to get the best possible light for walking to and from the meetings, but it could be misconstrued as astrological or occult.

Tales leaked out that Freemasons were initiated in rituals involving symbolic death. This was true. In one ritual, the candidate is led in blindfolded, with a noose ("cable tow") around his neck. He has been deliberately made to look ridiculous. He has one shoe on, one off, and one pant leg up, the other down. His shirt is laid open at the left breast, and the point of a compass is pressed against it threateningly. He cannot see it, but a sword or dagger may be threatening him from behind. He is symbolically slain, laid into a coffin, then raised up or resurrected.

It should be mentioned here that fraternities of all kinds have rituals intended to scare the candidate and break down his resistance to fraternal ideas and secrets that will be introduced. This is an aspect of a college fraternity "hell week," and it is an accepted, if controversial technique in military training as well.

The public could tisk-tisk at the rituals on the level of "boys will be boys." But the leaks also brought news of the oath that Freemasons took. It was hard to shrug off. As conveyed to the public, it was truly bloodcurdling. One account gives the penalty for a Freemason breaking his oath:

"...my Heart pluck'd from my Left breast, my Tongue pluck'd from the roof of my mouth, my Throat cutt, my Body to be torn to pieces by Wild Horses, to be bury'd in the Sands of the Sea where the Tide flowes in 24 Hours, taken up and burn't to Ashes and Sifted where the four winds blow that there may be no more Remembrance of me."

However, this gruesome language was not considered the worst aspect of a Freemason's oath, believe it or not. Rather, it was the fact that the oath-taker gave his foremost allegiance to his craft, and not to God.

This was to become the source of never-ending turmoil for Freemasons, a controversy that is still quite alive today. It was originally among the reasons that Catholics were not supposed to become Freemasons, but the Church issued many dire warnings regarding other aspects of Freemasonry over the years. In the meantime, several other religious groups and denominations, including some Protestants, have become anti-Masonic. In addition to religious issues, there are many other angles for viewing, with suspicion, a man who does not swear his primary allegiance to your cause.

So far, we have covered some of the early influences on Freemasonry. We can see that it bubbled with a surprising combination of ancient legends already, but that more influences would be tossed into the mix. Because Dan Brown likes to jump all the way back to the beginning with one of Professor Langdon's short history lectures, we will not be slouching in the back of the lecture hall; we'll be up front, keeping the professor honest. But now we turn to a chapter of Freemasonry that was *not* honest. It was, in fact, nefarious and subversive.

☙ Real Illuminati ❧

Nowhere does the conflict between the Church and the combined forces of science and reason come into sharper focus than in the story of the Illuminati.

For the purposes of Dan Brown's Langdon novels (*A&D*, *DVC*), the Illuminati serve very well indeed as the mysterious hidden enemy (the enemy of the Catholic Church, if not, strictly speaking, the enemy of the protagonists of each novel). But the Illuminati legend also confirms how Freemasonry can be corrupted. And the Illuminati legend has great influence elsewhere, such as the Mormon mythology that sprang up decades later.

Although Illuminati-like references to "enlightened ones" can be found in a number of ancient settings, such as Persia, Egypt, and Spain, the organized formation of the Illuminati occurred in 1776, when Adam Weishaupt, a Bavarian college professor, launched the "Order of Perfectibilists," renamed immediately as "Illuminati."

It is said that Weishaupt, a professor of canon law who had been educated under the iron hand of the Jesuits, was influenced by stories of Pythagorean secret cults (see Appendix A, Symbolic Systems). In the context of Jesuit excesses, there was fertile soil for a religious and philosophical movement that would replace divine powers of prelate and monarch with the powers of the individual man, of science and reason.

Freemasonry had already spread widely in Europe, although it was often well distanced from the original Blue Lodges of London. What Weishaupt found in Freemasonry was a structure, a framework that he could infiltrate and manipulate for his deeper purposes. (According to some, he considered the secrets of Freemasonry to be too openly available for his order.)

At the heart of the Illuminati was a belief in the ability of man to secure his own salvation through self-improvement. This "perfectibility" had many antecedents in ancient religions, was implied in much of the lore of Freemasonry, and was adopted as part of the Mormon religion, not to mention other modern sects. But Weishaupt's goals involved a strong anti-Church (anti-Jesuit) passion as well.

From 1776 onward some seven or eight years, the

spread of Freemasonry continued in various cities of Europe, and with it rose the Illuminati. The Illuminati received a great boost from the enlistment of a northern German gentleman of substance, Baron Knigge.

Any scheme of this kind had a head start from the basic organization of the Freemasons themselves, which had a system of Blue Lodges for the first three degrees, but did not have a central authority governing all Masons, and left room for a series of orders of higher degrees that piggybacked on the existing memberships. Baron Knigge took advantage of this by enticing members of Blue Lodges (indeed, the lodge leadership) into accepting the higher Illuminati degrees. However, it was a bushwhack—upon progressing up the ladder, an Illuminee was eventually required to sever his existing lodge ties.

The rosy picture was not to last, however. Dissent arose within the Illuminati, and from without there was pressure on civil and religious society, led by the vengeful Jesuits.

In 1784, the Bavarian Elector (the nominal king) issued an edict banning the Illuminati and soon thereafter, a second and third edict, until all Freemasons were also banned from Bavaria. Arrests were made and documents were confiscated. Weishaupt fled and was never arrested, but subsequently faded into obscurity.

However, the Illuminati had already demonstrated that they were looking to establish a New World Order, that they were going to subvert Freemasonry, and that they were going to be deeply secretive. Therefore, any conspiracy theorist could argue that the Illuminati have never died, but merely have gone deeper underground.

Precisely this conspiracy theory erupted within a few years of the disbanding. Books by John Robison and the Abbe Barruel came out around 1797 and were rapidly circulated throughout Europe and America. The books, poorly grounded in fact, exposed all the known dangers of the Illuminati conspiracy, and claimed the order was the direct spark of the French Revolution and Reign of Terror, not to mention linking it to the Knights Templar.

Both Jefferson and Washington commented at the time in defense of Freemasonry. But the seeds were sown and the Illuminati legend was to see many embellishments and reawakenings. Alarm at what the Illuminati plotted in 1776 would burst forth to startle new conspiracy theorists even two hundred years later. In 1967, for instance, the John Birch Society republished Robison's book, titled *Proofs of a Conspiracy against All the Religions and Governments of Europe, Carried On in the Secret Meetings of Free Masons, Illuminati, and Reading Societies, Collected from Good Authorities.*

The title says it all: Conspiracy is everywhere, and the Freemasons/Illuminati are the source. It's probably impossible for a modern conspiracy theorist to top it, except to embellish the edges with links to every conceivable secret society, every intelligence organization, every government, every corporation, every organization concerned with internationalism, every scientist, all of it "collected from good authorities."

Dan Brown in his Langdon novels simply adopts the conspiracy theories, in particular the idea that the Illuminati are still alive, and still plotting the downfall of the Catholic Church, not to mention world domination. The Illuminati constitute the core concept of the villains in *A&D*, and are inferentially in the background of *DVC*. Based on these books, I expect that Dan Brown will tell us that the Freemasons are nice guys and probably harmless, but they have been unknowingly infiltrated by the Illuminati, who are really the ones pulling the strings.

❧ The Rosicrucians ❧

Both *A&D* and *DVC* weave together symbols of the cross and the rose, and sometimes they are brought together. How they got together symbolically is certainly at least as old as the Protestant movement, since Martin Luther used a rose and cross as his emblem in the early sixteenth century, but the strongest ties of all would link the rose and cross to Rosicrucianism, a secret order founded in Germany a century later.

Since at its heart, Rosicrucianism could be construed as anti-Catholic, and its rise signaled a real outbreak of a war of ideas that has been going on ever since, it is a crucial theme of Dan Brown's Robert Langdon series. Before there was an order of Illuminati in 1776, there was the Rosicrucian order in the early seventeenth century, very much antagonistic to the Church. It isn't very accurate to amalgamate the two orders, but when Dan Brown does so, he gets to talk about secret brotherhoods reaching

back four centuries, which he paints as still alive and
powerful, but lurking in the shadows in both *A&D*
and *DVC*.

Rosicrucianism began with a myth. It was probably
invented by a German Lutheran pastor, Johann
Valentin Andrae, in works published around 1614 to
1616. It first appeared as a series of manifestos
published in Cassel, Germany, in 1614 and 1615,
announcing the presence of a brotherhood of
followers of a mystic figure. Then in 1616 came the
story of Christian Rosencreutz, who supposedly had
lived in the late fourteenth century.

Rosencreutz, it was said, had studied in Damascus,
Egypt, and Morocco before returning to his native
Germany and founding the Rosicrucian order of
monks in 1409. There was to be a total of eight monks,
who were to go out into the world, seek knowledge,
and return once a year, replacing themselves with their
successors when they died. As the tale went,
Rosencreutz died at the age of 106 and was interred in
a special tomb, which was lost until being reopened in
1604, allowing the rebirth of the order.

Whether anyone was suspicious at the time, the
response to the documents was immediate and
intense. Rosicrucian societies arose, and the rose and
cross symbol became popular all by itself. The
Rosicrucian groups combined a vision of social transformation, the study of alchemy, Kabbalah, and
mysticism with otherwise "orthodox" Christian
theology. The Rosicrucian groups blended into the
larger community of Christian Pietism that could be
found throughout Germany at this time. (They would

also migrate in waves to populate a certain area around Philadelphia.)

Rosicrucian thought owed a certain homage to writings that were translated around 1463 in Italy, having been preserved since the second and third century, called the *Corpus Hermeticum*. These were said to be the works of Hermes Trismegistus, but were surely written by a collection of authors, probably in Egypt around the time of the Gnostics. Resurrected under the auspices of a famous Italian family, the Medicis, the *Corpus Hermeticum* had the effect of encouraging a practitioner to investigate mysticism, alchemy, and even the occult while remaining devoted to Christian Scripture. It allowed scholars, physicians, and scientists to see their work as pursuing the "two books," the first being the Bible, and the second being the "book of nature."

The Swiss pioneer of medicine, Paracelsus (1493–1541) developed these ideas in pursuit of both medicine and alchemy. In a ripple effect, for about a century, many physicians and would-be wizards (often one and the same) continued to expand on Paracelsus, as well as attempting to integrate classic Greek medical writings. Among these was an Oxford-trained English physician, Robert Fludd (1547–1637), who absorbed these ideas and added some of his own. His practice in London was a combination of accepted medicine, mysticism, alchemy, and the occult. He used horoscopes of his patients as a diagnostic tool, and he may have hypnotized them as an aid to healing.

Fludd thus was like a well-primed pump when the Rosicrucian manifestos exploded onto the scene. Fludd

almost immediately began writing about Rosicrucianism in English and popularizing it among intel-
lectuals in London. Fludd and his medical followers felt
they possessed the "Key to Universal Sciences." Fludd
was, of course, a contemporary of Francis Bacon. Thus,
Rosicrucian ideas were widely circulated in Europe and
the British Isles, very quickly—within a year or two.

The symbology and its variations, such as "rosy
crux," "rose croix," or even "red cross," are with us
today. There are no less than eight societies in
America alone tracing their legends back to the
Rosicrucians. The Freemasons have several degrees
that are associated with the symbology, the most
obvious of which is the Scottish Rite's eighteenth
degree, Knight (Prince) Rose Croix. There is a putative
link between the Rosicrucians and the legendary
Freemason Albert Pike, even to the point of specifying
a trip to Europe wherein Pike was inducted. However,
scholars have found that a Massachusetts Masonic
group, seeking to form a Rosicrucian group in
America, actually selected Pike and sent him a letter
inducting him, as an honorific, leading to the
apocryphal legend. He never traveled to Europe.

One of the largest of today's Rosicrucian organ-
izations is the Ancient and Mystical Order Rosae
Crucis (AMORC), founded by H. Spencer Lewis in
1915. It is rumored today to have 250,000 members.
Lewis was also affiliated with a number of British
occult orders, including Aleister Crowley's Ordo
Templi Orientis, an amalgam of legends of the Knights
Templar, the Gnostics, the occult, etc.

Dan Brown's novels allow some latitude to the

various characters who are part of the "science and reason" side of the conflict, so that at times, they philosophically are more like Rosicrucians than Illuminati. A very good example is Leonardo Vetra in *A&D*, who combines devout Catholicism with a keen scientific mind.

Vetra, who was murdered at the beginning of the novel, was a devout priest who also happened to be a particle physicist. He became a leading scientist at the Conseil Européen pour la Recherche Nucléaire, home of the world's largest particle collider. Vetra and his daughter, Vittoria, have succeeded in producing a substantial quantity of anti-matter, which has been stolen to create a very powerful bomb intended to destroy the Vatican. Vetra is said to have proved "the existence of an energy force that unites us all," which the scientific press had labeled, "a surer path to God than religion itself."

According to a recent AMORC pamphlet, "The Rosicrucian teachings enable people to find themselves, turn their lives, and influence the universe. We are educators, students, and seekers devoted to exploring inner wisdom and the meaning of life. We offer an ancient time-tested system of study and experimentation which reveals the underlying principles of the universe. Our method offers practical tools applicable to all aspects of life. The Rosicrucian teachings allow individuals to direct their own lives, experience inner peace, and leave their mark on humanity."

It's fairly easy to recognize that these are statements Francis Bacon could have made some four hundred years earlier. It's an example of how the cross-pollination of ideas just never seems to end.

Freemasonry in its early years was surrounded with these controversies, and there were already rumors and lies being told by opposing or rival groups. But it was an era called the Age of Enlightenment, and large numbers of people, educated and not, were beginning to think that man could discover fundamental truths and pathways to God without having to subscribe to a hierarchy like that of the Catholic pope and priests, or of a king under a theory of divine rightness. In this environment, Freemasonry could grow.

❧ Masons of the Pre-American Revolution ❧

The fraternity took hold and was so popular that, by the 1730s, Freemasonry was being imported into America, with the founding of the first lodges in New York and Philadelphia. Later, there would be lodges in South Carolina and, eventually, throughout most of the colonies.

Freemasonry grew in colonial America even while it was encountering trouble in England and Europe from a wide range of enemies. Because Masons require belief in a god but do not specify whether it is a Catholic, Protestant, Hebrew or Muslim god, practically any well-entrenched religion could view it as a threat. In addition, monarchs felt threatened. The Roman Catholic Church was officially opposed to the group ever since 1738, when Pope Clement XII condemned Freemasonry and banned it from his faith. Catholics were forbidden from joining, under pain of excommunication. Later popes would reiterate the strictures.

At the time, America was very WASPish. It was non-Catholic, in both the sense that it was mostly Protestant, and the sense that there was anti-Catholic sentiment. (The fact that most had come to America to escape religious persecution meant that they were not going to start new religious wars between colonists, so mostly there was tolerance, but with occasional sharp exceptions.) The range of religious views among just the Protestants was huge, from Puritans and Calvinists, to Anglicans, Baptists, Quakers, Unitarians, and Deists. The net result, however, was that most of the men responsible for the birth of America were non-Catholic.

Many worthy colonists joined Freemason lodges, including a long list of the Founding Fathers, such as George Washington, Paul Revere, Benjamin Franklin, and John Hancock. Thomas Jefferson was not a Mason, but did strongly believe in avoiding a state-sponsored religion. It was no accident that documents like the Declaration of Independence spoke of "Divine Providence" and "Nature's God" instead of a specific deity. (However, there is an ongoing debate about whether this was a Masonic master plan or merely the confluence of fashionable ideas.)

Again, in America as in England, a young gentleman with hopes of "improving" himself would join a lodge because it offered a chance to associate with "the right kind of people." Colonial Freemasons were careful to make it clear that they learned morality in their lodges and practiced it in the form of civic service and charity. So it was fairly appropriate for a young man of 20, such as George Washington, or 25, such as Benjamin Franklin, to join a lodge as part of an urge to make respectable social "connections."

❧ Reason, Science, and Religion in Colonial America ❧

It's time to look at the ways that the Age of Enlightenment was reflected in colonial America. Since there was plenty of commerce between England and the colonies, Americans got a pretty good idea of what was going on in the mother country. Of course, lots of people in England figured the colonies were ignorant and unschooled. If this was true at first, it rapidly became untrue. America had already become a country of self-improvement in every sense, and imported European ideas only fed that movement. As Franklin would prove, it would not be long before American science would lead Europe, not follow. Franklin's achievements were simply spectacular, since he was entirely self-educated.

Freemasonry was at the heart of the matter, steeped in the philosophies of Enlightenment and imported from England, but with connections to the Continent.

Two of the most famous thinkers of the period were Benjamin Franklin and the French philosopher Voltaire, and they actually joined a Masonic lodge together in France in 1778 (however, Franklin had been a Freemason since 1731). To the Catholic Church, Voltaire was the very essence of a demon, and practically his entire literary career was spent in undermining the powers of the Church and the king (the two powers were as thick as thieves in France at the time). Voltaire and Franklin were brought together in 1778 publicly at the Royal Academy (of Science) in Paris, and the crowd would not be satisfied with a handshake, but demanded a full embrace.

Voltaire was himself very enamored of Isaac Newton, and as a young man was in London to witness Newton's funeral, at which the English scientist was honored almost as a deity. (Newton's funeral plays a part in *DVC*, on the erroneous assertion that Alexander Pope presided over it.) For Voltaire to honor Franklin, and vice versa, was to exchange the torch of science and reason to be shared in the Old and New Worlds.

Scientific thought from Galileo to Newton, by way also of Copernicus and Tycho Brahe, built on "heresies" that the Catholic Church could not countenance, such as the heliocentric theory of the solar system. But science held a deeper threat for the pope: The Church no longer had a stranglehold on interpreting the universe. Benjamin Franklin, a self-educated man, had risen to the pinnacle of science with no help from any church.

The lodge that Voltaire and Franklin joined in France was the Lodge of the Nine Sisters, which had become known as a freethinkers' lodge, somewhat radical among Masons, leading the challenges to the orthodox church and monarchy that would eventually erupt as the French Revolution.

Among many other scientific links, Franklin struck up a friendship with the cleric/scientist Joseph

Priestley. Because of his fame for the lightning and electricity experiments, Franklin was inducted into the Royal Society a year before his first official trip to England in 1757.

Priestley began a career in religion that turned away from strict Anglican beliefs toward Unitarian ones. But he also embarked on a scientific career that would make him a giant in the field of chemistry, particularly focusing on gases such as oxygen. Franklin met Priestley in 1766 and they became lifelong friends.

In 1780, when both men were famous as accomplished scientists, Priestley and Franklin became associated with the Lunar Society, a group of men in Birmingham, England, interested in natural science and literature. They were sometimes known as "the Lunatics" because they met in each other's houses on the Monday closest to the full moon. This was a practical matter, allowing them to return home by moonlight, and was adopted by many fraternal organizations, including some Masonic lodges. But it is easy to see how an occult connotation could be extracted from it.

Franklin returned to Philadelphia for the last time in 1785 and died in 1790. By about that time, Priestley had embarked on a religious path that would lead him to great troubles in England, where his brand of religious dissent was outlawed, and he was the subject of vilifying pamphlets and was burned in effigy. Adding to his unpopularity, he was an ardent supporter of both the American and the French Revolutions. In 1794, this became intolerable for him, and he left for America. He joined his son in

Northumberland, Pennsylvania, on the banks of the Susquehanna River, in a community of English dissenters. He wintered in Philadelphia, where he lectured and established the first Unitarian church in America.

Notably, both John Adams and Thomas Jefferson (non-Masons) made a point of coming to hear Priestley preach, and Jefferson later consulted with him before founding the University of Virginia.

Among other things that unite Newton, Priestley, Franklin, and just about any scientist of the sixteenth through eighteenth centuries, is an interest in alchemy. In quite a literal sense, Newton was an alchemist, and Priestley was one of the later thinkers who would edge themselves over from *alchemy* to the more respectable science of *chemistry*.

Alchemy descended from ancient times to medieval pursuits, based on the belief that all matter has a common origin and has the ability or potential to change its shape or form. (This basic definition is not all that far from the current most advanced view of the universe: string theory!)

The basic dream of alchemy was to find a key to transmutation known as the Philosopher's Stone, which would allow the changing of base metals into gold, the discovery of a universal cure for disease, and the means of indefinitely prolonging life. In the arcane definition, the Philosopher's Stone was said to be "a stone that is no stone" and was probably a liquid.

But there is a philosophical and religious context to alchemy that goes deeper, into the concepts of a belief in self-proven principles of the universe, of "per-

*The self-taught Franklin easily
proved Americans could excel at
science.*

fectibility," of a union of spirit and body, of sexual
hieros gamos or "alchemical marriage."

What a lot of people do not see is how these
influences swirled in American history. There were, in
fact, many examples of American alchemists' seeking
the Philosopher's Stone. Oddly, some of the early
religious sects—among them, Quakers, believe it or
not—became associated with these influences.
Always troublesome to authority, the early Quakers
were unfairly accused of being a "Family of Love" sect
(i.e., free lovers).

Further, alchemy was not always a pure stream, but
a mixture of real science and the occult, plus such
things as counterfeiting and various other con games,
magical healing, and the like. Early New England
(Calvinist and Puritan) Americans actually consulted
witches ("white" witchcraft) for many decades before

they turned against "black" witchcraft in the Salem trials. But there were many waves of religious immigrants, increasing in numbers, frequency, and variety. It was, religiously and philosophically, the spread of many beliefs and movements from England, France, and elsewhere that easily crossed the Atlantic and took root in the New World.

❧ Shaking the Cocktail ❧

An extreme example of a very mixed-up religious concoction is the famous religious commune at Ephrata, Pennsylvania. It held to genuine Rosicrucian beliefs with forms of alchemy, along with German Baptist (Dunker) faiths, Pietism, and even some practices that approached Judaism.

Ephrata's main strand of religious belief came through a mystic, Johann Conrad Beissel, who needed no text or Bible to preach, but merely closed his eyes and began to spout long, fiercely animated "sermons," or what would be called "rants" today. He had tried to be a religious hermit several times, but followers kept showing up at his cabin door. So he founded a sect that eventually grew to about three hundred, mostly German religious refugees streaming into Pennsylvania.

Beissel was described as "physically diminutive, emaciated, a living skeleton until his death, but possessed of such a magnetic personality that his influence, benign or malign, was felt by almost all with whom he came into contact."

Beissel preached strict, total celibacy, so a joiner

had to give up any marriage that he or she held. This carried an attraction to certain married women of the area around Ephrata. Thus, on more than one occasion, Beissel was attacked by an angry husband. Other times, a man might be severely disciplined for sleeping with his wife. Members of the order wore white robes and slept on narrow wooden platforms with stone pillows. Like ancient Jews, they rose at midnight to study Scripture and pray, and they adopted Saturday as their Sabbath, getting them in trouble with civil authorities.

Beissel believed in certain Hermetic traditions, including alchemical marriage (philosophically but not sexually), and in his later years he pursued real alchemy, searching for the Philosopher's Stone. In fact, his tenets were practically straight from Hermetic and Rosicrucian texts. In one legend, man was complete, being both male and female in spirit, before the conflict between the archangel Lucifer and God. Through celibacy, faith, and revelation, the masculine could reunite with the feminine to become a perfect spirit. The members of the Ephrata sect were therefore known as *perfecti*.

Beissel, raised as a baker by trade in Germany, was in fact a *widow's son*, born after the death of his father. It is said that as a young man he joined a Rosicrucian chapter that, because the order was banned, had to meet under the guise of a Pietist conventicle. His membership became known in Heidelberg where Pietists were persecuted, however, and he was forced to flee, eventually making his way to Pennsylvania. To those Pietists remaining behind in Germany, the group that had gone to America was called "the Woman Wandering in the Wilderness." Beissel intended to join them, but he wound up founding his own sect.

With only rudimentary knowledge of music, Beissel put together his own theory of harmony, wrote about two thousand hymns, and was the fiery choirmaster of the women of Ephrata. He saw music in a Kabbalah-like way, considering the musical notes to be "letters." Thus, a hymn was a coded form of divine guidance. Music was viewed in "Aeolian" or Pythagorean terms.

All over America, for most of its history, diverse religious groups have frequently seen a reason to proclaim the Second Coming, a new Messiah, or the End of Days. This was not particularly different from Europe and elsewhere, where new Messiahs and Millennia had been regularly announced for centuries. (It is a very real, very *courant* undercurrent among American religious fundamentalists today.)

Ephrata got a taste of this. In 1742, a comet was seen for several weeks in the night sky. The elders were convinced it meant the End of Days, and some of the brethren had to be restrained from killing themselves through starvation. Later, a dispute broke out when an elder detected hints that Beissel was preparing to declare himself a new Christ.

The Beisselianer, as they were known, practiced *agapas*, or love-feasts, tracing back to the earliest Christians. These were holy celebrations in which everyone, including servants and slaves, ate together and gave one another the kiss of peace. *Agape* is Greek for "love." *Agapa* was part of the mason's mark of the famous Scottish Freemason, Sir Robert Moray (see page 139, Sexual Overtones of Dan Brown).

The Ephrata brethren were followers of the apocryphal wisdom of Sophia—which is Greek for "wisdom" and figures in the plot of *DVC*, explaining Sophie Neveu's name. It is a significant part of Gnosticism.

❧ The Brotherhood of Zion ❧

Ephrata was strange enough, but within the commune there arose a subsect that readers of *DVC* will find downright spooky.

Around 1738, a secret society formed at Ephrata called the Brotherhood of Zion (I kid you not). This has a truly eerie resemblance to the Priory of Sion that figures so prominently in *DVC*, the brotherhood founded among the Templars that supposedly carries the bloodline of the Merovingian kings, through Leonardo da Vinci to the Illuminati, and continues to Jacques Saunière, Sophie's grandfather.

At Ephrata, the Brotherhood of Zion consisted of thirteen adepts who built themselves a circular chapterhouse that, it is said, was based on plans handed down from ancient Freemasonry. (In *DVC*, Dan Brown says the Knights Templar characteristically built round churches.)

The Ephrata brotherhood was headed by a Perfect Master, or Prior. It thus could be called a "Priory of Zion."

Later, the nuns of the cloister took on the name of the Order of the Roses of Sharon. Once again, we have the rose as a symbol, almost certainly linked to

Rosicrucianism. This would fit perfectly in a Dan
Brown setting.

The three-story Zion chapterhouse had a first floor
with a refectory and provision rooms, a second story
with no windows—just one candle in the center and
thirteen wooden cots radiating outward—and finally,
an upper floor containing the "mystical chamber,
where the arcana of the rite were unfolded." (Would
this make a great setting for a Dan Brown novel, or
what?)

To begin their spiritual journey, the thirteen
brothers entered the building and locked the door
behind them, then spent forty days in prayer. On the
fortieth day they were visited by seven archangels,
one of whom handed them a sacred parchment. On
the parchment was a "sacred pentagon" containing
the Ineffable Name of God. The Brotherhood chose
the Virgin Mary as their patroness, and showed their
dedication to her by shaving their heads like Catholic
monks. In fact, the nuns of the cloister also began to
shave their crowns in the same manner, known as a
tonsure.

They walked wherever they went, typically single
file, so the spectacle of white-robed monks and nuns
following Beissel looked to outsiders like a hen and
chickens, or a father with his children. Their spare,
vegetarian diet left them very skinny, and visitors to
their services were struck by the way the powerful
harmonies would emerge from a choir of emaciated,
spirit-like beings.

A very spooky legend has it that there are human
footprints on the ceiling beams of one of the Ephrata

buildings, put there one night at midnight when the Prior and another monk walked on the ceiling.

Although Ephrata seemed very odd to other Pennsylvanians at the time, it wasn't unique. There were dozens of strange religious communities in a colony that, after all, was intended as a haven for castaway religions. It certainly didn't stop Ephrata's commune from becoming a fixture in the area. Members were known for baking pumpernickel bread and sharing it with neighboring towns. In fact, Benjamin Franklin did the early printing work for Ephrata's hymnbooks and religious tracts and later, it was where foreign translations of the Declaration of Independence were made, to be sent to foreign governments.

But Ephrata was almost guaranteed to fail as a religious experiment. Combining alchemy and mysticism with celibacy is not exactly a winning strategy. But it was part of the ever-changing cultural mixture in the colonies.

This American stew of philosophy, religion, and science informed many of the formative stages of our Revolution. Just one example is found in one of the most famous phrases of all, the second sentence of the Declaration of Independence beginning, "We hold these truths . . ."

Jefferson drafted the Declaration based on many streams of thought (not the least of which was John Locke's concept of natural rights, plus heavily borrowed passages from George Mason, a prominent Virginian). But Jefferson turned it over to Franklin for editing.

Among Franklin's most powerful changes was to

amend Jefferson's "We hold these truths to be sacred and undeniable." Franklin made it "self-evident," avoiding any religious justification and instead drawing on Enlightenment traditions of Newton in science and Hume and Leibniz in philosophy.

In essence, Franklin brings independence into focus as a self-creating goddess, not requiring a religious parent in order to be born. It was a genuine nose-thumbing at all the monarchs of Europe, who needed some form of religious authorization to hold their crowns.

As we have seen, Franklin was in a unique position to say such an audacious thing. He was a Freemason, one of the world's preeminent scientists, and an excellent representative of Enlightenment thinking, both in America and in the world. If Dan Brown takes advantage of Franklin as a major figure in *The Solomon Key*, I would not be surprised or disappointed, although I think the subject has now been covered by the 2004 movie *National Treasure*, starring Nicolas Cage. This perhaps may thwart Dan Brown's employment of Franklin.

In *National Treasure*, the hero is an heir of Freemasons from the Revolution named Benjamin Franklin Gates. On the trail of a vast Templar treasure that was protected by the Freemasons, he follows clues, including codes and symbols, presumably created by the clever and wily Ben Franklin. One of the artifacts used to view hidden symbols on the back of the Declaration of Independence is a set of special filtered eyeglasses, constructed by Franklin and left in a niche at Independence Hall. The decoding of one important clue is done with ciphers keyed to the "Silence Dogood Letters," a series of anonymous letters to the editor that Ben Franklin wrote as a youth.

❧ The Mason-Influenced Revolutionary Conspiracy Begins ❧

I think it's funny when conspiracy theorists start talking about the original Masonic plot to take over America. Pssst! Didya know that a roomful of men started a big conspiracy in 1776 in Philadelphia?

For the record, yes, there was definitely a conspiracy among the fifty-six signers of the Declaration of Independence. They really plotted to overthrow the rule of the king of England and create a new form of government called a democracy.

Yes, it was secretive. The men in the room all knew that their signatures would get them hanged on the spot if they were captured by the British. For this very reason, the copies of the Declaration that they signed were not made public until about five months later. The document itself was read in public on July 8, 1776, but the identities of the signers were not revealed.

There were nine known Freemasons among the fifty-six signers (although some put the number of Masons even higher). The primary writer of the Declaration, Thomas Jefferson, was not a Freemason. The only other signer who became president was John Adams, and he was not a Freemason. Benjamin Franklin was a signer, a Freemason, a wily fellow, and a man of huge importance, but none of his pursuits smacked of a conspiracy to run the new country.

So it doesn't make sense to say that the Freemasons took over the United States from the start. But when it's time for Dan Brown to refer to this slice of history in *The Solomon Key*, I am betting he will play up the "Masonic conspiracy."

What really can be said about these people at Independence Hall is that they were all white men, men of substance who generally were Christians, almost all of them Protestants. However, some were Deists; some believed in other personal or idiosyncratic interpretations of mainstream religion. (Jefferson, for instance, once attempted to create his own Bible by simply tearing out all the pages of the standard version that he felt didn't belong.) They were thoroughly steeped in Enlightenment thought, and to the extent that this coincided with the philosophies of Freemasonry, they were steeped in Masonic thought.

Furthermore, although many, many Freemasons fought in the Revolution—and that included almost all of Washington's top commanders—they did essentially nothing conspiratorial to take over the country. In fact, Washington did not seek the presidency and would have been happy to retire to enjoy his beloved Mount Vernon. He set the paradigm for future democratic societies when he stepped down from the presidency at the end of two elected terms, instead of converting it into some form of constitutional monarchy, which his popularity would have allowed.

Freemasons were like any other soldiers, except that they would occasionally have lodge meetings and certain celebrations, such as the feast days of St. John the Evangelist (December 27) and St. John the Baptist (June 24). The Freemasons among the British soldiers brought their lodge paraphernalia with them also, so they would be conducting mirror-image celebrations. For a soldier, it was a way to elevate oneself; even a private could hobnob with a colonel as an equal brother in Freemasonry.

During the Revolution itself, there was a very significant Masonic procession among military men at West Point in 1779 that was led by George Washington. About one hundred Masonic brothers participated in the celebration of St. John the Baptist with speeches, songs, a sermon, and toasts. It was an opportunity to engage in a social event in a grand, refined manner. As the historian Steven C. Bullock points out in *Revolutionary Brotherhood*, within a few months this celebration generated a whole new raft of Masonic brothers. General John Paterson founded a new military lodge, with thirteen brothers, nine of whom were present at the West Point celebration. It was named Washington lodge, and had 250 members before the war was over. Such was the charisma of the commander in chief.

A big issue to remember about the American Revolution is that the people were not united during the long war. In any given colony or county, perhaps one-third of the population was glad to see Washington's army march into town, but another third would have been happy to see the British. Straddling the middle was the remaining third, hoping it would all just go away. Both Washington and the

Continental Congress had to walk a tightrope, financially and otherwise, to keep the Revolution going when about two-thirds of the population would have accepted defeat.

Even the leadership was not unanimous. From the New England colonies came people like John Adams, Samuel Adams, and Paul Revere, all of them firebrands who argued for independence long before the shooting started in earnest. Along with John Hancock, these were often merchants, artisans, bankers, shippers, and the like. From the Southern colonies came genteel landowners, who measured wealth in acres, not necessarily dollars. Like Washington and Jefferson, they were also slave-holders. Some of these men felt the relationship with the king could be repaired. Though philosophically more like the New Englanders in most things, Benjamin Franklin actually believed for many of the early years of the war that it wasn't winnable. He thought the colonies would make their point and then negotiate a peace settlement that would keep them in the Commonwealth.

One of the extreme oddities of American history was pointed out by Steven C. Bullock in *Brothers of the Revolution* while describing the procession that marked the death of Benjamin Franklin in 1790. This was the biggest funeral procession in America—in its day and for a very long time to come—with more than twenty thousand people along the route of march. Almost every group in Philadelphia turned out a contingent to be in the procession, and every single religion in the city, including Catholics and Jews, was also represented by clergy. There was really just one group missing: the Freemasons.

It turned out that, because of a schism that had occurred years earlier, Franklin's original Philadelphia lodge was not recognized by the lodges in the city at the time (it was a dispute that hung over the terms *Antient* and *Modern*). It was yet another example of how even the Freemasons, whom some imagine as disciplined secret society members and "conspirators," were not unanimous in anything.

Franklin wasn't a typical Freemason, in the same way that he wasn't a typical printer. A year before he joined the Masons, his *Pennsylvania Gazette* published an exposé of their rituals.

Franklin suffered a blot on his reputation when he failed to be forthright in stopping a prank that had fatal consequences. It seems a bunch of young Philadelphians (non-Masons) convinced a gullible apprentice that they were inducting him into the Freemasons. In one ceremony, he was blindfolded and given a "sacred" wine containing a laxative, was made to swear allegiance to the Devil, and told to "kiss the book" but actually was kissing the naked buttocks of one of the pranksters. When they assembled again in a cellar to give the victim a "higher degree," they tried to persuade him that he was seeing the Devil (a prankster dressed up in a cow's hide with horns). They lighted their faces using flaming pans of brandy, and one of these pans spilled onto the victim. He died within a few days. Franklin had not participated in any way, but he was shown a copy of the pranksters' imitation Masonic ritual in a pub one night.

If Dan Brown needs his contemporary-set plot to have connective tissue to the past, recent events provided an odd echo of that eighteenth-century prank when a real Masonic initiation ceremony went tragically wrong in 2004 in Patchogue, New York. The Southside Lodge there had a suborganization for selected members called the Fellow Craft Club. This social club, which was not sanctioned by the Grand Lodge of New York, had its own initiation rituals performed in a basement, where police later found a nine-foot guillotine and a setup designed to mimic walking a plank. An initiate was blindfolded and was told he was going to be shot. While one Mason fired a blank, another behind the initiate would knock down some tin cans. Unfortunately, the shooter, a seventy-six-year-old Mason, was carrying two guns, a .22-caliber handgun with blanks in his left pocket, and a .32-caliber gun with live rounds in his right pocket. He reached into his right pocket, pulled out the wrong gun, and shot the victim, a forty-seven-year-old fellow Mason, in the face, killing him, authorities said. He was charged with second-degree manslaughter and received a sentence of five years' probation.

⟡ Post-Revolutionary Excesses ⟡

It was the period *after* the Revolution that saw a great rise in influence in Freemasonry in America. In the towns and cities of the new nation, people were building a new social structure. And part of that structure was a fraternal system providing benefits like social status, business contacts, death benefits, and recreation.

Those in this new society had quite a number of groups to join, and more were founded on a continual basis. Not coincidentally, new groups would often just copy and adapt the symbols and rituals of the Freemasons, rather than try to invent their own. So if you wanted the real McCoy, you joined the Freemasons, if you could wangle an invitation (admission was controlled by the "blackball" system, in which one dissenting lodge member could veto a candidate).

You had a rich menu from which to choose among Masons, though, because there were York and Scottish Rites, "Antients" and "Moderns," and white (most of them) or black (the Prince Hall Freemasons).

In this golden age of American Freemasonry, many men took advantage of the prestige of membership and forged business deals primarily based on their brotherhood connections. Because of the basic pledge of mutual assistance, a Mason could arrive in a strange town and simply go straight to the local lodge to seek help in finding accommodations, or even obtaining a small loan.

Masonic lodges were benefactors to the community, and had resources to help with burial expenses for members. They were also places where two merchants could meet and make overt or tacit agreements to deal with each other, rather than non-Mason competitors.

Political life tended to be linked to Freemasonry, until it got to the point, in certain states, that a man could not become governor without being a

Freemason. Political candidates began to boldly refer to their status as a brother when seeking votes. In the extreme, there were even cases in which government authorities hinted that the Masonic lodge could take care of its own legal issues, such as disputes arising out of loans between brothers. Thus, had the concept been accepted, there would have been one court system for the ordinary people, and another for Freemasons.

But Freemasonry was showing signs of injury from its own success. By the end of the eighteenth century, there were already slanderous exposés circulating about their Illuminati and Jacobin (French Reign of Terror) connections. Now, men who did not get government contracts, business deals, or elective office began to see Freemasonry as the reason for their unsuccess.

But the focal point for anti-Masonry came when a man in upstate New York, William Morgan, was murdered in 1826 and the alleged perpetrators were set free.

An intemperate ne'er-do-well, Morgan attempted to use bogus credentials to become a member of the Masons. When the local Masons caught on, they rejected him and he became embittered. In revenge, he decided to publish what he had been able to learn of Freemasonry's secrets. With the help of local editor David C. Miller, he made arrangements to publish *Illustrations of Masonry by One of the Fraternity*.

Furious local Masons promptly murdered him. They were tried in court, but because the evidence was scanty and the body was not found, they were acquitted.

The Morgan murder case merited national attention. Soon, springing from New York and New England, there was a clamor of anti-Mason sentiment that grew so loud it became a political force in America. By 1832, it figured in the election of the president. The Anti-Mason Party was, in fact, the first appearance of a third party in the fledging United States. Its candidate took a drubbing though, and Andrew Jackson (a Mason) was elected president.

George Washington is the most revered of all American Freemasons.

By this time, some of the most unsettling rumors against the Masons had been born, both in Europe and in America. It was said that the Freemasons worshipped Satan, that they had a secret oath promising a dire death if the lodge's lore were revealed. In America, it was seen as offensive that the Masons were a secret fraternity that swore an oath of allegiance (a very specific focus of the Revolution had been against forced oaths). Some felt that one's first oath ought to be to God, and then to Country.

In the wake of the public outrage for several decades following the Morgan murder, Freemasonry suffered a large loss of prestige, as well as membership, and whole lodges were forced to shut their doors for lack of brothers. This trend was reversed later in the nineteenth century, and Freemasons reassumed their place more or less as equals in a larger congress of fraternal life in America. One of the major figures who helped to "rehabilitate" the Masons was the legendary Albert Pike.

❧ Albert Pike ☙

Outside of Freemasonry, hardly anyone knows about Albert Pike today, but in his time he was a giant—in practically every sense of the word.

Pike was a large man (300 pounds, 6′4″) with a powerful speaking and singing voice. He came to be a teacher, lawyer, newspaper editor and owner, judge, poet and songwriter, Civil War general, and a scholar of formidable accomplishment. He was essentially self-taught in all these things.

Born in Boston in 1809, he was accepted at Harvard but could not afford to go, so he became a country schoolteacher in the Boston area from about 1825 to 1831. Some say rumored affairs caused him to leave the area and head west.

His meanderings took him as far west as Santa Fe, in what is now New Mexico, in hopes of becoming a trapper. Although Pike got some experience that would serve him well, such as contact with various Indian tribes, he didn't succeed as a trapper.

Pike settled in Arkansas, where he began to expand his career horizons. Eking out a living as a schoolteacher again, a bit of luck with some writings of his earned him a position on a newspaper. He became an editor, then a lawyer and circuit judge. Upon admission to the bar in 1834, he married an Arkansas woman and they eventually had eleven children.

Pike combined his careers as lawyer, writer, poet, and even colonel in the Arkansas Guard. He was part of the Arkansas landscape through the coming of the railroads, of statehood, and of banking. One over-arching issue that demanded his attention over the next several decades was the slavery question. Pike, seeing states' rights as paramount, was very much a pro-slavery advocate, though not eager to jump at secession as the Civil War approached.

He was made a Freemason in 1850 and rose rapidly, marching through all the Blue Lodge degrees, then all the York Rite and then all the Scottish Rite degrees by the end of 1853. From 1854 through 1860, he worked on a complete rewriting of the rituals of the Scottish Rite.

He was also a major force in the American Party, also known as the "Know-Nothings," because they answered every question about their organization with "I know nothing." The Know-Nothings had staunch anti-Catholic and anti-immigrant planks. Pike was not anti-Catholic, but agreed with the anti-immigrant stance, and he saw in the Know-Nothings a chance to preserve the Union while preserving states' rights—i.e., slavery. (To be fair to a man of complexity like Pike, he might have been in favor of abolition if the North had not made slavery an excuse for attacking states' rights.)

When the Civil War began, however, Pike made a clear choice. He rose to begin military service for the South. He was named a brigadier general and, because he had experience negotiating with the Indians, he was

The enigmatic Albert Pike, famous among Freemasons.

assigned to bring them into an alliance with the Confederacy. He did this and formed a brigade composed of Indian soldiers. Their only serious battle was at Pea Ridge, Arkansas, in 1862 and it was a loss. Worse, reports were circulated that at least one Union soldier had been scalped. This was a terrible black mark against Pike and his brigade, as well as the Confederate cause, and he was eventually forced to hightail it into the Arkansas woods to avoid prosecution.

Pike found his way to a simple cabin along a creek in the Oauchita Mountains, where he refined the Scottish Rite rituals and wrote certain other ceremonies. There is a tale that Pike buried gold under the porch of this cabin and marauders learned of it. They planned to rob and kill him, but Pike, alerted by a neighbor's son, escaped in the dead of night with his money and most of his papers and books. The marauders burned his cabin anyway.

Pike managed to secure a pardon from President Andrew Johnson (a Freemason) after the Civil War, and he resumed his career as a lawyer in Memphis, but never found big success in law. He also wrote editorials for the *Memphis Daily Appeal*, where he had bought a share of ownership. By now, he had essentially abandoned his wife back in Arkansas.

According to allegations, Pike was among those who helped to found the Ku Klux Klan. It is alleged that he assisted the founder, Nathan Bedford Forrest, as chief judiciary officer and writer of the KKK rituals. Scholars and historians have not located anything to confirm these accusations. It is true that Pike wrote an editorial saying he didn't necessarily believe in the KKK, but if it were to succeed, it would have to be "efficient." He argued for a "secret association" for "mutual, peaceful, lawful, self-defence." He called for "one great Order of Southern Brotherhood...whose very existence should be concealed from all but its members."

That description fits the KKK, but it also fits the fabled Knights of the Golden Circle, the legendary keepers of the hidden treasure of the Confederacy, a group that I will discuss later.

Pike went to Washington in 1868 and lived in various places in and around the city while practicing law and building the organization known as the Supreme Council of the Scottish Rite of Freemasons, Southern Jurisdiction, where he was Grand Commander and, later, a kind of resident scholar.

He had by now completed the massive elaboration on the Rite's degrees, titled *Morals and Dogma*, which combines lore from numerous ancient and occult sources, including Egyptian, Hebrew, Babylonian, Gnostic, Hindu, and other legends, to name a few. This was published in 1871 and became the book that was handed to many thousands of Freemasons for decades to come. Today, it is a book that most Masons probably have heard of, but probably have never read. Pike's last great scholastic works were studies of the *Rig Veda* of the ancient Hindus, and the *Zend Avesta* of the ancient Persians.

Although his writings were vaguely recognizable as moral instruction, Pike's skill with words occasionally backfired on the Freemasons.

One notable example was when he spoke glowingly of Lucifer, meaning the morning star (ascribed to the planet Venus). By *Lucifer*, he meant "light," or "enlightenment." But anti-Masons seized on this mention as proof that Freemasons were Satanic (ignoring the other eight-hundred-odd pages in *Morals and Dogma*).

One point that Pike made, intentionally, was that the symbolism of Freemasonry ought to involve a bit of work, or else the student would not value the knowledge gained. At times, he indicated, the new Freemason would be told deliberate lies in order to later learn a fuller truth. Along with some other evidence of this type, conspiracy buffs have had all they need as proof that Freemasons are controlled by inner cliques—maybe even the Illuminati.

Pike had an eye for the ladies throughout his life, but in 1866 he was smitten by one young woman in particular. This was the sculptor Vinnie Ream, newly famous in Washington for her bust and statue of Abraham Lincoln. According to Pike's solemn avowal, it never went beyond holding hands and kissing. Pike would sit and read poetry with her. He wrote her some 2,166 pages of "Essays to Vinnie" before his death in 1891.

Pike was chronically poor, and came to depend on the Freemasons for income and shelter. A brick building in Washington at 433 Third Street, NW, was bought in 1882 and became the first House of the Temple, headquarters of the Scottish Rite for all of the Southern states. Pike and his large library soon took up residence there and he remained until his death. Pike was buried in an Episcopal cemetery, but in 1944 his remains were brought to the new House of the Temple at 1733 16th Street, NW, a magnificent marble structure built in 1911. Not far from the old House of the Temple, in Judiciary Square, a large statue of Pike was placed in 1901 at the behest of the Freemasons and the Daughters of the Confederacy. Thousands pass the statue every day without a clue about who Albert Pike was. They probably won't be ignoring the statue of Pike after they read Dan Brown's tales in *The Solomon Key*.

❧ Other Fraternal Organizations of Interest ❧

In *The Solomon Key*, I foresee a potential for Dan Brown to develop other fraternal organizations as friends or foes of the Masons, and as participants in actual or fictional conspiracies. The history of America is rife with the rise and fall of hundreds of organizations, some of which were in direct competition with the Masons.

For instance, a large and popular fraternity, the Odd Fellows, unlike the Freemasons, did not incur the enmity of the pope. Like Freemasonry, it also had its origins in England in the eighteenth century. It was brought to the United States in 1819.

The rise in America of the Ancient Order of Hibernians, an Irish Catholic secret society, was a direct result of the rise of the anti-Catholic movement, personified by the American (Know-Nothing) Party. Later, there were the Knights of Columbus, a fraternal group that was, in part, a Catholic Church-sanctioned rival of the Masons. This was part of a general pattern. As wave after wave of immigrants hit the shores of America, ethnic groups organized themselves for such basic things as survival and self-defense. The movie *Gangs of New York* is a gut-wrenching portrayal of this.

In the late nineteenth and early twentieth century, fraternal groups blossomed to more than three hundred organizations, many of which have since expired. They had names like Improved Order of Red Men, Knights of Pythias, Sons of Temperance, even the United Ancient Order of Druids, which claimed 14,600 members in an almanac of 1896. (At their height in England during the nineteenth century, the Druids claimed more than a million members.)

The Improved Order of Red Men are direct descendants of the Sons of Liberty, the Boston radicals who dressed up as Mohawks for the Boston Tea Party.

Late in the nineteenth century would come some hereditary organizations, such as the Daughters of the American Revolution and Sons of the American Revolution. A very early group of this nature was the

Society of the Cincinnati, begun in 1783 by the top leaders of the Continental military. It was partly to honor George Washington, in his role as an emulator of the Roman statesman and general Cincinnatus, and partly to provide death benefits to veterans' families in an era when nothing like that existed.

One huge reason for the rise of fraternal organizations, which counted some 5 million members at the turn of the twentieth century, was the establishment of mutual aid societies, the forerunners of modern life insurance companies. This stemmed almost certainly from the popularity of the Ancient Order of United Workmen, a group founded by a Mason, John Jordan Upchurch, in 1868. Each member paid $1 and was assured at least $500 when he died. On the death of a member, the membership was assessed another $1 each to replenish the fund.

Fraternal organizations also came to be major sources for works of charity, evolving today into what are called non-governmental organizations (NGOs).

In many cases, when a new group arose and its leaders cast about for rituals and myths, they borrowed from Freemasonry. Interestingly, a lot of organizations took on the name of the Knights Templar, or at least, aspects of their symbology.

One example is the Order of the Temple, or Ordo Supremus Militaris Templi Hierosolymitani. This was founded in France in 1804 under the approval of Napoleon and grew as a genuine attempt to recreate real, Christian chivalric Knights Templar, although without claiming a direct connection to the original order. It had schisms over the years, so there are perhaps eight or ten of these descendant groups, some calling the others "heretics." They are found in various countries, including the United States. One major splinter group is the Sovereign Military Order of the Temple of Jerusalem.

Thus, in a fictional tale by an author like Dan Brown, it would be easily workable to pose a rival group of Knights Templar, with Maltese crosses on their shields, swords in their hands, and conspiracy in their hearts.

❧ "Greek" Fraternities and Other Secret Social Groups ❦

Benevolent fraternal organizations aren't the only kind—there are the "Greek" college fraternities to consider, and it is intriguing to find Hermetic and Masonic principles at work, too.

The idea of Greek-letter college fraternities started in 1776 with the honorary society Phi Beta Kappa at William and Mary College, in Williamsburg, Virginia. Purely social college fraternities were founded in 1825 and 1827 with the first three (Kappa Alpha, Sigma Phi, and Delta Phi) at Union College in Schenectady, New York. The Greek fraternity movement spread throughout the United States in colleges. Notably, Delta Phis wear a Maltese cross as their emblem. Kappa Alphas originally called themselves "The Philosophers."

The first house of the Delta Kappa Epsilon fraternity—often nicknamed the "Dekes"—was founded at Yale in 1844. Members have included

Presidents Rutherford B. Hayes, Theodore Roosevelt, Gerald R. Ford, George H. W. Bush, and George W. Bush, as well as Vice President Dan Quayle. The first director of the CIA, Rear Admiral Sidney W. Souers, was a Deke. When George W. Bush was on the Yale campus in the 1960s, the Dekes were known as a drinking frat, and it was in the company of his Deke brothers that "Dubya" committed his notable acts of mischief.

But another Yale fraternity looms much larger in all theories of "good old boy" networking, and New World Order conspiracies. This is the legendary Skull and Bones, founded at Yale in 1832. Each year, only fifteen students at Yale are "tapped" to become members. It is a very exclusive society, but its members have included three generations of the Bush family, Sen. Prescott Bush, George H. W. Bush, and George W. Bush, not to mention Sen. John Kerry and many dozens of other men who have occupied high positions in government and industry.

Skull and Bones incorporates rituals of death and new birth into the lodge, the confessing of one's secrets (sexual history, in the case of Bonesmen), a solemn oath of silence, and other aspects that are direct borrowings from early Freemasonry.

Among other connections, conspiracy theorists say the early history of the CIA, an outgrowth of the OSS, was heavily influenced by a gaggle of Bonesmen. George H. W. Bush served as a CIA director. Further, it is alleged that Bonesmen were integral in the Council on Foreign Relations. Two brothers, William and McGeorge Bundy, served in the Johnson

Member: Delta Kappa Epsilon, Skull and Bones, Bohemian Club.

administration in the CIA and Defense Departments. McGeorge became president of the Ford Foundation. William Bundy went on to be editor of *Foreign Affairs*, the influential quarterly of the Council on Foreign Relations, often alleged to be part of a conspiracy to create the New World Order.

An oddity among secret social groups is the Bohemian Club. This draws a select swarm of men each year to a mid-summer "encampment" in a California grove of redwood trees. This weird society kicks off with a comic "Druid" ceremony in front of a 40-foot owl, where an effigy called "Dull Care" is burned, to signal the start of bacchanalian revelry (said to be a chance to drink, talk, and pee on the redwood trees). Scheduled on certain days are "Lakeside Chats" by prominent speakers from public, corporate, and political life. Nights are reserved for drinking and conversation. Attendees and speakers have included Henry Kissinger, Defense Secretary Donald Rumsfeld, Vice President Dick Cheney, former Secretaries of State Colin Powell and George P. Shultz, Supreme Court Justice Antonin Scalia, U.S. Rep. Newt Gingrich, *National Review* founder William F. Buckley, Jr., and both Bush presidents.

The fact that the current president can be linked to the Dekes, Skull and Bones, and the Bohemian Club, along with all of the interconnections to men of power and prestige that such affiliation brings, could be very enticing for Dan Brown to cover in his next book.

The Boy Scouts

Dan Brown often adopts an unconventional view of common societal fixtures. It's another long shot, but the Freemason-like aspects of Boy Scouting, along with some uncanny linkages to history, could attract Brown's attention.

Boy Scouting is a hugely popular fraternal movement, global in reach. Almost from the start, it had an approximately equal female arm, the Girl Scouts.

The Boy Scout movement was founded around 1908 by an Englishman, Lord Robert Baden-Powell. It experienced explosive growth in England, and doubly so when imported to America in 1910.

For the record, Scouting is not Masonic. But it has extremely strong parallels to Freemasonry that cannot be overlooked.

Scouts have special signs, handshakes, symbols, and mottos. There are three basic "degrees," Tenderfoot, Second Class, and First Class, the last earning a badge that shows a trefoil (fleur-de-lis, a symbol significant in DVC). There are a series of higher "degrees" (Star, Life, Eagle) and merit badges, reminiscent of York and Scottish Rite Freemasonry.

Within the Boy Scouts is an honorary organization known as the Order of the Arrow, which has its own secrets, such as initiation rites and passwords.

Practically the only strict requirement to join the Scouts is a belief in a supreme being, just like the Freemasons.

But it is the philosophy of Scouting that most closely aligns with Masonic tradition. Scouts are, above all, helpful to others, while being self-reliant at all times. A foundation stone of Scouting is the law "A Scout is a friend to all and a brother to every other Scout." Just like the Freemasons, he has a duty to help any brother in need. (Eventually, this allegorical lesson extends to a duty to help anyone in need.)

Scouting is based on a large number of different activities, starting with "woodcraft" skills, designed for fun, but with a hidden purpose: the building of character. Originally, one of the aims of Scouting was to create modern knights, young men of chivalrous character. The original name for merit badges was "Badges of Honour," and even today, the ceremony to award the Eagle badge is a Court of Honor.

Baden-Powell's Boy Scouts were not sprung from his mind alone. He had obvious borrowings from other youth organizations, including the Boys Brigade, Ernest Thompson Seton's Woodcraft Indians, and Dan Beard's Sons of Daniel Boone, as well as many other groups.

When it came time for creating the Cub Scouts, Baden-Powell leaned obviously and almost completely on the work of a good friend, Rudyard Kipling, whose stories of Kim and Mowgli, with their friends the jungle animals, contained practically everything that would be needed for symbols and lore. Kipling, who was a giant in literature and a long-standing

Freemason, wrote one of the best tales of Freemasonry ever, *The Man Who Would Be King*, brought to life in a movie version starring Sean Connery and Michael Caine.

Baden-Powell was a veteran soldier, a hero of the Boer War who had also served in India and Burma. He may never have become a Freemason, but he could have no higher pedigree than his father, the Rev. Baden Powell, who was a long-standing Fellow of the Royal Society and professor of geometry at Oxford University. No Freemason could have better credentials than these, particularly with the great Masonic reverence for geometry.

The Rev. Baden Powell wrote extensively on ways in which science and religion might be reconciled. (He was thus a precursor to a character in Dan Brown's novels, Leonardo Vetra, who was a clergyman-scientist seeking resolution of the same conflict.)

But the Powell family has connections going back much further in history. For centuries, they had been among the members of a craft guild called the Mercers. One of the most famous Mercers was Sir Thomas Gresham, founder of the very same Gresham College that first nurtured the Royal Society.

The Mercers are among what are called the Livery Companies of London. These were craftsmen who for centuries operated under royal licenses that allowed them to control trade by regulating who could become members of the guilds, as well as the fair prices for their wares and labors. Mention of "mercers" in London (meaning "merchants") goes back to about 1130, but actual records of the Mercers' Company date to 1348, when it adopted a new set of its ordinances. Mercers came to be seen as the fabric merchants, who exported English woolen goods, a lucrative trade, and imported silks and other rich cloth, also a lucrative trade. There were many guild companies in London, and for years they disputed their places in the royal pecking order. This finally was settled by an Order of Precedence in 1515 and the Mercers were put at the top—No. 1.

Many of these Livery Companies have lost practical connections with the trades themselves, and exist almost exclusively as charitable organizations. The Mercers last admitted an apprentice in 1888, for instance. In latter days, Baden-Powell's family saw the organization as honorable for its service to society.

Interestingly, the home of the real working masons of London, the guild called the Worshipful Company of Masons, is No. 30 in the Order of Precedence. This would have been at odds with what the masons believed—they would have said they were No. 1, of course. According to their Web site, "The company should not be confused with the Freemasons. Any possible connection was left behind centuries ago."

❧ Mormons ❧

This could be a side trip or dead end, but the "widow's son" reference by Dan Brown draws you to the aforementioned speech by Reed Durham. It practically welds the Mormons to the Masons.

This was a speech given in 1974 in Nauvoo, Illinois, one of the home bases of the Mormons before their migration to Utah. Reed C. Durham was a minor figure in the Mormon Church, and had been president of the Mormon History Society, but this speech became famous. His speech gives the top-level Google hit if you query the phrase "Is there no help for the widow's son?"

It seems clear to me that Durham merely intended to pep up an otherwise dusty meeting of the historical society. So he brought a few slides and notes, and gave a talk on the relationship between the Mormons and the Freemasons. He titled it after a quotation said to be from the Masonic legend of Hiram about the "widow's son."

As I scanned the text of Durham's speech, I could picture the historical association's members being blown backward in their seats. The tale involves the founder of the Mormon faith, Joseph Smith. It gives hints that can be followed down other trails, leading— I'm afraid—to the conclusion that Joseph Smith was a charlatan. (Durham's speech wasn't exactly public at the time, but underground copies were circulated and eventually a transcript was published, and can be found at several Web sites.)

For Dan Brown, I think the Mormon story could be a cherry ripe for the plucking. What some people perceive Dan Brown to have done to the Catholic Church, he may be about to do to the Church of Jesus Christ of Latter Day Saints.

In 1805, only a scant six years after George Washington's death, Joseph Smith was born in Vermont and later came to Palmyra, New York. At the age of twenty-five, he would found the Mormon Church.

Joseph Smith grew up within a folk tradition of magic and the occult, and displayed a number of talents, including a method of divining. Two "seer stones" were placed in a hat, and then the practitioner would put his face into the hat (the better to see what the stones would reveal). In this way, secrets could be revealed and buried treasure located.

Smith would come to use the technique as the local practitioner. Smith employed this scam as a young man, taking money from local farmers without finding a rumored "Spanish gold treasure."

Only a few years later, Smith would allege that an angel gave him the location of certain buried thin plates of gold, on which were written the word of God. After he translated the plates into the Book of Mormon and founded his church, the angel (conveniently) took back the gold plates. Smith said he had been taught how to read "reformed Egyptian" to be able to do the translations (see Appendix A, Symbolic Systems).

What Durham also noted was that Joseph Smith had borrowed heavily from the Freemasons not only in developing the Book of Mormon, but also in devising his religious rituals and symbology, and in designing Mormon works of architecture.

As we have seen earlier, the full phrase, "Oh, Lord, my God, is there no help for the widow's son?" is a Masonic plea for assistance from a brother Mason, traditionally given with arms raised "to the square," and it also has overtones relating to the original Temple of Solomon in Jerusalem. Legend has it that Joseph Smith started the plea with raised arms, but only got to "Oh, Lord, my God" when he was killed by a mob in 1844.

Meanwhile, in 1826, very near Smith-the-budding-prophet in Batavia, New York, there occurred the aforementioned case of Captain William Morgan, in which Freemasons were believed to have murdered Morgan for revealing the brotherhood's secrets.

Joseph Smith certainly heard about the Morgan case and possibly even knew Morgan; it is also possible that he had read Morgan's book. Joseph Smith's older brother Hyrum had joined the Masons, so it is highly likely that Smith had two routes to knowledge of "the craft" as he set himself to the task of "translating" the thin gold plates that he said were revealed to him by the visiting angel.

There are witnesses who say Smith sat in a cabin for about two years peering into the stones in his hat and talking aloud, with his wife, Emma, and others transcribing. The product, the *Book of Mormon*, was published in 1830. Smith went on to adapt many more borrowings from Freemasonry. In the early 1840s, when building his great temple in Nauvoo, Illinois, he festooned it richly with Masonic symbology. Smith used the language of symbolism to teach the principles of the "Mormon endowment."

Joseph Smith, Mormon Church prophet and founder.

Masonic symbols such as

the sun, moon, and five- and six-pointed stars were placed throughout the Nauvoo temple. On the weather vane was an angel, supporting a compass and square. Shortly after Smith was made a Master Mason himself, he began to outline rituals for initiating his Mormon priesthood involving the "keys of the Kingdom" as well as certain "signs and words," all of which clearly echo the Masonic rituals. Smith planned Mormon temple clothing that included aprons and sacred undergarments embroidered with the compass and square.

From a Dan Brown perspective, the Mormon story could be interesting also because of the way with which women are dealt. Smith originally had a place for women in the hierarchy, and all Mormons were to be considered part of the priesthood at some level anyway. When Smith died, his wife, Emma Hale Smith, could have been thought of as a natural bearer of the torch. Indeed, she was the protector of the "seed" of Smith in the form of his son, Joseph III, who would eventually lead a Reformed group of Mormons. But there really was little likelihood that Emma Smith would acquire the reins. They were seized by Brigham Young, who hammered out a male-dominated church. Young revised church histories in order to accomplish this.

This parallels the treatment of women and Mary Magdalene in Dan Brown's reading of the Council of Nicea in AD 325 and the early maneuverings of Peter and the other male apostles. In DVC, it is asserted that Mary Magdalene was probably the wife of Jesus and would have been the first leader of the Christians (i.e., pope), had she not been shouldered aside by Peter. The male-dominated hierarchy of the Catholic Church was later firmly cemented in place at the Council of Nicea, according to DVC.

Also, Joseph Smith practiced "spiritual wifery," or polygamy, eventually marrying some forty women. Many of his apostles followed suit (although some balked, and this was the source of rifts). Since Dan Brown showed a strong interest in religious sexuality (e.g., *hieros gamos*) in DVC, this undercurrent of Smith's life may be a great attraction.

The Smith family flirted with various forms of counterfeiting and monetary fraud, not to mention alchemy as a scheme for transmuting base metals into precious ones.

Durham's speech also describes in detail a magic amulet, or talisman, that was supposedly on Joseph Smith's body when he was killed by a mob in 1844 (but is now missing and its existence is denied by the church). Luckily, photographs were taken of it before it went missing. When Smith's brother Hyrum later died, he was said to have a "magic dagger," as well as certain coded documents called lamens, written in the manner of the Kabbalah and the occult.

The Smith talisman was similar to amulets that were known at the time as magical or, at least, the recognized paraphernalia of magicians. However, Smith's amulet differed somewhat in its markings. Interestingly, scholars have now discovered that his amulet has a defective symbol that shows up only in the first edition of the famous magic book Francis Barrett's *The Magus*. Due to a printer's error, the 1801 edition has a flaw in the *sigil* (symbol) for Jupiter. And other Smith family artifacts show a lot of borrowing from various occult sources. A novelist could use these differences to guide us to special clues and twists of plot.

Could it be that Dan Brown will use Joseph's and Hyrum's relics to provide the coded clues to find treasure? Perhaps, but as we will see, history provides other examples of ciphers and codes that would also suffice.

❧ Codes and Ciphers ❧

Let's talk about codes for a while. There's just no doubt that Dan Brown will play with codes and ciphers in his next book, given his propensity to work some form of code into every one of his first four novels.

By the time of the American Revolution, it was already established that refined and educated gentlemen might have a number of reasons for protecting messages. Correspondence was often easily intercepted, so a very important message might be coded. An ancient code system, attributed to Caesar, consisted of putting a short message into a square grid of characters. This is the "Caesar's Box" used in several Dan Brown novels. Well known was the "substitution cipher," in which the letters of the alphabet were merely rearranged and assigned numeral values (see Appendix A, Symbolic Systems).

But the Revolutionary War signaled the start in earnest of all kinds of codes, spying, secret communications, and even rampant propaganda and disinformation. George Washington supervised an

extensive network of intelligence officers (there was a "secret service" almost at the outset), and his Culper code ring was used to send secrets back and forth to field commanders. Meanwhile, master spy Benjamin Franklin went overseas to secure a treaty with France, as well as to gain intel about British and other forces, and Franklin sent back coded diplomatic messages.

The Culper code was a substitution based on a long passage of a mutually available document, in which each useful word was assigned a number. For instance, Washington himself was "711" and New York was "727." Franklin was "72." (The fledgling nation owed a debt to a female spy who died in British captivity, never known except as "355.")

Two types of secret ink were known to Washington and the Continentals. One was a simple invisible ink that was revealed under heat. The second they called a "sympathetic stain." The message was written in one chemical, and another chemical was used by the recipient to develop and reveal the message. Typically, the invisible message was written between the visible lines of a given document—hence the phrase "reading between the lines."

Thomas Jefferson, in his role as the third president, kept his diplomatic messages secret by use of a cipher device that he himself designed. It consisted of twenty-six wheeled alphabets on a common axle—a rudimentary form of the famous Enigma machine used by the Germans in World War II. The Jefferson cipher wheel was "reinvented" a couple of times, and saw service as the M-94 coding device from 1922 to World War II.

Jefferson also worked out a cipher that specifically armed Meriwether Lewis for his trip west with William Clark in 1803. It gave Lewis and Clark (both were Masons, by the way) a means to send secure messages back in the event the potentially hostile French intercepted them. Lewis had served Jefferson as a personal secretary, and had used another cipher to help Jefferson in picking out excess (and possible disloyal) Army officers when it was necessary to reduce the size of the standing Army.

Codes and spies go hand in hand, so we should remark on Nathan Hale. He was a twenty-one-year-old Revolutionary zealot with an itch to accomplish something, and his year of service as a soldier had not been exciting enough. So he foolishly volunteered to become a spy, even though advised that he was too naïve to make a good liar. He was arrested almost immediately on his first mission, and hanged promptly, and it is debatable whether his actual last words were the famous "I only regret that I have but one life to give for my country." In addition, there is evidence that the thought was not original, but rather, a quote from a published source of the time.

In any event, America honors Hale's spirit and zeal first and foremost, and then we honor him sometimes as the first famous spy for America. Because of this, there is a statue of Hale outside the original CIA headquarters in Virginia. In addition, notably, a copy of the statue can be found at Yale University, which was Hale's alma mater, and another copy can be found at Phillips-Andover Academy, which was George H. W. Bush's alma mater. Some conspiracy theorists also see a Yale connection in everything having to do with American intelligence services.

In 1885, there emerged a tale of a Virginia gentleman who buried a great treasure of gold and silver and jewels, hidden in the area of Bedford County. The legend has it that Thomas J. Beale (also known as Thomas Jefferson Beale) buried the treasure in 1819 or 1820 and on death passed to his friend, a Robert Morriss, three cipher-coded messages telling of the treasure. These messages employed a method of assigning numbers to the words in a document. The only message said to have been decoded was the one describing the amount of gold and silver. The document used to encode it was the Declaration of Independence, widely believed to have been penned by Thomas Jefferson, again of cipher wheel fame. The other two messages, consisting of an inscrutable series of numbers, have never been decoded, though many people have tried.

❧ Sexual Overtones of Dan Brown ❧

Before we move on, let's not overlook the subject of sex. In a way, DVC is all about sex. Throughout its pages, we learn that in earliest times man worshipped goddesses, and only in the past couple thousand years have male-dominated religions held power. At the very end of DVC, there is a strong hint that Robert Langdon may be sent on a quest to "restore the sacred feminine."

We are introduced in DVC to the concept that an inverted triangle represents a vulva, or womb, as well

Nathan Hale, a failure as a spy, is nonetheless honored with several prominent statues.

as the "chalice" or receptacle for the blood of Christ, i.e., a new way to define the Holy Grail as the bloodline of Christ, as carried in the womb of Mary Magdalene. The phallic symbol is the "blade" or upright triangle, not to mention all the obelisks and pyramids that abound in both *DVC* and *A&D*. Wedded, the two triangle symbols form the Star of David, or Seal of Solomon, sometimes construed as the Key of Solomon.

In *DVC*, Sophie Neveu is shocked to witness the ceremony of *hieros gamos*, or divine sexual union, as practiced by her grandfather and the Priory of Sion.

Besides being a symbology geek, Langdon isn't all that sexy. Langdon has relationships with two women that we know of. In *A&D*, he gets to know Vittoria Vetra and, after the exertions of running around Rome and saving the Vatican from destruction, they fall into bed together, with her promising to show him the sexual skills of a Hatha yoga master. In the whole of *A&D*, that's all we get about Langdon's sex life. In *DVC*, Robert and Sophie do not sleep together, but he gets a pretty good kiss at the end, plus a promise to meet a month later in Florence.

This leaves wiggle room for Dan Brown and Langdon. It may or may not come to pass that Langdon beds Sophie, either in *The Solomon Key* or another novel to come. One of the hidden issues is *hieros gamos*, which brings overtones of sexual union between a human and a divine. We learn that Sophie is evidently descended from the Merovingian royal heirs of Mary Magdalene's child, who would have had royal blood from the House of David, as well as divine blood of Christ. Is Langdon prepared for that—spiritually or otherwise?

Hieros gamos has roots going back at least to ancient Mesopotamia, where the king once a year coupled in public with a priestess prepared as a "sacred prostitute" in order to regenerate the land's prosperity and fertility.

It was thought that the priestess became divine in the ritual, becoming the goddess Inanna. This has an analogy in Christian rituals in which bread and wine become the body and blood of Jesus. It also has a very direct connection with *DVC*, in which there is an allusion to marriage between Jesus and Mary Magdalene, who was mistakenly labeled a prostitute.

Sexual union also belongs in Hermetic and *alchemical coniunctio* (alchemical marriage) tradition. An early work that makes this explicit is the *Rosarium Philosophorum*, published in 1550. It actually has drawings that show a couple uniting, spending time in a coffinlike box, then arising as a single, hermaphroditic individual.

It also should be mentioned that various secret societies, fraternities, and even religious groups in history have linked group sexual practices to religious belief. There was a noted club in England in the eighteenth century that worshipped the goddess Venus, and had sexual orgies in a converted monastery, where the "monks" said a satanic Black Mass as part of the ritual. Indeed, I have found an account like this that allegedly involved Benjamin Franklin when he was overseas. Since the origins of most fraternities involved men in bonds of brother-hood, there were potential allegations of impropriety if women were included (especially if these fraternal meetings took place after dark and involved drinking and carousing). The same kind of logic could also be used to spread rumors of homosexuality.

The mainstream of Freemasonry, at times cognizant of these pitfalls, has remained men-only, with provision for females to participate in affiliated organizations such as the Order of the Eastern Star. Having carefully distanced themselves from the early debauchery clubs, Freemasons in their lodge work generally study morality, rather than departing from it.

Part of the change in sexual attitudes over the long centuries has been the development of the concept of friendship, both male-male and male-female.

The famous Scottish Freemason Sir Robert Moray practiced a form of Christian stoicism. When his wife died, he made a seal that evoked the North Star, the constant star, as a symbol of his undying love for her. When he became a Freemason, Moray went to great lengths to design his customized "mason's mark," which was a pentacle (five-pointed star) with the Greek word *agapa* spelled between the points. This he translated as "he loves" or "love thou." Others said it more precisely meant "friendship." Thus, Moray was part of what was called a "cult of platonic friendship" of his era, which allowed for lots of talk about "love" between men (as in "brotherhood") and lots of nonsexual friendships with women. When at the court of Charles II, notorious for sexual immorality, Moray remained faithful to his dead wife. In early Christian times, an *agapa* was a "love-feast," a holy day when members of a sect would wash one another's feet and give one another the innocent "kiss of peace."

Fast-forward to 1866 and another famous Freemason, Albert Pike. Pike, then about fifty-seven, met a nineteen-year-old sculptor who had become famous for sculpting a bust of Lincoln and was working on a full-size statue. Pike was immediately smitten with the young woman, Vinnie Ream, and he began an intimate but allegedly platonic friendship with her that lasted to the end of his life. He lived to be eighty-one. The relationship endured throughout her subsequent marriage. They typically met once a week, when both were in Washington, and would read poetry together. They would hold hands, kiss, and caress, but never consummated their love, as the story goes. On a promise made in 1873, Pike began a series of "Essays to Vinnie," which came to five manuscript volumes of 2,166 pages in total. As Pike neared his end, he said, "No lie is on my lips.... If every man has at some time worshipped Anteros, he is to be pitied who has never worshipped Eros alone." This is a typical Pike-like allusion to a platonic distinction: requited versus unrequited love.

Chapter Four

BUILDING THE PHYSICAL TEMPLE: WASHINGTON THE CITY

I N CHAPTER THREE we laid out the groundwork for a kind of cosmic, virtual temple that exists in the common mind. The virtual temple exists as a construct of symbols and images, of scientific reasoning, philosophy, and religious faith. In the highest aspirations of a Dan Brown novel, this may be the most important temple that the characters react to, worshipping and pursuing ever-elusive truths.

It is now time to look at the physical temple. Already in *DVC* and *A&D*, Dan Brown has alluded to certain round-shaped structures as reminiscent of pagan worship sites, such as the Temple Church in London, where a major scene in *DVC* takes place. And in *A&D*, he has taken advantage of the cross-shaped floor plan traditionally found in cathedrals, extending it across the entire central city of Rome in a large cross-shaped symbol. It's only a small leap of logic to perceive an entire city as a temple of a kind.

Europe's great cities are old and have been rebuilt in sections, many times over. But I believe the evidence is everywhere to show that the creators of those cities strove with all their energies to make the physical city evoke the spiritual city. So it is with Washington, D.C., with the added advantage that it was conceived from the start as a great city, and all of its major architecture has been added in full awareness of what has come before.

I had been to Washington many times, but I gladly went again in 2004 to survey sites of interest for this book. It is a grand place and I have always enjoyed it, but the experience was heightened all the more when I factored in Dan Brown's books. Among other things, I kept looking at the facades of the buildings, at which way a given statue seemed to be facing or pointing, at inscriptions, and at all the depictions of gods and goddesses, Zodiacs, and a myriad of other symbols, which were everywhere I turned.

Let's hop on the tour bus, and get a good taste of Washington. I can promise you some stops that are not on the regular tour route!

Laying Out the City of Washington

There was a rosy period of Masonry when the Revolutionary War was over and Masons could bask in the glow that the revered Father of Our Country provided. The choice of a president was over before it began—only one person would do—and it was time to build a new country.

Congress voted for a one hundred-square-mile

federal district in 1787. George Washington picked out the land for the Federal District, or District of Columbia, in 1790, obtaining a grant of the land from the states of Maryland and Virginia so that he could have a ten-by-ten-mile square. He laid it out as a square diamond, with the corners pointing exactly north-south-east-west. Later on, in 1848, the land across the Potomac River in Virginia was given back, but it's easy to visualize the original tilted square on any map of D.C.

Why a square shape? Well, Washington was a former surveyor and a Freemason. If you leave a Freemason alone to doodle, you will probably get either a square or a circle out of him.

Congress picked a committee, which in turn picked city designer Pierre Charles L'Enfant to make the city plan, and engaged Andrew Ellicott for the surveying. Ellicott was assisted by Benjamin Banneker, a name not well known in history today, but a person Dan Brown might find intriguing. He was locally famous already as a free black man who was skilled in mathematics and astronomy, and later he published his own almanac after discovering that the almanacs available at the time were incorrect.

The surveyors set the southern cornerstone of the district on April 15, 1791, at Jones Point, Virginia. A minister gave a blessing, and a solemn Masonic ceremony was conducted (more about that later). They then set up markers at every mile, all the way around the diamond—forty markers in all.

L'Enfant, according to one account, leaned heavily on a plan that was developed in the 17th century for

L'Enfant created a grid system with long vistas, broad diagonal avenues, and many hidden shapes.

the post-fire rebuilding of the city of London by the famous architect Christopher Wren, prominent in the Royal Society and believed to have been a Freemason. He also had early direction from Thomas Jefferson. L'Enfant had disputes with the committee and walked off the job without completing his part, but his general plan was already well established.

There is a delightful myth that is often solemnly repeated: When L'Enfant quit and would not give up his documents, the story goes, Banneker saved the day by redrawing the city plans from memory. However, L'Enfant and Banneker did not work alongside each other, nor at the same time, so this story is surely a folktale, as attractive as it may be.

The L'Enfant plan involved a number of grand concepts. There was to be a grid network of streets running north-south and east-west. Overlaid on this was a series of broad diagonal avenues, one for each of the fifteen states in the Union at that time. These would cross at large intersections suitable for plazas and monuments.

Two broad vistas were laid into place. One looked westward from Jenkins Hill, which L'Enfant called "a pedestal waiting for a monument." This would be the site of the Capitol Building. The other vista looked south; it would be the site of the President's House, now called the White House.

The broad National Mall was part of the plan, but nothing remotely like today's mall was developed for the first hundred years. In the interim, it served for all sorts of things, such as a place to let pigs wander, a campground for soldiers, and the site of a large railroad yard. But it was always intended that a major monument would be placed at the intersection of the two vistas—and the only monument that ever made any sense would be one in honor of George Washington.

Washington was conceived of as an ideal city, but the real city had quite a few challenges to overcome.

First, there was a water channel, Tiber Creek, running through the district, connecting the Potomac with the Eastern Branch. This was eventually reshaped into the Washington City Canal, which ran right down what is now Constitution Avenue. Today it is completely gone from view, although water still flows under the avenue.

Second, everything generally west of the current Washington Monument was in the Potomac River. It was not filled in until the 1880s and 1890s, creating all the land on which we now find the Lincoln Memorial, the Jefferson Memorial, the John F. Kennedy Center for the Performing Arts, and many other structures. When the Washington Monument was first raised to the 150-foot level, you could have stood at its base and thrown a stone into the Potomac.

A grand illusion: The Capitol and the Mall appear to align precisely east-west.

Furthermore, it took a long time for Washington to be populated with the crowded blocks of government buildings, office buildings, and apartment buildings that it has today. For a long time, the broad avenues were obstructed by trees.

A famous quote by Charles Dickens describes Washington's aspirations versus its realities when he came for a visit in 1842: "It is sometimes called the City of Magnificent Distances, but it might with greater propriety be termed the City of Magnificent Intentions."

❧ Cornerstone Ceremony, American Style ❧

The first of these magnificent intentions was the Capitol building. It was begun on September 18, 1793, with a ceremony that set the tone for a lot of what was to come in the next two centuries.

A grand procession of dignitaries marched to the building site in full Masonic regalia, with drums and trumpets. A local newspaper account called it "perhaps the grandest Masonic procession ever." Presiding over the laying of the cornerstone was George Washington, who not only was president of the United States, but in this ceremony, was known as the Grand Master of the Masons *pro tem*, as well as the Worshipful Master of his lodge, Alexandria No. 22. In the procession was a ceremonial sword, as well as the Masonic Bible that Washington had used in his inaugural ceremony.

Washington spread mortar with a silver trowel that had been made for the occasion, and the cornerstone block, suspended from a wooden tripod, was lowered into place. The placement was witnessed by hundreds, if not thousands. However, it's a minor mystery: Nobody knows exactly where it is today. As we will see with the Washington Monument as well, we Americans seem to lose our cornerstones!

There were moments of prayer and silence such as one would expect in a Christian nation, but a highlight of the service was when Washington did something most Americans would consider very odd: He anointed the cornerstone with "corn, wine, and oil."

The corn, wine, and oil libation is highly significant. It's Masonic. It is an adaptation of an ancient system of consecration of a site, which would normally require four items: corn, wine, oil, and salt. For some reason, Masons in America have forgone the salt, although Masonic texts traditionally included it. (*Corn* is used in the European meaning, for any of several kinds of

grain such as wheat or
barley, not the New
World corn that is called
maize.)

If you consult a
Masonic reference book,
it will say the grain symbolizes "plenty," the
wine is "joy and cheer-
fulness," the oil is
"peace and unanimity,"
and the salt is "fidelity
and friendship." These

George Washington, Freemason,
laid the Capitol cornerstone
in 1793.

are what would be called the "politically correct"
meanings if they had to be explained today.

In fact, however, these four elements historically
represent libations to the pagan gods of earth, air, fire,
and water. They also represent the four directions of
the compass, i.e., the four winds. (For A&D readers,
think of ritual killings of four cardinals, the West
Ponente marker, the Fountain of Four Rivers, etc.)

This symbology goes back further than the Greeks
or the Romans or the Egyptians. It goes back to the
time before the gods even had individual names. And
coming forward in time, the twelve signs of the Zodiac
were subdivided into three groups of four, assigned
aspects of earth, air, fire, or water. They first were fun-
damentals of ancient astronomy and astrology, then
were adapted into their roles as gods and goddesses.

In DVC, Dan Brown explains that pagan is not a
lack of religion. It merely is a religion other than
Christianity, in the wake of the Roman Empire's

designation of Christianity as the official religion.

By this definition, the U.S. Capitol cornerstone ceremony was about as pagan as a ceremony can be. And this very ceremony, with only slight variations, has been part of practically every cornerstone laying of every major historic building in the United States. This is hugely significant for an author such as Dan Brown, who is always looking for the deeper, pagan meaning of symbols in plain sight.

One of the authors that Dan Brown is most likely to read closely as he works on laying the foundations of symbolic Washington is David Ovason. In particular, I expect Brown to study Ovason's *The Secret Architect of Our Nation's Capital*, subtitled *The Masons and the Building of Washington, DC*. Published in 1999, it has been a very influential book, especially among those who see conspiracies everywhere.

Long before there were any Dan Brown novels to read, Ovason began roaming the great buildings of Washington in awe at a single thought: There are an awful lot of Zodiacs and symbols of ancient gods and goddesses all around the city. Over the course of about ten years, Ovason counted some twenty-three major Zodiacs and more than a thousand lesser zodiacal and planetary symbols.

Seeking an explanation, Ovason explored the allusions that to him appeared to indicate that Washington was oriented astrologically, in honor of the goddess Virgo. Ovason also makes the short putt from Virgo to the Virgin Mary, and to Isis and Minerva. But throughout these discoveries, he kept coming across links to Masonic symbols.

A CLOSER LOOK

THE BIBLE AND THE TROWEL

ENGLAND has her crown jewels, including a fabulously gem-encrusted crown and scepter. These are the symbols of power that are passed on to the new monarch at a coronation. They are kept in a special chamber in the Tower of London. America has a trowel and a Bible, both of them kept by the Freemasons.

When George Washington presided over the laying of the Capitol cornerstone in 1793, a set of symbolic tools was made especially for the occasion, including a marble gavel and a silver trowel. After the ceremony, he gave the gavel to the lodge that had served as the local host of the occasion, Lodge 9 of Maryland, and the trowel to his own lodge, Lodge 22 of Alexandria, Virginia, where he had been a Past Master.

The trowel was silver with an ivory handle. As time went on, it became almost impossible to perform an important American cornerstone ceremony without having Freemasons and this trowel in attendance.

To mention just the major Washington occasions, there were the cornerstone ceremonies of the Smithsonian Institution, Washington Monument, House of the Temple (Scottish Rite), Masonic Temple of the Grand Lodge of D.C. (now the Museum of Women in the Arts), U.S. Supreme Court, National Cathedral, Library of Congress, U.S. Dept. of Commerce, National Education Building, Jefferson Memorial, U.S. Post Office Building, and the State Department Building. It was also used at the

ABOVE: Not a scepter, but a silver trowel, used first by George Washington at the cornerstone laying of the Capitol.

George Washington Masonic National Memorial in Alexandria.

Later, an exact replica was made that is now used at most ceremonies, but the real trowel was again used at the two hundredth anniversary reenactment of the U.S. Capitol cornerstone ceremony in 1993. The trowel resides at the Washington Masonic National Memorial, under the care of Lodge 22 of Alexandria.

When George Washington was about to be sworn in as the first president in 1789, the location was New York City, the capital of the country at that time. A platform was built at the city hall on Wall Street and the dignitaries were assembled, including the entire Congress of the United States (a much smaller group than today, of course). That's when they noticed that they did not have a Bible for the ceremony.

But not to worry. Since the presiding officer for the occasion was a Masonic Grand Master, New York Chancellor Robert Livingston, an immediate solution came to mind. A fellow Mason (among many present) was dispatched down the street to a coffee house where St. John's Lodge No. 1 held its meetings, and the lodge's elegant 1767 King James Bible was brought.

Washington placed his hand on the Bible, which was randomly opened to Genesis, chapters 49 and 50. He swore the oath, then reverently kissed the book. A bronze statue of Washington marks the spot to this day, at what is now the Federal Building on Wall Street.

The same Bible has since been used at four other inaugurations: those of Warren G. Harding in 1921, Dwight D. Eisenhower in 1953, Jimmy Carter in 1977, and George H. W. Bush in 1989, who had it opened at random.

In honor of his father's presidency, it was also to have been used for the inauguration of George W. Bush in 2001. An honor guard of three Masonic officials brought the Bible to the ceremony. But there was rain at the scheduled time and a last-minute decision was made (reportedly by Vice President Dick Cheney) not to subject the book to risk of damage. A Bush family Bible was substituted, and kept closed.

President Ronald Reagan had a family Bible at his inaugural, opened at a verse that his mother, Nelle Reagan, had highlighted. When he was sworn in for his second term in 1985, groups of conservative Christians urged him to open the Bible to the same verse. The passage is II Chronicles 7:14, which reads: "If my people, who are called by my name, will humble themselves and pray and seek my face and turn from their wicked ways, then will I hear from heaven and will forgive their sin and will heal their land."

Besides the obvious urge for people to repent, the verse is said to have deeper meanings. Although it actually applies to Israel, it could be seen as applying to America as a "chosen people." In addition, it is tied to support of

George Washington and George H.W. Bush swore oaths on this Bible

Israel, since it is believed that a Second Coming will take place in Jerusalem.

As plans were being finalized for George W. Bush's second inauguration, the same Christian groups were asking him to do the same as Reagan, and to use a family Bible, not the Washington Masonic Bible. Although we're waiting for confirmation, it appears Bush did as requested. In some circles, this would be seen as a symbol that President Bush is fulfilling prophecies of the coming End Times. In both *DVC* and *A&D*, Dan Brown refers to millennial prophecies or events that are being anticipated.

As Ovason says in his book, he did not mean to claim that the Masons had some kind of secret grip on the building of the city, or by extension, the operation of the government. But that's the way people construed him. Unfortunately, Ovason's book provided all the fuel necessary for some truly bizarre conspiracy theories, by interpreting the street layout so as to see an inverted pentangle—a symbol of Satan—and proceeding to find other Satanic meanings in the symbolism Ovason had highlighted.

But symbols there are. Washington is a city with ample symbology on practically every building façade or cornerstone. Although the Constitution had made it clear there was not to be a state religion, the official artwork, such as the paintings on the Capitol dome and walls, has a profusion of Zodiacs, Greek and Roman gods, Egyptian motifs, Christian references, and numerous images that still defy contemporary critics' ability to understand or decode.

Certain recurring themes cry out for attention (see page 52, Traditional Symbols of Freemasonry). Consider the Masonic symbols of compass and square (the tools). Looking at them for evidence of male and female symbology, you can readily see the phallus and vulva, or as Dan Brown likes to put it more delicately, the blade and the chalice. Notably, in the Masonic symbol, they are united. This is no accident, and to Dan Brown it surely brings up the notion of sacred marriage, not to mention the *hieros gamos* ritual. In a Masonic sense, the combination of equilateral triangles forms a six-pointed star, having the same meaning as the Chinese yin-yang. In the context of

Dan Brown's *DVC* it has essentially the same meaning, but with hints of the sexual as well.

Speaking of sex symbols, there is no more phallic symbol in existence than the Washington Monument, and the Capitol dome can be viewed as breastlike. Also, the Washington Monument sits in the center of the city like the world's biggest sundial. For a novelist's purposes, if you choose the date and time correctly, you could have the monument's shadow point toward practically anything in Washington.

But to Masons, the compass and square have a multitude of meanings, not just the six-pointed star. The compass can be used to draw a circle, expanding three-dimensionally to a sphere, and the square to draw a square, or three-dimensionally, a cube. To a Mason, the circle represents the heavens; the cube, the earth.

Squares, circles, spheres, and cubes are "hidden in plain sight" all over Masonic structures and in fact, throughout the architecture and art of Washington. If you just wander around the major buildings and look at the floor occasionally, it will become obvious that a circle within a square, or vice versa, seemed like the "right" motif to many of the city's builders and designers.

Nowhere is symbology a better playground for a Dan Brown book than at the openly Masonic buildings and monuments of Washington. The list would start with the House of the Temple, at 1733 16th Street, NW, about thirteen blocks north of the White House. This is the home of the Supreme Council 33° of the Ancient and Accepted Scottish Rite of

Freemasonry. It has two massive sphinxes guarding the door. The steps are tiered in sets of three, five, seven, and nine, so you are hit with Masonic symbology before you even enter the building.

Once inside, black marble columns support a soaring ceiling in a cavernous temple atrium, leading to a richly appointed lodge room. In a special alcove, the remains of Albert Pike, the revered Mason, are interred. The Temple houses a large library full of priceless books of Masonic and other historical significance. Large museum rooms dedicated to famous Masons occupy a labyrinthine basement, with special focus given to the Founding Fathers, Burl Ives, J. Edgar Hoover, and several U.S. astronauts.

A loose secret is that astronauts Aldrin and Armstrong, first to set foot on the moon, had a Masonic lodge flag secreted in their inner clothing. Since the American flag was unloaded only after they had stepped onto the surface, the actual first flag to be carried onto the moon was the Masonic one. This flag was brought back from the moon and is on display in a case at the House of the Temple, along with thousands of historic artifacts. In addition, there are other rooms in the basement, crammed with other relics and

A Masonic flag was the first flag actually carried onto the moon.

treasures far too numerous to be displayed. One can only imagine what Dan Brown might conceive of in this "secret" archive.

The Washington Monument itself is considered Masonic in design for a number of reasons, not the least of which is the form of a pyramid at the top. Just after Washington's death in 1799, the Congress had hopes that his family would allow him to be interred in the city, at the place where his monument would eventually be built. In anticipation of this plan, a crypt was constructed deep beneath the Capitol Building, where George and Martha were to have been interred while a monument was under construction. It didn't happen, but if this original plan had gone to fruition, there would be a large pyramidal tomb in the center of what is now the National Mall.

Washington's family never consented to disturb the instructions of his will, so he remains in a mausoleum at Mount Vernon. But in 1865, a catafalque was hastily built to support the coffin of Abraham Lincoln, and it came to be stored in the Capitol's crypt, emerging only on rare occasions when a figure of importance lies in state. The latest occasion was President Ronald Reagan's body lying in the Rotunda in June of 2004.

At 3rd and D Streets, NW, in Judiciary Square, we find a statue of Albert Pike. Pike is the only Confederate general to get a full outdoor statue in the nation's capital, but it was his prominence as a scholar and leader of the Freemasons that earned him a spot for his statue. Pike was a major source for the rituals and lore of Scottish Rite Freemasonry.

Albert Pike's many facets could make him a central

figure in *The Solomon Key*, since he combined knowledge of so many arcane subjects—including Freemasonry's deepest secrets—and had so many strange connections historically. His appearance in later life was the very personification of Merlin the wizard, with flowing shoulder-length hair and beard and a ponderous expression. Dan Brown used Leonardo da Vinci to create codes and secrets for *DVC*; he could use Pike the same way in *The Solomon Key*.

One structure that is actually in Alexandria, Virginia, must be included in the list of openly Masonic buildings, the striking George Washington Masonic National Memorial, built by the Masons to honor their most famous member.

Since Dan Brown weaves religion into his plots wherever possible, it is appropriate to look around Washington for a religious setting, such as a church or cathedral. Washington has many of these, but it should be mentioned that the National Cathedral, prominently placed on a hill northwest of the central city, has a rich collection of ornaments and stonework, the equal of any major cathedral of Europe. Like European cathedrals, it has subterranean vaults and crypts, reminiscent of catacombs. The cathedral's rich symbology may be interpreted in various ways, including Masonic ones, of course. Gargoyles and grotesques abound (including one of Darth Vader, as you can learn by poking around the National Cathedral Web site). One could reasonably expect Dan Brown to include at least a chase scene through these American catacombs in *The Solomon Key*.

*The National Cathedral is equal to Europe's finest. The
lower level holds crypts.*

David Ovason, astrologer and symbologist, whom I
mentioned earlier as the author of *The Secret Architect
of Our Nation's Capital*, believes that the city's Federal
Triangle is an imitation of the formation of the three
stars of the constellation Virgo as they aligned on
August 10, 1791. This linkage to Virgo (the Virgin)
would be of great allure to Dan Brown, calling to mind
not only the Virgin Mary, but also Venus, the chalice,
the rose, and the "sacred feminine." These are all
themes from *DVC*, linked together by Dan Brown in a
way that startled his readers.

One truly weird theory floating around the Internet
holds that Washington is laid out with an inverted
pentacle shape, symbolic of Satan or Baphomet, and
that this demonstrates a link to the alleged dark side of
Freemasonry. The most popular Web site that illustrates
this theory goes on to link the Washington symbology to
terrain formations on the planet Mars. To me, it seems
odd that conspiracy theorists scour the street plan for a
pentacle, when the Pentagon itself across the river is

such an obvious symbol. Another Web site develops the street plan into eight or nine symbolic themes, including shapes like pyramids, hexagrams, and pentagrams, but also phallus and vulva, compass and square, the Tree of Life, and even the cross-section of the Great Pyramid at Giza in Egypt. If you adopt the Great Pyramid theory, you perhaps should dig for treasure underneath the Potomac, somewhere between the East Potomac Golf Course and Reagan National Airport. By the way, good luck with that!

❧ Portraits and Paintings of George Washington ❧

We have covered a lot of the must-see monuments, as well as some that are not on most tour maps, and even some spots that are little known to city residents. Now it's time to take on the topic of artwork. Our favorite cousin, George Washington, makes a very good subject to concentrate on, and here we will talk about the many paintings of him.

In his time and in the years that followed the Revolution, Washington was almost deified by a grateful population. He had led the fighting, then tried to retire to his plantation. He had come back as president for two terms, then retired again. He had only a few years to enjoy retirement before he died in the waning days of 1799. He was laid to rest in a mausoleum in Mount Vernon with both Masonic and religious rites.

Everyone wanted a portrait of him. Washington sat for many portraits, even though he really hated it, including some at the pleading of the Freemasons. He was presented with gifts such as ornate Masonic ceremonial aprons, including one from the Marquis de Lafayette, made by Lafayette's wife.

George Washington sat for a number of portraits well before the Revolution. Being especially proud of his commission as a young colonel in the Virginia Militia, he was willing to pose in uniform. But during his years in command of the Continental Army and later as president, the demands and pleas for portrait sittings reached an unbearable level. He had become too famous, in the way that a celebrity today is gawked at and photographed endlessly.

Quite a number of famous artists gave Washington their best shot, including John Trumbull, Charles Willson Peale, and Gilbert Stuart. However, they almost universally ended up making him look stiff and uncomfortable (however, because he really was uncomfortable, it may have been complete realism as art).

In the eighteenth century there was no way to mass-produce or copy a painting, so the artist who got a subject to sit for him had a huge advantage. If the subject would indulge, the artist would make lots of sketches and extra poses, so that he could put out varied canvases and collect more commission fees for years to come. Then other artists would copy the originals, and the copies would spread, eventually reaching artists who did engravings for printed books, and thus, finally, the general public would get a hint of what a great man looked like.

First in fame among the great painters of

Gilbert Stuart's likeness of a slightly perturbed Washington, later adapted for the U.S. dollar bill.

Washington was Gilbert Stuart. He came along relatively late, when Washington was just about fed up with painters. When Stuart tried to make small talk at the first sitting in 1795, Washington wasn't buying it. As Stuart described it, "an apathy seemed to seize him, and a vacuity spread over his countenance, most appalling to paint." If you look carefully, you can see a grumpy look on Washington's face, despite Stuart's best artistic technique. The dollar bill has an adaptation of Stuart's work as the portrait.

Over the succeeding years Stuart cranked out at least 104 portraits of Washington, mainly in three major poses. The full-length view was very prized. It is known as the Lansdowne version. One such copy hangs in the White House, and we have First Lady Dolly Madison to thank for that. She saved the painting from being burned when the White House was torched by the British in 1814. She bravely remained behind until the last moment, considering this a sacred duty.

Charles Willson Peale painted Washington first in 1772. The two men became friends, before either one of them could know what history had in store. Peale became a Mason in 1774. He joined the Continental

Army in 1776, serving with Washington in several battles, as well as during the tough winter at Valley Forge in 1777–78. He thus was in a position to get Washington's likeness several times, including 1779 in his general's uniform. This version was promptly copied by Jean-Baptiste Le Paon and spread throughout Europe as the Continent's first glimpse of the man.

William Joseph Williams, a lesser artist, managed to get Washington for one of his last sittings in 1793, at the urging of Washington's "brother" Freemasons. The result shows him in Masonic regalia of a past master of Virginia, looking fairly grim.

One of the many artists who assisted the immigrant Italian painter Constantino Brumidi, commissioned often for works in Washington, was the painter Albion Hurdle. In 1840, he painted a standing post-humous portrait of Washington in full Masonic regalia. Hurdle, like Washington before him, belonged to Alexandria Lodge 22, and the painting hangs there now. It is much revered among Freemasons.

Washington's aura was hardly diminished in 1875 when the Capitol dome was decorated with its *Apotheosis of Washington*, a depiction of George Washington ascending to heaven, godlike, accompanied by heavenly maidens.

The fresco was painted by Constantino Brumidi, who is unknown today by most Americans but was a renowned artist at the time. He was an immigrant who had painted a number of government-commissioned works, with the *Apotheosis* considered to be his masterpiece. It called for Washington to be flanked by two goddesses, Liberty and Fame, as well as thirteen virgins in a circle, representing the first states. However, as the story goes, Brumidi had befriended some of the local working girls in Washington and he needed some fresh faces, so he used the local prostitutes as models.

Thus, one of the closest things America has to a "sacred" piece of art is actually a group portrait of some prostitutes!

This is another bit of legend and myth that would feed into Dan Brown's themes of the sacred feminine and the accusations of prostitution against Mary Magdalene. In *DVC*, Dan Brown explains that long ago a pope made a mistake in reading the Bible, and equated Mary Magdalene with a prostitute mentioned in a following verse. For more than a thousand years, Magdalene was considered a redeemed harlot, until very recently when the Church corrected its mistake.

❧ Sculptures and Monuments of George Washington ❧

It was common knowledge throughout America that a monument to George Washington would be erected in the center of the Mall, but people took it for granted, so the project fell between the cracks for years at a time. The concept was broached within weeks after Washington's death and one plan for it was almost adopted by Congress by 1801, but there were fits and starts, and construction did not begin for decades.

Unwilling to wait, the nearby city of Baltimore erected a very fine statue of Washington atop a grand-looking 178-foot column. The cornerstone was laid in

1815 and it was completed in 1824. American-trained architect Robert Mills, of Charleston, South Carolina, won the design competition and was going to build a massive column resting on a base with balconies at several levels, inscriptions, and a crowning statue representing Washington, dressed as a Roman warrior, riding in a horse-drawn chariot. Due to costs, this idea had to be scaled back to a simpler, more graceful column and, thankfully, the statue eventually sculpted was a standing portrayal of Washington in a much friendlier pose.

In an eerie echo of Francis Bacon's symbolism of pillars, the American author Herman Melville described Baltimore's monument: "Great Washington stands aloft on his towering mainmast in Baltimore, and like one of Hercules' pillars, his column marks that point of human grandeur beyond which few mortals will go."

Embarrassed by Baltimore's successful monument, Congress took steps to move the Washington project along, but it still fizzled at times, and the cornerstone was not laid until 1848. Even then it lapsed several times until the nation was again embarrassed in 1876, the centennial year, to have a mere 150-foot stump of a monument. The monument was finally completed in 1884.

The thought of a chariot-driving Washington had occurred to a number of people, since it was the style of the day to compare a revered person figuratively to a Roman emperor or a god. Thus it was that Antonio Canova, considered the greatest Italian sculptor of his day, made a statue of Washington in 1818 complete with curly, Caesar-like hair and Roman armor. The statue stood in the Statehouse in Raleigh, North Carolina, until a fire destroyed it in 1831, but it was replaced at long last in 1970. Although it eventually became a source of pride for North Carolinians, in its day it was unliked and occasionally ridiculed. Washington's loyal French friend the Marquis de Lafayette said it looked more like Lafayette than Washington.

Not so with an excellent portrayal done by another great artist, Jean-Antoine Houdon of France, who took care to spend two weeks with Washington in 1785 at his home in Mount Vernon, studying his features and measurements, and making a face mask. According to one story, Martha Washington walked in just before the cast hardened and George grinned slightly, giving him a "Mona Lisa" smile. Houdon made a terra-cotta bust of Washington as a gift to him that still resides at Mount Vernon today.

Somewhat earlier, in 1770, the American artist Benjamin West had broken long tradition by painting a famous British general in his own uniform, instead of in Roman garb. When asked his opinion about the statue in progress, Washington leaned in favor of the Continental uniform for himself, so that is how Houdon portrayed him, and it was quite successful. The pose, however, was that of the famous Roman Cincinnatus, who left his farm to become a general, then returned to it and resumed a simple life of peace— just like Washington.

Houdon went back to France to complete the statue, which was delivered in 1791. (To see it today, however, you must travel to Richmond, Virginia, where it stands in the statehouse rotunda, which is unfortunately undergoing renovation.) Washington himself got to see the statue and pronounced it "a good likeness." Lafayette was more enthusiastic: "That is the man himself. I can almost realize he is going to move."

Houdon's work shows Washington wearing his uniform but holding a civilian walking cane with his right hand. Washington is warmly portrayed as a man, not as a god, but the theme is classical. Behind him is a farmer's plowshare. He rests his left hand on a bundle of rods called a *fasces*, the Roman symbol of civil authority. The bundle has thirteen rods, standing for the thirteen original colonies, and arrows are shown in between that likely refer to Indians or the idea of America as a wild frontier.

Treatments of Washington, and other figures, thus illustrate the conflicted nature of America art. Seeking respect, American art imitated classical European art for a time, and this meant posing people as gods or Romans, as well as adorning buildings with images of mythical beings. Any stroll around the city of Washington gives plenty of support to any assertion that Dan Brown might make of the "pagan" origins of the capital.

From my personal point of view, George Washington's essence is captured beautifully in the statues of him mounted on a horse, in his uniform. This was the way his troops saw him, always calm and fearless in battle, a leader who had often been under fire yet had never been wounded.

The equestrian statues can be found in many places, both in the city of Washington and elsewhere in the country. One is at Washington Circle (23rd and K Streets, NW). Another interesting one is on the grounds of the National Cathedral, often missed by visitors. It has a story of its own. In the 1950s a wealthy donor contributed enough to build the center tower of the cathedral, but on one condition: that an equestrian statue of Washington be placed near the west entrance to the grounds. The donor was insistent that the horse modeled be a special one—the famous Man O'War, one of the greatest racehorses of all time.

One statue of George Washington became a white elephant. This was a statue commissioned by Congress in 1832 from the American sculptor Horatio Greenough, a Harvard-educated artist steeped in the neo-classical style. Greenough worked in Rome and Florence at the time. In 1841, his statute arrived in Washington, where Congress had ordered it placed in the newly refurbished Rotunda of the Capitol.

Greenough had chosen to give Washington a Zeus-like appearance. The statue is naked from the waist up, muscled, sitting regally with one hand aloft and the other holding a sword. Greek gods adorn the base. It is the personification of Washington as a pagan god, and again, a perfect illustration for a Dan Brown novel.

The ten-foot high, twelve-ton statue was unveiled in place and the members of Congress got a look at what they and the taxpayers had paid for. Practically everyone hated it. It was also poorly lighted, sitting in the very center of the Rotunda so that light came straight down from above, giving it a gloomy appearance.

"Luckily," after about two years the floor began to sag and crack, and it was necessary to remove the statue. It was hauled out to the east yard of the Capitol and sat there for many years, suffering the indignities of the weather and the pigeons. Someone eventually recognized that it would be disgraceful to allow the statue to decay further, so it was moved in 1908 to the west wing of the Smithsonian Institution.

Greenough's statue: When they thought of George Washington as a god, they really meant it!

This wing had many exhibits over the years, but for a time, Washington presided over the Marine Invertebrate Exhibition! Oysters, clams, and starfish, oh my! The room didn't even have electric lighting until 1956.

In 1962, this version of Washington was given its present home in what is now known as the National Museum of American History, on Constitution Avenue. The lighting is much better, but George as Zeus still looks weird. Please forgive me, Cousin George.

In a very interesting twist of history, there were members of Congress alive in 1866 who remembered the Zeus-Washington fiasco when it came time to commission a statue of Abraham Lincoln. Some months before Lincoln's assassination, he was approached by friends who asked that he help a poor young sculptor's apprentice by sitting for a bust, since she showed great talent. The young woman, Vinnie Ream, did a fine bust of Lincoln, completed just days before his death.

She parlayed this, along with good looks and a vivacious personality, into a bid to make the life-size statue of Lincoln for the Congress. After considerable debate, the senators took a chance and put their trust in the nineteen-year-old. This time the results were wonderful. When unveiled in 1871, some of Lincoln's old friends said it was like looking at the man himself. The Lincoln statue still holds a place of honor in the Capitol Rotunda.

Vinnie Ream would soon become the platonic "friend" of the legendary Freemason Albert Pike. They had a relationship that lasted some twenty-five years (see page 139, Sexual Overtones of Dan Brown).

The most important monument, of course, is the Washington Monument, completed in 1884—widely considered to be Masonic in design. On completion it briefly became the world's tallest structure and the tallest structure to be built in Washington (until the National Cathedral). The monument stands 555 feet. By some, the number 5-5-5 is seen as symbolic in itself, since to Masons, five is a special number and threes of anything are special. A noted authority on Freemasonry tells me that in fact nothing about 555 is significant in a Masonic sense. But, like so many other legends, it has been repeated so often that it has acquired the patina of truth.

But the monument building did not stop. In 1932, the Masons themselves—rarely as unified in any previous project in their history—built the magnificent George Washington Masonic National Memorial on a high hill overlooking Alexandria, Virginia. No one who arrives in Alexandria can fail to feel the imposing presence of the Memorial; it is a commanding structure. The Memorial stands 333 feet (3-3-3, get it?) on the highest point in sight for miles.

It is, simply put, a temple for George Washington. The main hall is a masterpiece of marble columns and murals, housing a massive three-story bronze statute of Washington, dressed in full Masonic regalia. There is a re-creation of the original lodge room where his lodge, Alexandria No. 22, met. It contains many Washington relics. Many special symbolic rooms abound, including one devoted to the Knights Templar, and another containing a richly detailed replica of the Ark of the Covenant. There is a mural depicting the ruins of the Temple of Solomon, among many dozens of pieces of symbolic art.

As such, the Washington Masonic National Memorial could be a perfect backdrop for Dan Brown's novel, since one can run from room to room chasing the symbolism of ancient history and Freemasonry.

❧ The Improbable Obelisk ❧

Of all the tales swirling around statues and

monuments, the story of the Washington Monument is truly a tale of intrigue and mystery, tied to the Masons and even to a conspiracy.

While Washington was still alive, it was proposed that there be a monument to him, with an "equestrian statue." Originally, there was a proposal to put him in a six-horse chariot, but later, he was to be seen on horseback, or standing. A pyramid one hundred feet square at the base was proposed and came close to being picked for construction.

But when the serious effort to build the monument began, the design that was chosen in 1836 was a kind of pantheon to the Founding Fathers, a round colonnade structure that would house statues of many famous founders, with Washington the central and greatest figure. Sprouting from the top of this rotunda was to be a large obelisk, six hundred feet tall.

It was an ugly design and would have been way too costly. Even after the design evolved into the general obelisk concept, it was modified many times for aesthetic and structural reasons until its final completion in 1884.

The monument's original cornerstone, a marble block of twenty-four tons, was laid July 4, 1848, amid formal Masonic ceremonies, as related in the monument's published history, which can be found at the monument's Web site, run by the National Park Service: "The cornerstone was formally laid by Grandmaster Benjamin B. French of the Grand Lodge of Free and Accepted Masons of the District of Columbia. He wore the same Masonic apron and sash that had belonged to President Washington, and wielded the same Mason's gavel that had been used by him when he laid the cornerstone of the U. S. Capitol on September 18, 1793. French applied the Masonic square, level, and plumb to the northeast corner and pronounced it sound. He then poured vials of the traditional Masonic symbols over the cornerstone. They consisted of corn, invoking the blessing of plenty upon the Nation; wine, for the joy ever to be found in our broad land; and oil, the healing oil of consolation." (Again, this is a sanitized explanation of pagan libations.)

Mysteriously, although the cornerstone was large and publicly laid, its exact location was forgotten and was covered by construction, so today no one really knows where it is.

In 1854, the construction of the monument was languishing as it had many times, when a series of decorative stones were contributed from around the U.S. and abroad. According to the government's account: "Among the stones received from foreign governments was one from Pope Pius IX. It was a block of historic marble from the Temple of Concord in Rome and was approximately 3 feet long, 10 inches thick and 18 inches high. The gift infuriated the American Party, a splinter group popularly known as the 'Know-Nothings.' The party was hostile to foreign-born Americans and to the Catholic Church. The Know-Nothings vowed that the Pope's Stone, as it came to be known, would never become a part of the Washington Monument."

It is important to understand the significance of the Pope's Stone to the Know-Nothings, as well as other

Americans who were sympathizers with the movement. It was far more than a mere decorative piece of marble. Not without some justification, they saw the Vatican (especially when allied with scheming European monarchs) as a machine of world conquest. The Pope's Stone to them represented the planting of the Vatican flag in America—surely an invasion of Catholic crusaders would follow, forcing everyone to convert at swordpoint.

This significance would be doubly meaningful to Dan Brown, who has already painted the Catholic Church as an imperial force in both religion and politics. Particularly in A&D, the forces of the Illuminati and of science are arrayed against the hegemony of the Church.

But the tale of the Washington Monument continues: "On the night of Monday, March 6, 1854, between the hours of one and two a.m., as the night watchman was standing guard alongside the incomplete monument which by then had reached a height of 156 feet, a group of four to ten men rushed out of the darkness, surrounded his shack and piled stones that were scattered throughout the swamp-like area against his door. The intruders then stole the Pope's Stone from the lapidarium on the grounds, loaded it into a handcart, and trundled it from the scene.

"The watchman could not explain to the investigating committee of the Society why he waited almost two hours before sounding the alarm, or why he failed to drive off the intruders with his shotgun. He was fired from his job by the Society and a $100 reward was posted for return of the stone and for information leading to the arrest of the culprits. No arrests were made and the stone was never recovered. The incident disgusted many Americans and contributions took a nosedive.

"It was believed for years that the stone was dumped into the Potomac River near Long Bridge, but it was never found. Some years ago a report was published that it was buried at the intersection of P and 22nd Streets near the border of Georgetown. Investigation of this rumor by an enterprising reporter who interviewed a work gang of the Potomac Electric Light and Power Company, then digging in the vicinity, failed to uncover either the Pope's Stone or any further information on the subject. One of the most current rumors, particularly among Catholic tourists visiting the monument, is that the Pope's stone was smashed by the Know-Nothings and that the fragments were ground up in the mortar used for setting the stones of the monument."

In 1982, through the efforts of a Seattle area priest, a replacement stone was sent in the name of the then-pontiff Pope John Paul II. It was placed at the 440-foot level. But strangely, mention of this was omitted from the National Park Service's published history of the monument.

Other stones have had mysterious provenances, including a stone from ancient Carthage that was contributed in 1854 but somehow misplaced in 1890 and found in 1950 in the elevator pit. Combine all the stones that have gone missing in Washington (such as the aforementioned Capitol cornerstone or the

*One of the many Masonic stones that line
the Washington Monument.*

Washington Monument cornerstone mentioned above), and it certainly seems to form a pattern.

Through infiltration, the Know-Nothing Party also seized control of the Washington Monument Building Society for a period, until Congress stepped in and took over. Thus, the anti-immigrant Know-Nothings, as secretive as you could get in a national political party, were at one time in control of one of our country's most important monuments. Could they have dug a sub-basement and stored secrets or treasures there? It would certainly make a great plot twist for a Dan Brown novel!

The Washington Monument is a striking symbol that stands out for so many reasons, but several other structures in the city may look more "conventional" while displaying symbology that is "hidden in plain sight."

❧ Pantheons ❧

Let us pursue just one Dan Brown-esque line of reasoning about architecture (perhaps over-pursuing, of course). Take the circle and square—or, at least, start with a circle:

As Dan Brown relates in *DVC*, the Knights Templar were known for building "round churches," one of which (Temple Church in London) figured prominently in one of *DVC's* culminating scenes. But the Temple Church actually consists of a round portion and a rectangular portion.

If we go looking for something similar in architecture, we suddenly see a multitude of structures in which something round is married to something squarish.

But much more significantly, this insight yields a chain spanning history and geography. In BC 27, a temple was built in Rome called the Pantheon. This was destroyed but rebuilt in AD 125. Its concept was a gesture by Marcus Agrippa to bring together the people of the Roman Empire in the worship of the gods of their choice, since they did not worship the old Roman gods, or did so under different names. The concept of a Pantheon is thus a temple for multiple gods.

The structure of the Pantheon married a round portion with a rectangular portion. The round portion was a coffered dome with a hole in the top called an oculus. The rectangular portion was a portico, or porch. This structure is the oldest surviving architectural relic from the Greco-Roman world.

Since the seventh century, the Pantheon of Rome has been used as a Christian church. Dan Brown is very fond of pointing out cases in which the Church built on or took over pagan sites, replacing pagan gods with Christian equivalents, such as saints. In *A&D*, the first, mistaken attempt that Robert Langdon makes to thwart the Hassassin is to race to the Pantheon, where readers get a thorough lecture about the building, not to mention the pagan antecedents of Christianity.

The pantheon concept was brought forward many times, but certainly it blossomed in Paris very strikingly. The Pantheon of Paris was built on a site chosen in AD 507 for his burial basilica by the Franks king Clovis I, first of the line of Merovingians (and descended from Mary Magdalene, if you believe *DVC*). The current structure was begun in the reign of Louis XV to honor Saint Genevieve, but it was turned into a temple to honor the "gods" of the French people after the Revolution.

The earliest of these "gods" was Voltaire, Freemason and friend of Benjamin Franklin, as mentioned earlier. Voltaire's remains were taken there in 1791 in a grand procession (but were later stolen and reportedly thrown in the trash). Famous Frenchmen buried there are Victor Hugo, Jean Monet, Marie and Pierre Curie, and Emile Zola. The floor plan of the Paris Pantheon is actually cruciform, but the prominent form of the building is a dome with a portico.

In the New World, the most famous and visible Pantheon-like structure may be the U.S. Capitol.

Jefferson considered the Pantheon design a perfect structure, so it was a natural choice for his own memorial.

Begun in 1793, it is dominated by a dome with a portico (actually, a portico on each of two "fronts," east and west). In the ceiling of the central dome is the aforementioned Constantino Brumidi fresco of Washington, rising godlike to heaven. Originally, Greenough's statue of Washington (see page 171) was to sit at the center of the Rotunda, but it was poorly received and it cracked the flooring. But other statues of great Americans remain in the Capitol, as though in a temple to multiple gods.

Thomas Jefferson, already a great student of architecture, spent time in Paris as the American ambassador. He was profoundly influenced by the classic structures he saw there, and it marked a watershed in his architectural career. At one point in his travels, he sat for half a day staring at a Roman temple, the Maison Carrée at Nîmes. After his return, Jefferson designed buildings for the University of

Unused National Pantheon design of the Washington Monument.

Virginia, the most famous of which, the Rotunda, is clearly inspired by the pantheons of Rome (which he never saw) and of Paris.

Because Jefferson considered it the "most perfect" of building designs, when it came time to build the Jefferson Memorial in the early 1900s, a pantheon was the natural and logical choice (although there was a fairly long and bitter controversy over it). Thomas Jefferson is, of course, the "god" enshrined there.

Originally, the design of the Washington Monument was not at all what we see today.

According to published descriptions, the design by Robert Mills chosen in 1836 "was a blend of Greek, Babylonian and Egyptian architecture. Its enormous circular base was a temple-like building 200 feet in diameter and 100 feet tall. Around the rotunda were to be 30 massive columns, 12 feet in diameter. At the outer ring statues were to be placed of the signers of the Declaration of Independence, Revolutionary War heroes, and Washington himself. From the center of the rotunda was to rise a four-sided obelisk, or shaft, to a total height of 600 feet."

Mills called it a "National Pantheon." Again, the design elements were a squared form married to a circular form, housing multiple gods.

❧ Treasure Hunt Fever ❧

Our tour so far has led us around Washington looking at structures that rise from the earth, but my gut feeling keeps leading me to think about the idea of buried treasure in the context of Dan Brown's next book. This breaks down into two questions immediately: *What* would the treasure be, and *where* would it be buried?

We can contemplate the *what* for a while:

There is a treasure, and an association with American history, which we will deal with in more detail shortly. It relates to a Civil War group, the Knights of the Golden Circle. If the plot of Brown's next book were to follow these native "knights," the treasure could be a fabulous amount of gold and silver coins and bullion, the entire wealth of the Confederacy at the moment that it decided the cause was lost.

But we can consider other ideas. The most serious treasure of all might be the one associated with the Temple of Solomon, which could include not only untold wealth in gold, silver, and gems, but also the Ark of the Covenant.

It should be mentioned that relics of huge significance were rumored to have been buried in the Rosslyn Chapel in Scotland, and could have been transplanted to America, fictionally speaking. These include not just the Ark of the Covenant, but also the genuine Stone of Destiny (a.k.a. the Stone of Scone), and even the mummified head of Christ. Of course, Dan Brown in *DVC* intimated that the Holy Grail, a term for the relics of Mary Magdalene, was (at least at one time) buried beneath Rosslyn Chapel.

Another intriguing thought is the modern, scientific incarnation of the ancient term *alchemy*. Suppose, for example, that the buried treasure is merely the true secret of the transmutation of metals (e.g., from lead into gold) or matter into energy at room temperature, etc. Last but not least, of course, is the treasure of the secret of eternal life, but this would tread very closely on the popular movie *Indiana Jones and the Last Crusade*.

The movie *National Treasure*, mentioned earlier, took a lot of the themes of importance to Dan Brown and wrapped them around a legend of Templar treasure, said to be a combination of the treasure of the Temple of Solomon, plus artifacts from many other parts of history, such as scrolls from the legendary Library of Alexandria. It welded the Templars to the Freemasons, weaving in some ciphers and technology by Benjamin Franklin, and placed the treasure trove deep beneath Wall Street's Trinity Church in New York.

In this context, works by a couple of authors deserve mention. So far, many of the themes of Dan Brown's novels have closely aligned with themes in *The Hiram Key*, by Christopher Knight and Robert Lomas. In the book, after a long series of credulity-stretching linkups, the writers arrive at the conclusion that a treasure vault similar to the one in *National Treasure* is hidden beneath Rosslyn Chapel, waiting for some use of the Solomon Key to open it. Among other things, it would contain the "Nasorean scrolls," which they say are likely to deal with "the story of Jesus the Christ, the secret ceremony of resurrecting the living and the importance of building the human spirit as though it were a temple." In a subsequent book, *The Second Messiah,* the same authors explore the Shroud of Turin as being the shroud of a tortured Knight Templar, Jacques de Molay, who they assert was a second Messiah, descended from a long line of Jewish "High Priests of Yahweh," of an order called Rex Deus.

These books are on the nonfiction shelf, but they rely on some very strained chains of "fact" and supposition. But it would not be the first time that Dan Brown picked such books as the basis for his novels. In *DVC,* Brown leaned heavily on *Holy Blood, Holy Grail,* by Michael Baigent, Richard Leigh, and Henry Lincoln, along with *The Temple and the Lodge,* by Michael Baigent and Richard Leigh.

Well, here is my modest guess: I think the treasure is probably something related to the genome of Jesus, as carried through the vessel of Mary Magdalene, which figuratively is the Holy Grail. From *DVC* we know that Sophie Neveu is a descendant of this bloodline and therefore a "goddess" as well as a "chalice." It also could be that some form of cloning, or manipulation of DNA, will provide the right amount of the "nano-technology" that Dan Brown tends to need in a novel as well. Additionally, I would expect that the treasure would also be portrayed as having a value beyond reckoning. Could it be that the genome carries the potential for immunity from all known diseases, for instance?

As to *where* to find the treasure, I will hazard just one fanciful guess at the end of this chapter, but it is truly a long shot because I cannot be sure Dan Brown will pick up any or all the clues that I see. So I would urge everyone to treat the city of Washington as a giant hide-and-seek playground, and look for clues in all the buildings and all the symbols and codes.

❧ Look High, Look Low ❧

One of the great aspects of Washington as a treasure yard is that it has plenty of things to contemplate underground. A real source of city pride is the Metro subway system, the envy of many cities around the world. If you are going to write a novel and it is your style to keep it compressed in time to within twenty-four hours or so—as Dan Brown is wont to do—then it would help if your characters could hop on the Metro to get around the city. Brown used this in London in *DVC*, but it was a very strained usage—in fact, Sophie and Langdon ran right by their destinations in order to use the "tube."

But in addition, there are subterranean aspects to a lot of the major Washington structures. The new approach to the Washington Monument is now underground. There are little-known "stalactites" hanging in the basement of the Lincoln Memorial, making for a very spooky atmosphere. As discussed before, in the Capitol building there is a crypt that was intended to store the bones of George and Martha Washington, but was never used for that purpose. Instead it now stores the catafalque used to support the coffin when a great person lies in state in the Rotunda. In the bottom of the National Cathedral there are crypts, and the bottom of the House of the Temple is literally a treasure trove of historical items.

There are well-known tunnel passageways between the House and Senate office buildings and their respective chambers, and all sorts of leftover Cold War-era fallout shelters and evacuation paths (and, presumably, many new ones in the post-9/11 era). Hidden away under Washington somewhere are the remains of an earlier trolley system.

In the 1980s, a tunnel was dug under the Russian Embassy in Washington, so that the FBI and NSA could jointly spy on the communists. An embarrassingly public airing of this in March of 2001 led Vice President Dick Cheney to say, "If it were true that such a tunnel were dug, I couldn't talk about it anyway."

Is that the only secret government tunnel under Washington? Well, if it were true that there were more tunnels, I couldn't talk about them anyway! But Robert Langdon might!

Along with spooky places like this come certain legends. For instance, there are as many as five or six ghosts attributed to the Capitol, including a soldier who salutes you and disappears. In the National Statuary Hall, a guard once saw all of the statues come alive. There is the ghost of a "demon" black cat, seen at times in the White House or in the Capitol basement, a harbinger of some bad event like a stock market crash or an assassination. The cat comes bounding at you, growing huge and ferocious as it makes a final leap at you and then vanishes. In the Library of Congress, a uniformed police officer has been known to help people lost in the library stacks find their way out, then he disappears.

❧ Figures of Power ❧

The layout of a Masonic lodge room bears scrutiny in the context of Washington, D.C. Finding a perfect overlay is not easy, but the actual resemblance is striking enough, and may very well suit a Dan Brown novel. Among other things, Dan Brown may be able to guide Robert Langdon around the center of town by giving him clues as though they were positions in a Masonic lodge.

In a lodge, the Worshipful Master sits elevated in the east, the Senior Warden in the west, the Junior Warden in the south, and no one sits in the north, because "no light" comes from that direction (i.e., no source of knowledge or enlightenment).

An attempt to apply a similar template to Washington is tantalizing but a little bit frustrating. Not coincidentally, the core of the city's layout is a cross, and this is surely going to mean something to Dan Brown. (After all, in *A&D* he contrived to make the murders occur on arms of a huge cross in Rome.)

It was originally intended that the two broad vistas would focus on the Washington Monument, but that monument had to be shifted slightly due to soggy soil, and, in fact, the western and southern arms of the cross would have been impossible to build without later projects filling in the Potomac River.

The Capitol building sits in the east, topped by the Statue of Freedom, a representation of the republic as a classical goddess. She faces east and is not what most Masons would call a "Worshipful Master," but she does hold the right position in the "lodge," elevated above the rest.

If you accept the Lincoln Memorial as the western end of the formation, then Abe sits in the west, making a fine figure of the Senior Warden. In the south (across the pond), Thomas Jefferson is standing, looking north directly at the White House—he could be the Junior Warden. This would leave the White House in the northern position of the lodge (from which no light comes). It's sort of an empty suit—er, seat.

If one thinks of "seats" of power, Washington is loaded with them, including the seat of government, the centers of all the cabinet agencies, etc. Practically every major interest group has its headquarters here, as well as many corporations that are wedded to government work. Looked at in this way, the shining Arlington suburb of Rosslyn, Virginia, on the west bank of the Potomac (on the extended western arm of the cross), could be seen as the western seat of power in a lodgelike setting. This cluster of steel and glass towers today houses some of America's major corporations.

Some strange statuary connections involve Nathan Hale, as mentioned earlier. Hale's statue can be found at his alma mater, Yale University, which is also the alma mater of George H. W. Bush and George W.

Bush. Another statue of Hale stands at Phillips-Andover Academy, the alma mater of George H. W. Bush, and the great rival school to Dan Brown's alma mater, Philips Exeter. Another statue of Nathan Hale stands at CIA headquarters; George H. W. Bush was a CIA director.

There are plenty of indications that the statue of Kryptos, located at CIA headquarters, will figure in Dan Brown's next book. Not only are there clues about it on the dust jacket of *DVC* and on the danbrown.com Web site, but there is a growing "buzz" about it on the Internet. Kryptos, which means "hidden," was created in 1990 by artist James Sanborn. The "statue" is actually a series of objects, the biggest of which is a scroll-like copper screen pierced by 865 characters of a coded message, divided into four parts. There is also a series of other pieces to the sculpture set, strewn along a walkway and in a courtyard of the CIA's New Headquarters Building.

This truly enigmatic sculpture presumably poses a mocking challenge to America's best spies and code-breakers who walk by it regularly. Since it has line after line of cryptic characters, it certainly lends itself to use in a Dan Brown novel. For instance, merely by inventing an encrypted message, tagged to the codes of the sculpture, Brown could create a clue to make Robert Langdon rush onward through the plot.

It took eight years before the cryptographic community began to unravel any part of the main message, but in 1998 a CIA analyst, David Stein, solved the first three parts. A year later, Jim Gillogly, a California computer scientist, also solved these parts.

The last part has some ninety-seven characters still to be solved. However, even if the entire message were decoded, it might not be easily interpreted, according to the artist. One passage in part three appears to come from a 1922 description by archeologist Howard Carter of what he saw when he first peered into King Tut's tomb. Another passage says, "Who knows the exact location? Only WW." The identity of "WW" remained a small mystery for some years, but Sanborn in early 2005 confirmed that it stands for William Webster, CIA director at the time the sculpture was dedicated.

The CIA required that Sanborn give Webster a sealed envelope containing the decoded message. This was done at the dedication ceremony. Webster, nine years later, told a reporter that he had read the message, but had simply forgotten what it said, since it was "philosophical and obscure." In a wry twist, Sanborn revealed in a Wired News interview in early 2005 that he had not given Webster the entire message anyway. He had omitted the last part, he said, because "that's part of trade craft, isn't it? Deception is everywhere." Ed Scheidt, former director of the CIA Cryptographic Center, who helped Sanborn with the code systems, has hinted to reporters that in the last part, the English may be "masked."

Since Dan Brown used

The statue of Kryptos at CIA headquarters still taunts codebreakers.

"only WW knows" on the dust jacket of *DVC*, it is clear that he was relatively current in his knowledge of the Kryptos codes when his book was published in 2003.

❦ *Rebel Treasure* ❦

Shadow of the Sentinel, a 2003 book by Bob Brewer and Warren Getler, brings out a complicated but rich trail leading to the promise of gold surpassing the Beale treasure. The book has been retitled for its more recent paperback edition and is now called *Rebel Gold.*

The book details the education of an amateur treasure hunter, Bob Brewer, who spent his youth in the Ouachita Mountains of Arkansas, where his grandfather and uncle, both experienced woodsmen, kept pointing out certain beech trees with strange symbols carved on them. He was told cryptically that they had something to do with "Spanish treasure."

As Brewer grew up, he pursued the meaning of the carvings and began to recognize that the woods were also full of other signs. He learned to find certain buried iron implements that caused a compass needle to dip, and eventually, after deciding that there appeared to be a system at work, he discovered a jar of gold and silver coins. With still more effort, he became somewhat skilled at reading the signs and finding small caches of treasure.

He also discovered there once was a secret organization called the Knights of the Golden Circle (KGC). These were Southerners who formed their bonds circa 1845 and became part of the Secessionist movement as the seeds of the Civil War sprouted. The KGC were seen publicly as the Copperhead movement in certain Northern states, attempting to turn states like Indiana and Ohio against the Union. They claimed responsibility for insurrections in New York and other places.

Driven underground, the KGC remained organized but were invisible later in the Civil War. As the South recognized that its cause was lost, the KGC were entrusted with vast quantities of rebel gold and told to bury it in depositories in the West.

In a very strange linkup, the book claims that the outlaw Jesse James was a member of the KGC and was a trusted leader of expeditions going west with the gold. In another odd association, the book alleges that the Ku Klux Klan was deliberately spawned by the KGC to become a hated public enemy that would predictably be put down in the years after the war. This was said to be a way of keeping attention diverted from the KGC, which had intentions of eventually rising again and creating a New World Order.

According to *Rebel Gold*, this had a lot to do with the Masons, and one famous Mason in particular, Albert Pike, whom I covered earlier. Not only was Pike a complex and enigmatic man, but he also represents a connective link of huge significance—if it could all be proved. Pike had well-documented relationships with the Freemasons and the Know-Nothings, as well as merely speculative links to the Knights of the Golden Circle and the Ku Klux Klan.

According to tales unearthed by Getler and Brewer, the KGC enlisted Pike as one of their deepest undercover agents. Perhaps he even was the mastermind of the group. In true conspiracy logic, the lack of direct evidence is proof of just how good Pike was at keeping his cover!

In historical fact, Pike went on to become a huge force in the growth of the Scottish Rite of Freemasonry. He not only helped to build the organization in Southern states after the Civil War, but also became the Grand Commander of the Mother Supreme Council.

Enter Jesse James, who the authors say was a thirty-second-degree Mason, although this is unsupportable, according to Masonic authorities. According to the book, the KGC through Pike had infiltrated the Masons and subverted Masons to their purposes. Thus, James was assigned to carry one or several large convoys of treasure and bury it. As the story goes, he made maps full of symbology, including lots of Masonic signs.

Bob Brewer, through long study, eventually discerned a huge geometric pattern to the signs and discovered that they centered on an area in the Superstition Mountains in Arizona. A kind of Masonic grid, based on a squared diamond shape with inscribed circles (i.e., the circle and the square), has intersections that seem to betoken treasure "hot spots." Unfortunately, although he made some minor finds, Brewer hit a major snag when all of the really promising spots turned out to be under the care of the U.S. Bureau of Land Management, where treasure digging is forbidden.

I noticed that *Rebel Gold's* grid pattern, which has clearly recognizable outlines of a Maltese cross as

*KGC treasure pattern superimposed on the District
of Columbia. ("Hot spots" are where the lines
intersect.)*

well, can be rescaled and superimposed on the city
of Washington (specifically the original District of
Columbia). It may be a stretch, but it's the kind of
symbology that Dan Brown is likely to find intriguing,
since it links the Knights Templar, the Masons,
Washington, and hidden treasure. My map, with
overlay, is shown above. I would also recommend that
you check out *Rebel Gold* to get a sense of the KGC
symbology.

Again in Brewer's maps, we see plenty of symbolic
keys and codes, and often, it takes a systematic
knowledge to "get" hints, such as a convention in
which certain clues must be read backwards in order to
make sense. In short, the most cryptographic of
Masons would love it, and so would the code-loving
Dan Brown.

⋙ *Geography* ⋘

Finding treasure, of course, always gets down to knowing where to dig. Of interest in a Dan Brown context would be the carrying westward of the latitude of Solomon's Temple, arriving in America and crossing the Southern states. This latitude line figures in several legends. But it is interesting that certain navigational fudge factors have been applied wherever necessary to deal with this "line" of reasoning.

For instance, it was an early notion of the Mormons that their Nauvoo Temple in Illinois was erected on a latitude line taking the Temple of Solomon's latitude and adding ten degrees. This breaks down, though, because Jerusalem is at 31° 46' N and Nauvoo is at approximately 40° 30' N.

However, for those who wish to round off the latitude of Jerusalem to thirty-two degrees, we can immediately recognize the Masonic significance: There are thirty-two degrees that can be earned through the Scottish Rite.

If a boat bearing the Lost Tribes of Israel (among other mythical concepts) were to sail west along the latitude of the Temple of Solomon, it would make landfall in America at Ossabaw Island, not far south of Savannah, Georgia. (Lost Tribe legends also include the idea, popularized in the eighteenth century and picked up in his Mormon mythology by Joseph Smith, that the Indians are really the Lost Tribes.)

Again, if one is willing to allow some rounding off, the thirty-two-degree line runs very close to Savannah. It also carries on through many Southern states through towns too numerous to mention (but Midland, Texas, is one).

But that's based on thirty-two degrees. When one remembers that it is possible to be awarded a thirty-third degree in the Scottish Rite—and the numbers three, thirty-three, and variations thereof are symbolic to Masons—then it's time to think about latitude 33° N, which happens to come ashore in the United States not far from Charleston, South Carolina, a city of significance to Scottish Rite Masons. It was, in fact, the place where the Scottish Rite itself was founded in America in 1801.

Turning from latitudes to longitudes, in *DVC*, Dan Brown wrote about various national prime meridians, including the so-called "Rose Line" going through Paris. In historical fact, the French clung to their line as the world's prime meridian long after most of the world had acknowledged the Greenwich prime meridian. In 1884, when a conference finally settled the matter, there were actually about a dozen countries claiming a prime meridian.

What was uncovered by Brewer and Getler in *Rebel Gold* was an eerie confluence of geography. They concluded that the supposed lode of gold treasure of the fallen Confederacy was buried in the Superstition Mountains, around the latitude line of 33° N. But further, they discovered that, if one took the prime meridian from Washington, D.C., as the zero point— which was correct when maps were drawn in 1851— then their treasure site lies at approximately 33° W longitude as well. It was a 33-by-33 crosshairs.

Drawing crosshairs on the city of Washington is

more of a challenge. Washington has one of the greatest optical illusions of any major city. It is the way that the Washington Monument falls between the Capitol and the Lincoln Memorial, its reflection centered in the Reflecting Pool. It is carefully designed to lead the viewer to believe that these structures are perfectly aligned on an east-west axis. They are not.

As I have noted earlier, due to the soggy soil where the Washington Monument was intended to be built on the banks of the Potomac at the time, the monument had to be shifted slightly to the east and to the south of the exact intersection where the Capitol and White House vistas cross.

In 1804 the marker that was placed at the correct crosspoint was a much smaller obelisk—about knee height! It was a short, squat stone with a blunted top, with a cross cut into it. The marker was put there at the behest of then President Thomas Jefferson, who was eager to establish the United States as equal in science and technology with any other country, so he decided it would indicate the U.S. prime meridian, the zero longitude for all of our maps for many years thereafter. Since the spot was at the time on the banks of the Potomac, it became known as the Jefferson Pier Stone. Barge crews would toss a line around it to hold on while waiting to use the city's canal. The original stone went missing in 1874, but the replacement stone placed in 1889 remains.

Do not be confused with the "Zero Milestone" that is to the north, on the Ellipse with a view of the White House lawn. This was placed in 1920 as a way of imitating the golden milestone of ancient Rome, the

centerpiece of the statement "All roads lead to Rome."
If the U.S. Zero Milestone idea had taken hold, it
would mark the starting point of all the federal
highways. Everyone ought to be glad this notion died,
or we would be passing markers on the Interstate like
"Mile 2,746" somewhere in the Southwest!

As it is, visitors to Washington have to learn that
the Capitol Building is the zero point of the street
system, making the quadrant—NW, NE, SE, SW—of
crucial importance when telling a cab driver your destination.

Also, it's a mere quirk, I suppose, but the center
point of the District of Columbia is not at any of these
points mentioned above. It is near the Organization of
American States, a block or two north and west of the
Jefferson Stone. Although I have sought some advice
from geography experts, at this point I simply don't
know why!

However, based on the importance of center points
and orienting geographical lines in the actual city of
Washington, as well as Dan Brown's use of a "Rose
Line" or prime meridian in DVC, I feel certain there
will be an important geographical clue of this kind in
The Solomon Key.

Moreover, just as Dan Brown did not confine
Langdon and Sophie to the mere city limits of Paris in
DVC, there is no reason to believe the Washington
city limits will imprison Langdon in the next book,
either. It is only a few miles to some very significant
places of interest.

I will lay out here just one little idea of mine, which
was stimulated by the clues I had found by the summer

Stubby little Jefferson Pier Stone marks the center point of the two great vistas.

of 2004. It led me to a place just outside the city limits. But this is just one of hundreds of ways to think about the philosophical and physical clues you can find that apply to Washington, so I have no doubt at all that people will come up with other, very valid ideas as well. What is wonderful about this hunt is that you can become your own guide. And you get to see some beautiful art and architecture, and think elevating thoughts—and you really have Dan Brown to thank for all that.

✤ Rosslyn in the New World ✤

The last time Sophie Neveu and Robert Langdon are together in *DVC*, they are at the famed Rosslyn Chapel in Scotland. This is known as the "Chapel of the Codes" because of the many symbols carved into the stones of the chapel. Since Rosslyn was built by the Templars and was a showpiece of the craft of masonry, it is a natural anchor for Dan Brown's stories of Langdon as he returns to America for his next adventure.

Lo and behold, if one stands atop the Capitol

building looking west, past the Washington Monument, past the Lincoln Memorial, to the opposite bank of the Potomac, one's gaze falls on the suburb in Virginia known as Rosslyn!

This "suburb" actually comprises a cluster of steel towers housing the headquarters of some major corporations. Could this be more than coincidence, or will Dan Brown plant a clue or a treasure in this New World version of Rosslyn?

We can even pursue some coincidences a little further here. Within sight of Rosslyn lies a small island in the Potomac. From its purchase in 1717 through the 1790s it was owned by the family of George Mason, a very prominent Virginia patriot who has only recently gained the honor he deserves. It was George Mason's writing that contributed some of the most eloquent phrases of the Declaration of Independence, brazenly borrowed by Thomas Jefferson from Mason's Virginia Declaration of Rights, penned only a few months earlier.

The island in the river was long known as Mason's Island. This could give us a pun, since George Mason was not a Freemason. But John Mason, his heir, built a beautiful house and plantation on the island, and entertained there some of the most famous gentlemen of the time, including James Madison and Thomas Jefferson.

The island later fell into government hands and eventually was set aside as a hiking and picnic park in which to honor Theodore Roosevelt—who was a Freemason. A massive bronze statue, memorializing Roosevelt in the middle of a fiery speech from his bully pulpit, stands in a cool grove of trees at the highest point of the island.

Notably, the bridge that crosses the Potomac north and west of the island is Key Bridge, named after Francis Scott Key (a Freemason), who wrote our national anthem.

I found this place by thinking of three words—Rosslyn, Mason, and Key—many months before Dan Brown's publisher announced the title, *The Solomon Key*. I visited it on a hot summer day and found the setting to be downright temple-like.

Will Dan Brown have us follow clues like "a Key" and "a Mason's isle" to reach a staging point in our scavenger hunt? Is the treasure buried where Roosevelt is gazing? (Will I find a hole there the next time I visit the spot?)

In addition, I believe I have found yet another eerie coincidence. A small, friendly memorial has recently been erected to George Mason in a little garden in the shadow of the much bigger Jefferson Memorial, not far from a bridge that most Washingtonians call the 14th Street Bridge, but which is formally the George Mason Memorial Bridge. The memorial consists of a cluster of benches upon which sits a bronze statue of George Mason, pausing amid his reading of Cicero and Rousseau. His tricorner hat and cane are leaning nearby. Mason, in an amiable gaze, is looking off in a northerly direction—vaguely toward Mason's Island.

THE JOURNEY ENDS —
FOR NOW

O**UR TOUR TOGETHER** is over, but the treasure hunt is really just beginning.

At the start of this book, we were looking at just a few clues, such as the "Widow's Son" quotation and the "Solomon Key" hint. We also could extract as many clues as we wished from Dan Brown's two Langdon novels. Then all we did was follow the connections, wherever that led, crossing centuries, crossing oceans, and crossing cultures as necessary.

There are a few big ideas that we have been tracking. They are already richly portrayed in *DVC* and *A&D* in their European context, but they can be developed further in the next Dan Brown book, and carried to America, a place where ideas have often taken root and flourished.

The idea that a person can be in direct contact with God without any intermediaries, and can hope to improve him- or herself spiritually, is a product of the

Enlightenment, with contributions from Hermeticism, Rosicrucianism, and other schools of thought. Americans have a very long tradition of self-improvement and religious independence.

The idea that before Christian saints there were pagan gods and goddesses—a rich and vast theme for Dan Brown—is lavishly reflected in our capital's art and architecture. Despite our constitutional division of church and state, our buildings have divine figures galore taken from all the world's religions and astrology.

The idea that there is an almost-unresolvable conflict between science and religion still lurks in America. From creationism on the one hand to the specter of human cloning or environmental disaster on the other, it seems there will always be fuel for the campfires of both armies.

The idea that deep conspiracies are at work, a fundamental element of all Dan Brown's plots, is certainly alive and kicking. It's found on thousands of conspiracy theory Web sites and is put forth in all seriousness by certain political and religious groups. The top of the list has always been some incarnation of the Illuminati, but we have seen why Freemasonry always gets tarred with the same brush.

But Freemasons, and hundreds of other organizations we now call NGOs, are also at the core of our American urge to help other people. American generosity sometimes goes unnoticed as a "big idea."

The idea that "History is written by the victors," one of Dan Brown's favorite aphorisms, is important, too. Along our tour of history, we have learned to separate real history from bogus, invented history—to the extent that it's possible.

We have built, first, a temple of the mind. It is uncompleted. It isn't even strictly defined by just one floor plan, such as the fabled Temple of Solomon. Rather, it is your temple, and you are free to design it any way you like. It can be as individual as you like, and it can incorporate any ideas you like. Some rooms may be stuffed with treasures, while others may have just a few items, or be bare. It merely depends on how many tokens you picked up as we scampered along the corridors of history and philosophy.

It's perfectly all right if some rooms are empty, because you can spend the rest of your life populating your temple with treasure, if you wish. You can do this every time you visit a museum or a monument, read a book about the Founding Fathers, or go to a movie and notice there are symbols and deeper meanings everywhere.

We have taken a glimpse of the physical temple that is the city of Washington. We focused mainly on Cousin George, but only as a prime example. There is a lot to learn about all of the Founding Fathers and you will find a huge amount of this lore in Washington. Even if you have never read a Dan Brown novel, you will find it a rich treasure yard of art, architecture, and history. But when your senses are sharpened by the magic of Dan Brown's fiction, then it becomes a truly spiritual experience.

But go early. If Dan Brown does for Washington what he did for Rome and Paris, it is almost guaranteed that there will be pilgrims streaming to our capital with copies of *The Solomon Key* under their arms. So you may want to take your own survey tour before the crowds get there.

SYMBOLIC SYSTEMS

THE HARVARD professor of "symbology" Robert Langdon is instrumental in Dan Brown's novels as he opens the reader's eyes to all the many ramifications of symbolism. Indeed, there are so many references to symbols, richly described and pasted together into word-collages, that a reader can easily become confused. On a single page, Dan Brown may refer to a Tarot symbol, a Greek symbol, an Egyptian one, and so on. Quite commonly, the obvious symbol is one matter, but its deeper, hidden meaning is the real clue for Langdon to interpret.

One of the best ways to fully appreciate Langdon's references is to break down the symbolism into its various traditions and cultures. There are actually numerous entire *systems* of symbolism, which I will cover broadly in this appendix. It is my aim to touch on most of the systems that Dan Brown embraces, while also exposing some little-known facts and unusual ways of looking at them.

❧ Hieroglyphics ☙

A favorite theme of Dan Brown is the way the Christian Church so often suppressed and supplanted "pagan" beliefs while these old "pagan" beliefs continued to make themselves felt in various ways. It's a somewhat surprising extension of this idea, but hieroglyphics are a great example of this point. Also, hieroglyphics represent hidden secrets to Freemasons and many other groups as well.

It will be up to a linguist to say what is the longest-living written language, but the language of hieroglyphics surely has to be a candidate. It is long-dead now, but it lived a long time. There are hieroglyphs that have been dated to as early as 3150 BC, and they were used all the way to the end of the fourth century AD.

Originally this picture-language had practical functions, but it eventually came to be used mainly for the really big, important writing: inscriptions on the walls of great buildings, such as temples and pyramids. Two other Egyptian languages were developed in parallel, Hieratic and Demotic, which were used for documents and commerce. Later, the living Egyptian language became Coptic.

Egypt's long, glorious history of pharaohs—and hieroglyphics—started its decline about 2,400 years ago. The Persians conquered Egypt. Then Alexander the Great vanquished the Persians, but his empire fell apart on his death in 323 BC. So control of Egypt passed to Greeks and the dynasty of Ptolemy. Greek thought moved in and flourished, to some detriment of the Egyptian. Eventually, control was given over to the Romans.

In due course, Rome came to consider itself a Christian empire. The old Egyptian gods and symbols were declared "pagan." The Egyptian languages were outlawed and documents were destroyed, in the late fourth century.

In the blink of an eye, historically speaking, all knowledge of how to read hieroglyphics disappeared.

In the Middle Ages and centuries afterward, scholars remained interested in the hieroglyphic language, but still couldn't read it. It wasn't that the language was terribly complicated. It was because the glyphs represent phonetic sounds that had not been uttered as a spoken language for a thousand years. Revivals of the works of the Greeks were not of any help. To guess what a phonetic language sounds like, you need to be able to make the sounds.

But there's always a pseudoscholar around when you need one. Enter one legendary "scholar," Athanasius Kircher, a German Jesuit who got such a reputation for knowledge that he was invited to Rome's prestigious Collegio Romano and eventually founded a school and museum of his own in Rome. His many studies in science and mathematics were legendary, but he was also known as the foremost Egyptologist of his era. He published a major work in 1652, *Oedipus Aegyptiacus*, which was widely circulated.

A lot of Kircher's work on Coptic was accurate, but

he basically fooled himself and his audience into believing he could translate hieroglyphs. For example, the Egyptian text reads, "Osiris says," but Kircher translates this as, "The treachery of Typhon ends at the throne of Isis; the moisture of nature guarded by the vigilance of Anubis." You go, boy!

Kircher argued that ancient Egyptian was the language of Adam and that Hermes Trismegistus, the legendary source of Hermeticism, was actually Moses. (Later, when writing about China, he said Confucius was actually Moses and/or Hermes.) Since there was no one to contradict him, Kircher got away with this kind of thing for a long time.

Kircher collaborated in real life with another of Dan Brown's polymath geniuses, Gianlorenzo Bernini, one of the stars of Brown's *A&D*. Kircher helped Bernini "translate" the hieroglyphs on the obelisks that Bernini used in his Baroque re-creations of Roman churches and piazzas, including advising on the Fountain of the Four Rivers in the Piazza Navona, where one of the critical murder scenes takes place in *A&D*.

Kircher was not the only one to pretend he had figured out hieroglyphics. Fast-forward about two centuries to the beginnings of the Mormon Church, when founder and prophet Joseph Smith told his followers that he had been given the knowledge of how to read "reformed Egyptian" and had been shown "golden plates" that contained the Book of Mormon, which he had translated.

Smith's followers constantly had to deal with critics and disbelievers. So in 1835 they warmly greeted a traveling Irishman, Michael Chandler, who drove into their town carting a load of Egyptian curiosities. For a small fee, Chandler would let you look at four genuine Egyptian mummies, as well as a number of scrolls of papyrus, with hieroglyphs on them.

In America and Europe, there was a certain flow of "culture" going on, and mummies were a part of it. The word *mummy* actually stems from a word for bitumen (asphalt), which was an ingredient used to wrap mummies at one time in Egyptian history (although the Egyptians actually preferred a certain resin if they could get it). In the nineteenth century, it was believed that rendering down a mummy by heating it would yield a supply of bitumen, which, at that time in America, was considered a medicine. People actually would take doses of ground-up mummy powder! Mummies began to appear in traveling shows like Chandler's and, among high society, mummies even were featured at macabre house parties where the guests would unwrap them, as curiosities.

The Mormons immediately brought the papyri to Joseph Smith, expecting that he would demonstrate that he could read them. They were not disappointed. Smith told Chandler it would take some time to fully translate the documents, but he could already make out certain symbols from memory. Chandler even wrote a kind of affidavit for the Mormons, saying he had observed that Joseph Smith could decipher the hieroglyphs. (Chandler could not possibly have known this, of course.)

The first period of "translation" was productive,

and Smith got about ten pages of manuscript from the papyri, saying that the works were really the ancient Book of Abraham (upon which the book of Genesis itself was based), along with the Book of Joseph. Over the years, Smith paused and restarted the work, leaving it unfinished at his death in 1844. But the Mormons eventually declared the Smith-translated Book of Abraham to be Scripture. The original papyri were lost from sight, believed to have been destroyed in a fire.

Until 1966, that is, when a professor of Arabic studies found them in a museum vault in New York. In due course, genuine Egyptian scholars got to compare Smith's work to the real sources, the Egyptian *Book of the Dead*. In one example, the true text says merely, "after." Smith translates this as, "But I, Abraham, and Lot, my brother's son, prayed unto the Lord, and the Lord appeared unto me and said unto me: Arise and take Lot with thee; for I have purposed to take thee away out of Haran..." You go, boy!

Joseph Smith had missed history by only a few short years. It was in 1799 that the Rosetta Stone was discovered, brought back to England in 1802, and the text was circulated among scholars. Progress was made by a young Englishman, Thomas Young, who published his work in 1819, but the real breakthrough was made by a Frenchman, Jean François Champollion, who published his work in the late 1820s, but in French, so that it is unlikely to have reached Joseph Smith in a form that he could read.

To pound home the lesson here, when accurate history isn't available, there will always be people who

are willing to just invent it. People like this have left a
crisscrossed trail of occult ideas and odd theories
throughout history. The ideas and theories have
themselves become part of history, and Dan Brown is a
master at treasure-hunting these oddities and spinning
them alchemically into golden fibers of his novels.

~ Kabbalah ~

People who have not delved into the Kabbalah tend to
dismiss it as a complex system of mumbo-jumbo.
Recently, it has become part of pop culture, with
people like Madonna announcing that she has been
studying it for years, and many celebrity Kabbalists
hanging out at fashionable New York and Los Angeles
centers for Kabbalah studies. But one of the real
"secrets" of the Kabbalah is the way it can provide a
great sense of fun, a satisfying hunt for knowledge, and
a meditative experience that is certainly calming and
may also be healing.

The Kabbalah is an ancient Hebrew system for
seeking enlightenment and a pathway to God, by
studying Scripture and interpreting hidden meanings
of letters and words. By tradition, it is said to date back
as far as 1800 BC, when one of the Kabbalistic texts,
the *Sefer Yetzirah* (Book of Creation), was written by
Abraham. There may be no way to confirm this
antiquity, but it surely dates back to several hundred
years before Christ.

Because Kaballah is ancient, because its scholars
were found in many parts of Europe, Africa, and the
Middle East, and because its arcane knowledge was

much sought by non-Jewish scholars, the Kabbalah has begotten many philosophical offspring. Kabbalah shows up in Renaissance occult handbooks, and appears in certain underpinnings of Freemasonry.

Freemasonry starts with the idea of spiritual light (not to mention actual light), shining down and providing knowledge and inspiration. The Kabbalah stems from exactly the same idea. There are numerous other connections.

Certain principles of Kabbalah can be expressed in a diagram known as a tree, or Tree of Life. In the diagram, ten centers of spiritual energy take on the names of *sephirot*, or angels. Pathways connect these centers, and the pathways from top to bottom are maps of how light flows from heaven to earth, or how enlightenment flows from God to man.

The pathways have been assigned letters of the Hebrew alphabet, and each of the letters also has a numerical significance. Associated with the diagram are also the names of God.

Ancient Hebrew has no vowels, so it traditionally requires the help of a rabbi to read Scripture. One of the names of God is expressed by four characters, YHVH, which represented the Ineffable Name of God that was never to be spoken. The four-letter representation is known as the Tetragrammaton. Non-Jewish scholars nonetheless insisted on making a name that could be uttered, so it comes down to us as "Jehovah." Hebrew scripture substituted the word "Lord" instead, or *Adonai*.

The Tetragrammaton has been co-opted many times over. It may appear in various Christian church

settings, plus it often appears on Freemasonry aprons
or tracing boards, and on symbols of the occult, such
as amulets or talismans.

An often-cited example of numeric association in
Kabbalah, known as gematria, is this one: The
Kabbalah uses *ilan* as the word for "tree," and this is
written *aleph-yod-lamed-nun*. *Aleph* has a value of 1, *yod* is
10, *lamed* is 30 and *nun* is 50, so the word adds up to 91.

The word *malakh* means "angel." It is written *mem-lamed-aleph-kaf*, and the addition is 40 plus 30 plus 1
plus 20, adding up to the same number: 91.

The Tetragrammaton is *yod-heh-vav-heh*, adding up
to 26, and the substitute word *adonai* or "lord" adds up

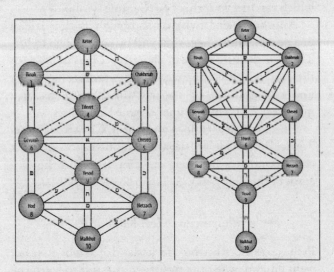

*Gra diagram, left, and Ari diagram, right, map out points on the
Kabbalah's Tree of Life.*

to 65, so that together, they add up to 91. A Kabbalist finds it no coincidence that 91 expresses linkages of the words for tree, angel, and Lord God.

Since the Kabbalah has had so many contributions over the centuries, there are many differences in interpretation, and even the diagram may differ. One diagram seen practically everywhere is called the Ari Tree, and it has one of the *sephirot* dropped down from the main array by a single path. However, another— perhaps older—diagram is the Gra Tree, in which the array forms a compact interlaced pair of hexagons.

If you are the sort of person who seeks to find it, you can discover an inverted pentangle in the Ari Tree, which can fuel your theory of Satanic symbology.

Another weird twist of Kabbalah is that it can provide the utterances that will bring a Golem to life. This is a creature made of clay that comes to life with the correct word sequence, fights to protect its owner, and can get out of control (like Frankenstein's monster). This isn't fantasy to true Kabbalists.

One adept of astrology and Tarot, Christine Payne-Towler, has made an elegant demonstration of exact correspondence between the Gra Tree and the face cards of the Tarot, as well as astrological symbols.

❧ *Pythagoreans Meet Kabbalists* ☙

Pythagoras, born on the Greek island of Samos, it is said, went far and wide on a twenty-year quest to learn the secrets of mathematics and geometry, perhaps traveling as far as India. When he returned, he founded a secret religious society devoted to numbers.

In fact, the concept or deity, Number, was their god. To join, you had to give all your possessions to the group, and pass an initiation. Women were allowed—a real switch from so many fraternities throughout history (such as the Freemasons, who do not admit women).

Pythagoras lived from about 560 to 480 BC, but his thinking made its way, probably through Plato's Academy, into the works of later Greeks, among them Euclid (325-285 BC). Euclid worked at the famous scholarly mecca of Alexandria, Egypt, in its heyday, and thus some of his writings were preserved and later revived in the European Renaissance.

The famous Pythagorean theorem, expressing properties of a right triangle, later became known as Euclid's 47th Proposition. All genuine craftsmen in the building trades—such as masons—would surely

*This depiction of a 3-4-5 triangle is a
Masonic symbol and an elegant
mathematical proof.*

come to know the practical use of it, in the 3-4-5 triangle. If a craftsman just remembered this one "secret," he could re-create a square (ninety degree) angle, anywhere he might be, using the most rudimentary starting point, such as a knotted piece of rope to measure with.

It is easy to see how the elegant simplicity of this theorem would strike someone as god-given and mystical. But this is merely a small example of what the number worshippers began to learn. The Pythagoreans also discovered a numeric relationship between harmonious tones on a lyre string. They believed this principle extended into the cosmos, and thus they were talking about "the music of the spheres."

It is no wonder that they attempted to keep it all a secret known only to the properly initiated.

However, legend has it that the Pythagoreans and the early scholars of the Kabbalah actually shared their secrets. It was a natural fit, since Kabbalists were also worshippers of numbers, in a special way, because they believed that numbers associated with the Hebrew letters revealed powerful divine secrets. This knowledge could have come from Pythagoras's travels eastward, since the major center of Kabbalah at the time was Babylonia. But it also is possible that the Pythagoreans and Kabbalists found their mathematical secrets independently, or both derived them from some contact with India.

The Pythagoreans could start with simple things and arrive at the most complex and intricate proofs. For instance, there is a simple triangle that can be made with a dot on the first row, two dots on the

Tetractys helps a Pythagorean count from 1 to 10—and is also an object of worship.

second, three dots and then four dots. This is called the Tetractys, because the dots add up to ten, which was considered the holiest number. One can make a lot more sophisticated expression of the Tetractys (see left).

In fact, the Pythagoreans assigned principles to their numbers. For instance, 1 is unity, the number of reason; 2 is diversity or opinion and also is the first true female number; 3 is harmony and male, as well as the sum of unity and diversity (1+2); 5 is marriage, as well as the sum of the first male and female (2+3). The number 10 represents the universe.

Pythagoreans also thought of other numbers as prime, perfect, or amicable, among other properties. A prime number has no other factors except itself and 1. A perfect number is one in which all of its possible divisors added together equal the number. For instance, the number 6 is perfect because 1+2+3 equals 6. The next perfect number is 28 (1+2+4+7 +14). The next perfect numbers get much bigger, quickly: 496, 8,128, and 33,550,336, to name a few.

Two numbers are said to be amicable if each is the sum of the divisors of the other. A famous example is 220 and 284, discovered by the Pythagoreans. The divisors of 220 are 1, 2, 4, 5, 10, 11, 20, 22, 44, 55, and

110, adding up to 284. The divisors of 284 are 1, 2, 4, 71, and 142, adding up to 220.

The next step is a crucial one. From merely being amazed at these number relationships, you begin to conclude that there is a divine influence. Moreover, you may conclude that using these numbers will let you borrow some of the power of that divinity.

In the case of 220 and 284, amulets were made with these numbers, offering the wearer love and friendship. In Arab numerology, you wrote 220 on one piece of fruit and 284 on another. You ate one piece and gave the other to the object of your affection, binding you together in love.

Kabbalah study can follow the trail farther, by assigning the letters *resh-kaf* to 220, giving the word *rakh*, and the letters *resh-peh-dalet* to 284, giving the word *rapad*. The first is "tender" and the second is "prepare a bed of love." In a kind of Morse code, lovers could send the message "220—tenderness" and get the reply "284—a bed of love has been prepared."

These are playful uses of Kabbalah, but when the numbers combine with the letters to give meanings to sacred words, it becomes powerful and compelling. Kabbalah can also be assigned to the signs of the Zodiac, leading to more interpretations of the kind that govern people's lives.

❧ Almanacs and Zodiacs ☙

The origin of the printed almanac comes from an item that the clergy of the Middle Ages carried in their belts (girdles), it is said.

The almanac was a piece of vellum (a fine lambskin parchment) folded somewhat like a road map and hung at a priest's waist. One of its primary functions was to help in determining the feast days of the Christian calendar, such as Easter, one of the "movable feasts." Since the Church was the keeper of astronomical knowledge, it was the reference for such things as the seasons (equinoxes and solstices) and lunar cycles.

The common people wanted different things from their almanacs. For instance, the almanac's record of the Church's feast days of the saints was an attempt to supplant the celebrations by the common people of

Priests of the Middle Ages carried symbol-filled almanacs, or girdle calendars, on their belts.

pagan gods and goddesses. In addition, the astrological journey of the sun, moon, planets, and stars was part of the belief system of the times. To the common man, these signs of the Zodiac were powerful forces and were a fact of life, despite what the Church dictated. They simply *belonged* in the almanac.

The minute the printing press came into use, during the latter fifteenth century, the people began to ask for what they wanted, and they wanted their almanac. It was a vital tool to help them with their daily lives, in such matters as choosing when to plant and reap, or to plan for an upcoming hard winter.

No printed almanac was successful without a "Zodiac Man." This annotated drawing was often the only medical guide that a frontier family had.

As the almanac was refined in later centuries, there was one page that was absolutely vital—no printer could sell an almanac without it. This was the illustrated page called the Zodiac Man. It simply showed a naked man surrounded by the twelve signs, with lines indicating which of the signs governed which part of the body.

To some extent it represented recognition of "pagan" symbols and gods. And the Zodiac Man, it seemed, also fueled popular belief in the occult. But it had a "practical" purpose as well: medicine. If there was going to be any printed home reference for folk medicine, it was this single page. If one of your family members got sick, you consulted the Zodiac Man to decide what foods or herbs (or spells) to administer.

One of the most successful of all English almanacs was *Rider's British Merlin* (the almanac itself took the nickname of the wizard).

When Benjamin Franklin launched his *Poor Richard's Almanack* in 1732, it had the Zodiac Man, as well as lots of other successful elements of a good almanac, since Franklin borrowed from about four other examples of the genre. One was *Poor Robin's Almanac*, which was published for many years by William Winstanley in England.

Franklin started out with a monster of a publishing joke and controversy. His closest rival in almanacs was a printer named Titan Leeds. In introducing himself as "Poor Richard," Franklin said he had to convey the sad news that his good friend, Leeds, discovered the astrological signs of his own impending death on a date and hour certain. When Leeds published a scathing counterattack in his own almanac the following year, "Poor Richard" took it not as proof of a mistake, but as a scam, since he was certain that his good friend Leeds (now supposedly dead) would never say such things about him! This back-and-forth continued for about eight years until Leeds really did die, and Franklin got the last word.

⋘⋙ Tarot ⋘⋙

While the advent of Tarot cards is often seen as a Renaissance development of around 1450, there are many indications that it really stems from lore that is at least two thousand years old.

There are seventy-eight cards in most Tarot packs—twenty-two in the Major Arcana (Major Secrets) and fifty-six in the Minor Arcana. The Major Arcana are the "face" cards, always seen loaded with symbolism.

Long before Dan Brown brought up the Gnostic tradition in *DVC*, there were known linkages of Tarot to Gnostic thought, as well as the Kabbalah and, of course, to astrological signs, which date back to the dawn of civilization.

The first printed Tarot cards showed up in the early fifteenth century, but Tarot historians talk of earlier hand-painted decks going back as far as 1200. If, however, the Gnostics and Hebrew Kabbalah are brought into the equation, then the origin really shifts back to about the fourth century AD.

The great *DVC* theme of "goddess" worship can be found reflected in several cards of the Tarot. When the

Phonetic Letter	Tarot No.	English Alphabet	Hebrew Letter	Kabbalah Value	Astrology Symbol	Arcana Name
Alef	1	A	א	1	♈	Magus
Bet	2	B	ב	2	☽	Priestess
Gimel	3	C	ג	3	♂	Empress
Dalet	4	D	ד	4	☉	Emperor
Heh	5	H	ה	5	♈	Pope
Vav	6	V	ו	6	♉	Lovers
Zayin	7	Z	ז	7	♊	Chariot
Chet	8	Ch	ח	8	♋	Justice
Tet	9	T	ט	9	♌	Hermit
Yod	10	I	י	10	♍	Wheel
Kaf	11	C	כ	20	♀	Strength
Lamed	12	L	ל	30	♎	Hanged Man
Mem	13	M	מ	40	♇	Death
Nun	14	N	נ	50	♏	Temperance
Samech	15	S	ס	60	♐	Devil
Ayin	16	Ayn	ע	70	♑	Tower
Pe	17	P	פ	80	☿	Star
Tzade	18	Ts	צ	90	♒	Moon
Qof	19	Qk	ק	100	♓	Sun
Resh	20	R	ר	200	♄	Judgment
Shin	21	Sch	ש	300	♃	World
Tav	22	Th	ת	400	♈	Fool

All the major symbolic systems can be combined into one table of correspondences, gathering up centuries of mysterious lore into a Rosetta Stone of symbols.

deck is one like the famous Visconti Sforza deck, the High Priestess clearly signals the legend of the female pope, not to mention the earlier Magdalene. There are interpretations of themes like reincarnation, the fall from the Garden, and so on.

Essentially, the symbolism was a way to veil ideas that could not be openly discussed in front of the powers that be. These powers included the prevailing orthodox strains of Judaism and Christianity, working to obliterate, at various times, the previous pagan gods and goddesses, or Gnostic, Egyptian, or

Babylonian traditions, and the like. So the Tarot was, once again, a way to "hide it in plain sight."

There isn't just one kind of Tarot (nor one kind of Gnosticism or Kabbalah, either), so the interpretations differ, but on the previous page is a table of correspondences that shows one way to relate numerology, Kabbalah, and the Major Arcana of Tarot.

This table is extracted from the work of Christine Payne-Towler, a scholar in astrology, Tarot, and Kabbalah who has been studying these broader connections for thirty-five years. Along the way, she has gained an outstanding reputation as an adept. Calling the Tarot "the flash cards of the Western Mysteries," Payne-Towler has herself taken orders as a bishop in the Home Temple of the Holy Grail, and in the Gnostic Church of St. Mary Magdalene, which "exists for people of every background and faith whose soul longings are directed towards finding a balance between the Divine Feminine and Masculine in Christianity." She and some associates also practice what they call "Pansophic Freemasonry," a form almost unique in allowing men and women as members.

❧ Magic Squares and Circles ❧

One of the ancient mysteries is the mere arraying of numbers or letters to form a square. These not only are part of pre-Christian numerology, but also can be connected quite firmly to a Founding Father—Benjamin Franklin.

Franklin was known for a lot of amazing things, then and now, but hardly anyone took him for a great mathematician. Let this be a lesson to you: Never take Ben Franklin for granted!

New discoveries show Franklin was a real master of the math specialty of discovering what are called magic squares.

The idea of a magic square can be expressed in numbers easily (see square below). If you add up any row, it totals 15; if you add up any column, also 15, and any diagonal, also 15. This is a 3 x 3 magic square, using all the numbers 1 through 9.

Magic squares are of interest in almost every great culture, including Chinese, Islamic, and Indian. The concept can also be found in a long trail leading back to the Greeks, the Hebrews, and even the early Christians.

Overleaf, top, is a magic square that appears in an Albrecht Dürer engraving called *Melancolia-I* (1514), made using the work of an Italian mathematician.

This is a 4 x 4 square, using all the numbers 1 through 16.

In cultures in which meanings are attached to the numbers, things take on a mystical overtone. For instance, overleaf, bottom, is an Islamic square using the numbers 18 through 26.

This square adds up to 66, which is the numerical

2	9	4
7	5	3
6	1	8

Magic square of the numbers 1 through 9, adding up to 15.

Top: Albrecht Dürer's magic square, using the numbers 1 through 16. Bottom: Arabic magic square for God totals 66 in each row.

value of the word *God* in the eastern Arabic system called Abjad.

Okay, it doesn't look too difficult to make a magic square, does it? Given time, you could probably come up with any of these examples through trial and error.

However, it can get more challenging. Serious mathematicians for centuries have taken up the magic square, and created some rather large ones. In Franklin's time, two books were available to him to describe such ideas. One of them showed all 880 possible squares of 4 x 4. Franklin saw this as a way to relieve boredom —at least, for a guy like Franklin. In the same manner that anyone else might make doodles, Franklin used his time during boring Pennsylvania Assembly meetings to craft 8 x 8 magic squares, and larger.

When he saw another book, *Arithmetica Integra* by Michael Stifel (1487–1567), Franklin realized there was a bigger challenge. Stifel had produced a magic square that was 64 x 64. Franklin rose to the challenge,

6	32	3	34	35	1
7	11	27	28	8	30
19	14	16	15	23	24
18	20	22	21	17	13
25	29	10	9	26	12
36	5	33	4	2	31

S	A	T	O	R
A	R	E	P	O
T	E	N	E	T
O	P	E	R	A
R	O	T	A	S

Top: Magic square of the sun.
Bottom: Sator-Rotas Square—
Christian or Mithraic?

and he came up with a 64 x 64 that improved on Stifel's square, which met "only" 34 conditions. Franklin's met 96 conditions.

But Franklin was not done doodling. He came up with the novel idea of a magic circle. This was a series of concentric and eccentric circles with radial numbers. Franklin's work would have been an astounding accomplishment, had it been known, but much of it went unnoticed until it was recently discovered by a Villanova University math professor, Paul C. Pasles, who is preparing a book that will tell the full story.

One thing to notice: Franklin was a Freemason, and, as we have seen elsewhere, Freemasonic symbology involves squares and circles. This could explain why he saw a magic circle as a perfect complement to a magic square.

But Franklin's achievement isn't quite the end of the story of these squares. For one thing, there is an old one called the magic square of the sun, shown at upper left on page 229.

This is a 6 x 6 square, whose rows and columns add up to 111. But more significantly, the total of the whole square is 666. While 666 has always been taken to signify the "number of the beast" (Satan), in fact, some scholars say, the magic square of the sun was assigned to Apollo, the Greek god of the sun. The scholars also say that there are ways to find Gnostic meanings in it. In late Roman times, the sun god was Mithras, called *Sol Invictus* or the unconquerable sun. Mithras appears to be of special interest to Dan Brown and makes several appearances in *DVC*.

The concept takes a very strange twist when alphabetical letters are entered in the same arrays. At the lower left on page 229 is perhaps the most significant of all. This is known as the Sator-Rotas square.

This is an amazing array that reads the same across, down, upwards, and backwards. It also has another aspect, possibly just a strange coincidence, but very meaningful to Christians for centuries. The letters can be rearranged into a cross-shaped figure, giving [*Alpha*] Pater Noster [*Omega*], reading across and down. To make this work, you have to construe some of the "spare" letters "A" and "O" as the Greek letters *alpha* and *omega* (see page 231).

This outcome appeared mystical to many people, and they came to assume that the squared array was a kind of vehicle to carry the coded message, *Pater Noster*, sandwiched between *Alpha* and *Omega*. *Pater Noster* is the "our father" in the Latin version of the Lord's Prayer, recited by Catholics for many

```
        α
        P
        A
        T
        E
        R
α P A T E R N O S T E R Ω
        O
        S
        T
        E
        R
        Ω
```

*The Christian acrostic derives
from the Mithraic Sator-Rotas
Square.*

hundreds of years. The *Alpha-Omega* is understood as a reference to a biblical message that God is the beginning and the end.

For a long time—possibly more than a thousand years, the linkage of the *Pater Noster* array to the Sator-Rotas square gave this a Christian significance. It became a custom to put this square of letters over the doorway of a house, to keep the residents safe and healthy. The bottoms of drinking glasses were inscribed with it, as were amulets.

Others used a different theory, assuming that an array like this was surely part of the Kabbalah. Indeed, in some magic books, called grimoires, the characters were shown in Hebrew. As a magic talisman the Sator square is found in Hebrew in the *Clavicula Salomonis*, or Key of Solomon, one such grimoire.

But there came a startling discovery in 1937 during the excavation of Pompeii, which was buried in volcanic ash in AD 79. There on the wall of a bathroom was scrawled a Sator-Rotas square!

Scholars did a double-take, realizing that *Pater Noster* no longer made sense, since it was a Latin phrase, and the early Christian writings were mainly in Greek. Besides, there hadn't been enough time since the death of Christ for the Gospels to have been written when Pompeii was destroyed. So scholars were forced to look deeper into history and have recently developed a different story.

It is now thought that the Sator-Rotas square comes from the cult of Mithras and was imported into the Roman Empire, years before the birth of Christ, by Roman legions coming back from Persia. One of the great mysteries of history is to determine conclusively what the array would have meant to a devotee of Mithras.

Aside from the Sator-Rotas square, which appears on plenty of magic amulets, there is an entire compendium of magic word-squares, used in various books of magic, sometimes using false claims of antiquity. Soon, it was possible to make squares to solve lots of problems, like sickness, unrequited love, and so on. Some of the squares, it was said, could be used to summon and control demons.

All of these ideas of magic and superstition were imported by waves of immigrants to the United States, beginning with the earliest settlers. Churches, whether strict or libertarian, could not erase the enduring folk and alternative occult cultures.

One case in point was the family of Joseph Smith, a Vermont family that moved to western New York. They were at times spirited Christians, but they also had lots of folk and magical traditions. When Joseph Smith, the founder of the Mormon faith, was killed, he was wearing a magic talisman dedicated to Jupiter, a god significant to his birthdate. It was also said that the Smiths (including Joseph's brother Hyrum) carried *lamens*, which were common in their time. These were pieces of parchment on which spells and incantations (and magic squares) were written. The Smith family also treasured a "magic dagger," inscribed with the symbols of Scorpio and Mars.

❧ Music ☙

There is a vast symbolic realm that bears mention here, the world of music. There are aspects of music that are very ancient, other aspects that permeate the history we have been discussing in this book, and some very modern aspects.

So far in his novels, Dan Brown has largely overlooked music. This is puzzling, because he has a highly musical background. Brown grew up in a household where his mother played church organ, and he learned keyboard as a youth. He was a group singer and when he joined the Amherst College Glee Club, it gave him the opportunity to go on a world tour, a pivotal point in his artistic life, as he later recalled. After college, he continued to play keyboard, sing, and write his own songs, showing enough promise that he was encouraged to go to Hollywood in the early 1990s to seek a music career. His CDs hardly sold, though, and he turned to writing novels.

Dan Brown's father was a teacher of mathematics and was a source for a lot of the discussion of Fibonacci numbers, the golden ratio Phi, and the like, that can be found in DVC. Thus, it would seem only natural that young Dan would be exposed to the legends that the Pythagoreans studied—worshipped, really—the discovery of math in harmony.

Although the Pythagoreans could not have known the exact frequencies, they were able to tune stringed instruments, the precursors of lyres, and discover that a musical tone and its octave tones had a relationship of halves of the length of the string. In other words, if a string is tuned to E on a modern guitar and you fret it at the high F, your finger is at the midpoint of the string. To get to the next E an octave higher, you would fret at the midpoint of the remaining string length.

What's more, they discovered that other harmonious steps, in a system we now call the musical scale, lend themselves to incredibly simple ratios. These are ratios such as 6:8::9:12, which also can be used to derive 8:9, thus yielding all the steps in the scale.

These simple facts are taken for granted today, but really, when you come to grips with the full implications, probably the only correct thing to do is fall to your knees in adoration of the Great Architect of the Universe, who built this into the fabric of the cosmos.

An excellent description of the astoundingly simple ratios of harmony is found in *Jesus Christ, Sun of God*, by David Fideler, who also delves into the gematria of the harmonious numbers.

Pythagoras lived and died five centuries before Christ. Fast-forward to an early father of the Christian Church, Clement of Alexandria (c. AD 150–216), who was deeply aware of the earlier Greek and Gnostic traditions that associated numbers with deities, and knew how they also applied to music. He was fraught with meaning when he described Christianity as the "New Song," implying it was an extension of Hellenistic beliefs.

Music, like other thematic streams in this book, is a mighty river, flowing timelessly and gathering many smaller streams unto itself. For a very long time, the main repository of formal knowledge of this river was the Catholic Church.

And it began very early. For instance, the earliest ecclesiastical chanting modes were defined by Ambrose, Bishop of Milan, in the late fourth century. The system was improved under the direction of Pope Gregory in the late sixth century, which is why everyone popularly calls them "Gregorian chants," completing forgetting Ambrose. Later, in the Renaissance, the eight Gregorian modes were given Greek names, such as Ionian or Doric, merely as a means of reference.

Around AD 774, Paul the Deacon composed a simple hymn for St. John the Baptist's Day. (As we have seen, this is a day of significance to Freemasons and Templars.) In approximately AD 1020, the monk Guido of Arezzo extracted the first syllables of each line of the St. John hymn, to obtain *ut, re, mi, fa, sol, la*:

Ut queant laxi
*Re*sonare fibris
*Mi*ra gestorum
*Fa*muli tuorum:
*Sol*ve polluti,
*La*bii reatum, Sancte Johannes

It took another six hundred years or more to modify this and come up with what we recognize today as: *do, re, mi, fa, sol, la, ti, do*. An excellent description of this history of the scale can be found at a Web page, www.standingstones.com/modeharm.html.

This is certainly a rocket ride through music history, but it shows that the very ancient beginnings of a formal understanding of music can be linked to today's musical scale—with an implied homage to St. John the Baptist every time someone sings it.

Although it is an unfair truncation of music history, we can now fast-forward again to the Baroque period. One of the more notable, but unsaid things to be known about the Baroque period was that the composers and musicians took the Gregorian heritage of eight modes, which had survived through the medieval and Renaissance periods, and chucked six of them. The two modes remaining in common use, Ionian and Aeolian, were renamed the "major" and "minor" scales.

Interestingly, traditional Celtic music still carries forward some of the other modes, whereas the vast majority of music we listen to today does not. It is "secret" musical knowledge that is "hidden in plain sight." Any musician who wishes to explore the Dorian or Mixolydian modes will have no trouble finding references.

There were many great Baroque musicians and composers, but the acknowledged giant of the age was Johann Sebastian Bach (1685–1750). Bach grew up in Germany in a time when there was still great religious strife and many of his countrymen were emigrating to America. His surroundings had previously been the home of many Rosicrucian and Pietist movements, but he and his large extended musical family were grounded in Lutheran and/or Calvinist society, which fostered and nourished him throughout his career. Later, the same general region would give rise to Adam Weishaupt, founder of the Illuminati. But there is no reason to believe Bach was either Rosicrucian or Masonic in his beliefs. He largely remained within orthodox religion as he knew it. In general, he is most remarkable for the intellectual power that his music displayed. However, one of Bach's musically talented sons, Johann Christian Bach, was a Freemason.

The form called a *canon* was a specialty of J. S. Bach's. In a canon, a musical theme may be started, then joined by a second voice rendering the same theme but raised by five notes on the scale, or depressed by four notes. Or, the theme may be played "upside down," or it may even be played backwards. The real challenge is to achieve harmony while all of these variations are being expressed. A more relaxed form was called a *fugue*, but it could still be made very complex. Bach was a master of the canon and the fugue, and could compose them for many parts, in his head, on demand.

Indeed, in about 1747, Bach made a celebrated visit to Frederick the Great, king of Prussia, who was himself an accomplished musician. Frederick challenged Bach with a complex theme. Bach immediately delivered a three-part canon on the theme, followed by a six-part canon of his own, astonishing his audience. He later went home and composed in the king's honor a piece of great complexity called simply *A Musicial Offering*, containing a six-part fugue.

All of this is described in a singular book, *Gödel*,

Escher, Bach: An Eternal Golden Braid, by Douglas R. Hofstadter, written in 1979 and widely read in the 1980s.

Hofstadter, one of our era's most notable polymaths, floored his readers by combining talk of mathematicians (Gödel et al.), artists (M. C. Escher et al.), and musicians (Bach et al.), in pursuit of a concept he called "strange loops" that eventually rendered out (after some seven hundred pages) his best guess as to what the basis for artificial intelligence might be.

Hofstadter described in detail how Bach made a minor puzzle out of the *Musical Offering*. He did not write down each and every note, but left it to the king to flesh it out according to the canonical conventions. At one point, Bach instructed: *Quaerendo invenietis* (by seeking, you will discover). For a non-Freemason, Bach had a lot of the same love of veiling the truth.

Bach had many musical tricks up his sleeve, according to Hofstadter, including writing his own name in the musical notes, and composing a very special piece that contains the ability to warp back on itself and rise in key. Hofstadter nicknamed it the "Endlessly Rising Canon," and saw it as an example of the self-referring "strange loop" of the kind expressed in art by M. C. Escher (as in the artist's drawing of one hand drawing another hand, drawing the first hand).

Bach's era closed around the time of his death in the mid-eighteenth century. A new musical era was rising—the Classical—with the "father of the symphony," Franz Joseph Haydn (1732–1809). Socially and politically, it was also the Age of

Enlightenment, and the next giant of the period was Wolfgang Amadeus Mozart (1756-1791). Both Haydn and Mozart were Freemasons.

The flamboyant Mozart wrote one of the most flamboyantly Masonic pieces of music ever crafted, *The Magic Flute*, an opera that is agelessly popular.

Like Bach before them, Haydn and Mozart both enjoyed planting little tricks into their music. Haydn is famous for the *Surprise Symphony*, for instance, which was deliberately written to lull the king to sleep, then wake him with a jolt. Mozart, in *Don Giovanni*, wrote into the score the sound of the musicians tuning up.

The aforementioned Douglas Hofstadter grabbed odd ideas like Bach-like canons that play the same backwards and forwards, and juxtaposed them with artificial recursive sequences of DNA, the genetic coding of life. At the time, it would have been outlandish to suppose that sequences of DNA could be manipulated in that way. He perhaps would have been gratified two decades later to see researchers actually coding secret messages into DNA, as a means of preventing counterfeiting, among other uses. Like DNA, music is sequential data.

Music is a peculiar symbolic system because is not only written, but audible, so there are almost infinite ways to use it to impart hidden meanings. Consider, for instance, the great opening theme of Ludwig von Beethoven's Fifth Symphony, which drums out the letter "V" in Morse code. It could be extended to pass an entire message in Morse code, making any number of tonal changes that would be ignored in decoding, because it would be the rhythm that carries the data.

Consider modern cases where, for instance, people played Beatles songs backwards to discover what were rumored to be concealed messages. Consider my own composition, a thankfully short cacophony called "Play Me," an example of another (albeit silly) way to code with music.

If one were to apply a layer of ciphers to written music, it would be relatively simple to hide a message in the string of notes. And with today's computers, the average person could encode vast quantities of secret data within a piece of music by audio compression and other techniques.

So far, nothing like these coding schemes have surfaced in Dan Brown's novels, but we surely can't rule them out in *The Solomon Key*, given Brown's musical expertise.

Play Me, by David A. Shugarts

THE SINCLAIR FAMILY

A T THE very end of *DVC*, it is revealed that Sophie Neveu is the daughter of a Plantard and a Saint-Clair, making her twice descended from the line of Merovingian kings and therefore descended from Mary Magdalene and Jesus.

The *Plantard* reference links to a forger of the 1950s, Pierre Plantard, creator of the false documents of the Priory of Sion, who tried to tie himself into a genealogy he didn't deserve. The Plantard lineage no doubt is bogus. The Saint-Clairs, however, are real.

The Saint-Clair family's holdings just south of Edinburgh in Scotland were of supreme importance in *DVC*. The land included the town of Roslin, but the name became Rosslyn when applied to the castle and the chapel that was built there by the Saint-Clairs.

Upon settling into their lands in Scotland, they changed their name to Sinclair. This can make for confusion in following the family through history. It's important to watch out for variations, including not only Saint-Clare and Sinclair, but also Sinkler. In addition, the family turns up practically everywhere, including the United States and Canada.

According to legend, the Saint-Clair family of France supported William the Conqueror, the Norman Frenchman who invaded England in 1066. But the real source of their landed rights came when William Sinclair helped Malcolm III regain the Scottish throne, opposing the Normans. It was Sinclair's son, Sir Henri Sinclair, who became the first heir of Rosslyn.

Henri Sinclair accompanied Godefroi de Bouillon on the first Crusade in 1096 and was present for the fall of Jerusalem. He became a Knight Templar when the order was founded in 1118. The family has been associated with the Templars ever since, with many of the generations serving as Templar knights in battle. Indeed, they twice provided the Templars with Grand Masters.

The Templars were in full force during the twelfth and thirteenth centuries, but they were ambushed by Philip the Fair on the famous date of Friday, October 13, 1307. They were officially disbanded in 1317. However, they were said to figure in an almost mystical victory when Sir William Sinclair came to the aid of Robert the Bruce against the English at Bannockburn in 1314. It was one of the greatest Scottish victories of all time, with mainly foot soldiers going against thousands of mounted English knights at a ratio of three to one. At a turning point in the battle, some five hundred cavalry came down on the English, who turned and fled in terror. It was said that the sight of these mounted Templars was enough to rout the English.

This battle was fought on June 24, Midsummer's Day, a day of significance in pagan times and in Christian tradition, marking the birth of John the Baptist, a patron saint of Freemasons. Prior to the fight, the Scots got down on their knees to pray to a peculiar gilded box called the Monymust Reliquary, said to contain the bones of a saint.

Arrayed opposite the Scots were the English. Their king, Edward I, at first made a joke about the Scots begging for mercy, but then was informed that they were merely seeking divine assistance. The Reliquary, decorated with Pictish symbols including rough circles and rectangles, looked like a miniature Ark of the Covenant. Some writers conjecture that this, combined with the signs of the Templar crosses in an unexpected attack of cavalry, won what scared the English into headlong retreat.

Readers of DVC have been briefed on the legend of Rosslyn Chapel, built around 1450 by the Sinclairs but unfinished. It is called the "Cathedral of Codes" by Dan Brown because of the Templar and Masonic symbology carved into its decoration and woven into its design. Likewise, the Sinclair family figured very prominently in the history of Freemasonry. Masons, Templars, and Sinclairs are tightly interwoven through nine centuries of history.

Eerie coincidence (or not): Dolly, the famous sheep that was the first mammal to be cloned from an adult of its species, was created at the Roslin Institute, a biomedical facility in the village that is the ancestral home of the Scottish Sinclairs.

The Sinclairs were well-traveled. The most significant legend involves a Henry Sinclair, born in 1345, who became known as Prince Henry. The Sinclair family already could trace its roots back to Vikings, but this connection was further strengthened when Henry Sinclair married into the royal lineage of Sweden and Norway. He was twenty-four and lord of Rosslyn when he was named also the earl of Orkney and lord of Shetland by King Olaf VI of Norway.

Prince Henry happened to be in the Faroe Islands around 1396 when he learned there was a shipwreck. It was the custom of the time that shipwrecks would be pillaged, but Henry arrived in time to save and befriend the commander, who happened to be a Venetian voyager and mapmaker, Nicolo Zeno (brother of a famous Venetian admiral, Carlo Zeno, "The Lion").

With the help and expertise of Nicolo Zeno and his son Antonio, in 1398 (almost one hundred years ahead of Columbus) Prince Henry set off in twelve ships for a voyage west, to Greenland, Nova Scotia, and even New England, as the legend has it. Accompanying them were two hundred to three hundred soldiers (depending on the account), who are assumed to have been Templars. Also, there were a number of Cistercian monks, known for their ability to farm. Clearly, there were thoughts of conquest and colonization.

Later, a Zeno grandson brought out a "narrative" of the voyage, as well as a map that seems to show cities and other identifiable points in Nova Scotia and Newfoundland. The explorers allegedly made friends with the Micmac Indians, and may have reached settlements begun decades earlier by Europeans who had been shipwrecked.

However, much of the story of Prince Henry in the New World is the result of embellishments and assumptions.

Nowhere is this more apparent than in the ancillary tale of the "Knight of Westford." Prince Henry and some of his band purportedly managed to travel up the Merrimack River in Massachusetts, where one of the Templar knights, Sir James Gunn, died. They inscribed a memorial to him on a rock face on a high bluff near what is now Westford, Massachusetts, according to legend. A learned writer interpreted this inscription as showing a knight, with a broken Templar sword, and the Gunn family crest. But an archeologist from Harvard later visited the bluff and found a T-shaped mark of no particular significance, and a local story that two boys had put it there in the 1800s.

There is another legend, with much more physical evidence, of a buried treasure in a carefully booby-trapped "money pit" on Oak Island, Nova Scotia. Supposedly buried deep in the pit was a stone inscribed in Masonic code, about riches that were buried deeper. Since the pit was engineered so as to fill up with water from a tunnel connected to the sea, no one has discovered the treasure, even though expeditions by treasure hunters have been made regularly since 1796.

The Henry Sinclair legend satisfies a major

requirement of a "big picture" conspiracy that would explain what happened to the biggest treasure of all time: the Templar treasure. In this scenario, the Templars escaped from the south of France after the arrests of 1307. They went in ships to Scotland, where an excommunicated king was not cowed by the Catholic Church and could give the Templars a home. The treasure later went with Prince Henry Sinclair to Oak Island, and then perhaps to somewhere in the American colonies. In the recent movie *National Treasure*, the treasure is portrayed as a staggering combination of the complete contents of the Temple of Solomon, plus treasures of the pharaohs, as well as documents from the Library at Alexandria. The movie has it all buried beneath Trinity Church in lower Manhattan.

While gold and riches cannot be sniffed at, Dan Brown in *DVC* hinted that the real treasure could be secret documents, relics (bones) of Mary Magdalene, or things primarily of religious, spiritual, and historical significance.

There are two very strange stories associated with the Sinclairs, in both of which hearts are separated from their bodies. In 1330, Sir William Sinclair, loyal Scottish knight and warrior, was among the small army that took the heart of Robert the Bruce on crusade. Bruce, on his deathbed in 1329, realized he would not be able to go on a crusade (as his grandfather had before him). He got his best, most loyal knights, led by James Douglas, to pledge that they would take his heart to be buried in the Church of the Holy Sepulchre in Jerusalem. The embalmed heart was put into a small silver casket that James Douglas wore around his neck.

The knights didn't reach Jerusalem. They chose to stop in Spain to fight the Moors and there were out-maneuvered and killed. Sir William Sinclair and his brother died in this battle. The heart of Robert the Bruce was eventually brought back to Scotland.

Fast-forward to 1998. Alisdair Rosslyn Sinclair, forty-seven, a true descendant of the Sinclairs and well aware of his birthright as a Templar, traveled to Jerusalem from Amsterdam, where he had been sub-sisting as a guitar maker. As he tried to leave Israel, airport officials found some $5,000 worth of deutschmarks in a false bottom of his suitcase and he was detained. According to accounts, he was found strangled from his shoelaces in the airport lockup. His body was autopsied in Jerusalem and shipped home to his family in Scotland about a month later. However, when authorities in Scotland performed a second autopsy, they found Sinclair's heart was missing!

After a demand from Scotland, the Israeli authorities produced a heart, which they said had been removed for tests to determine whether Sinclair had been a drug user.

According to one conspiracy theory involving anticipation of the End of Days, the Templars have never given up hopes of returning to power in Jerusalem, although there are nefarious forces aligned against them. Conspiracy theorists feel it was inevitable that a Sinclair heir imprudent enough to visit Jerusalem would be murdered.

In a Dan Brown context, this is not as far-fetched as

it may seem. After all, there is talk in both *A&D* and *DVC* of a millennial event of some kind that has been anticipated by the Illuminati but has not yet materialized. Could it be the Templar reconquest of Jerusalem?

DEATH AND
RESURRECTION

S OME ASPECT of religious, spiritual, or physical resurrection is almost certain to come up in Dan Brown's next novel. If Brown takes a deep dive into Freemasonry, he simply cannot escape the ritual of figurative death and rebirth as part of the initiation of a Master Mason (not to mention initiation into Skull and Bones). But there are many more implications and connections.

One of the theories that Dan Brown has floated in public is that Jesus survived the Crucifixion. This is certainly provocative and, if pursued in *The Solomon Key*, would start a whole new level of antagonism between Brown and traditional religions. However, ideas of the same kind have surfaced regularly for hundreds of years. Giordano Bruno, for instance, was burned at the stake in 1600 for saying, in essence, that Jesus was merely "an unusually skillful magician." This outrageous thought probably stemmed from

Bruno's study of early Hermetic and occult writings.

In this thread of thought, alchemy could tap into the spiritual lifeforce, giving a wizard or magus the power to heal and, yes, even to resurrect. Despite these mystical connections, Bruno is actually celebrated today as a man of *science*. Many of the early scientists were in fact alchemists and students of Hermetics. Likewise, the early history of medicine is actually a history of alchemy, witchcraft, the occult, astrology, and the like, with occasional lapses into science.

Nowhere is this better illustrated than in the events of the last days of George Washington. The medical treatments he received bordered on witch-doctoring, and notions of resurrection figured in the aftermath of his death.

The former president and general was enjoying, at last, his retirement to his beloved estate, Mount Vernon. Still robust at age sixty-eight, it was his practice to ride out onto his lands, daily if he got the chance. On December 12, 1799, he rode around his farms from about 10 a.m. to 3 p.m., as the weather turned nasty, with wind, hail, rain, and then heavy snowfall. But Washington did not change clothes when he got home, saying he believed his greatcoat had kept him dry. The following day, he was somewhat hoarse and the snow continued, so he spent most of the day indoors. In the afternoon he did, however, take the time to go out into his large backyard on the Potomac River bluffs and mark some trees for cutting. As he went to bed for the night, his personal secretary, Tobias Lear, suggested that he take something for his "cold." Washington replied, "No, you know I never take anything for a cold. Let it go as it came."

At about 2 or 3 a.m., George awoke Martha Washington to say that he was very unwell, having "taken an ague" (this was a fever of a kind). Martha saw that he had great difficulty speaking and breathing. She wanted to get up and rouse the household, but he told her not to, fearing that she would catch a cold herself. So she stayed in bed with him until just before daybreak, when a servant came and they could get a fire lit.

They sent word for the first doctor, while they also prepared a home remedy and called for one of the plantation's overseers, Albin Rawlins. Washington, who had suffered many a serious illness in his life, had been subjected to the practice of "bleeding" a patient to remove harmful substances in the blood. He believed in it and even had the apparatus available to perform this procedure. He was certain that whenever the first doctors arrived, they would prescribe it. So he got Rawlins, who had shown skill at the technique, to do it for him.

When Rawlins opened the wound, the blood did not flow enough, so Washington told him, "More, more." Martha was against it, saying she did not think bleeding was the proper solution, but Rawlins obeyed George.

The home-brewed elixir was a mixture of vinegar, molasses, and butter, and it might have been soothing for a sore throat, but Washington couldn't swallow any of it. When he tried, he convulsed and almost suffocated.

The first doctor summoned was James Craik, of Alexandria, Virginia, who had been with Washington for every major battle in the Revolutionary War and was a trusted physician. Dr. Craik had earlier advised the family that another doctor, Gustavus Brown, who was just across the Potomac from Mount Vernon, should be called in an emergency. Remembering this, Martha also sent for Dr. Brown.

Dr. Craik arrived first, sometime after 9 a.m., and his first action was to bleed Washington again. He prepared a new gargle—this time with vinegar and sage tea—but again it almost suffocated the patient. At around 11 a.m., fearing Dr. Brown would not arrive in time, Dr. Craik sent for Elisha Cullen Dick, another Alexandria doctor and a Freemason. Then Dr. Craik bled Washington again!

Dr. Brown and Dr. Dick arrived shortly after 3 p.m., examined the patient, and conferred. Dr. Brown believed the malady was "quinsy," which is a tonsil infection. Dr. Craik concurred, but not forcefully. Dr. Dick, who at age thirty-seven was much younger than the other physicians, disagreed. He felt the problem was not quinsy but a violent inflammation of the throat membranes. Interestingly, both Dr. Craik and Dr. Brown had been educated in Edinburgh, Scotland, whereas Dr. Dick had been born and educated in Pennsylvania. Dr. Dick proposed a tracheotomy. He had learned that this operation had recently succeeded in England, but it had never been attempted in America. The other two physicians demurred, and the tracheotomy was not attempted.

The doctors were not without ideas, however. At

various times, they tried soaking Washington's feet in warm water and wrapping his neck with flannel dipped in a salve, wrapping his neck with a poultice of dried beetles, administering an enema, giving him doses of calomel (mercurous chloride, a poison), twice giving him a tartar emetic (intended to induce vomiting, but it only produced an involuntary discharge of the bowels), and applying "blisters and poultices of wheat bran" to his legs.

After the tracheotomy discussion, the doctors returned to the bedside and George Washington was bled one more time! It was a big draw of blood, too—thirty-two ounces. Dr. Dick expressed opposition at the time, and a month later, Dr. Brown wrote of his regret at this last bleeding, which he came to believe was the ultimate cause of death.

Modern doctors have analyzed the surviving records. Their findings vary, but they believe that the total amount of blood taken was as much as half of his body's total supply, which by itself may have been sufficient to kill him. However, the modern doctors generally believe the cause of death was a severe swelling of the epiglottis, brought on probably by strep bacteria, but possibly by diphtheria or even flu. This condition is still very serious and potentially fatal, even today.

Around 8 p.m., Washington called his three doctors together and said, "I thank you for your attentions but I pray you take no more troubles about me. Let me go off quietly. I cannot last long."

George Washington, like other people of his day, considered resurrection or reanimation to be possible.

According to one source, Washington actually gave credence to a theory that Jesus himself was physically reanimated from a death-like state (rather than ascending to heaven). And Washington had on at least one occasion witnessed one of his own slaves at Mount Vernon coming back to life after apparently dying. Also, practically everyone in those days had heard of people being buried when mistaken for dead. Some were true stories and some were "urban legends" of the time.

For this reason, Washington's last few sentences did not seem at all strange to the people attending his deathbed. They viewed it as a sensible and practical thing when he said, "Have me decently buried, and do not let my body be put into the vault in less than three days after I am dead." He obtained an acknowledgment from Lear. "Tis well," he said.

He felt for his own pulse, laid back, and succumbed at 10:20 p.m. Dr. Brown went over to the bedroom clock and cut its pendulum cord so that it would never tick again.

(The clock, still reading 10:20, and the blood-letting instruments are on display at the Washington Masonic National Memorial in Alexandria.)

But that is not the end of the story—a fourth doctor had been summoned. Dr. William Thornton arrived on December 15, the day after Washington died. By then, Washington's body was frozen.

Thornton's presence at Mount Vernon was incongruous, since he was hardly a practicing physician. He was born and reared in the British Virgin Islands, studied medicine at Edinburgh, and received his MD in Aberdeen, Scotland. But his career in medicine was not what made him most famous. He settled in Philadelphia and became a citizen in 1788. In 1789, without any formal education as an architect, he won a competition to design the Philadelphia Library Company's new building. In 1792, he applied slightly late for a much more important competition: the design of the U.S. Capitol building. Even though his sketches were late, Thornton was given shrift by Thomas Jefferson, who oversaw the competition, and the Thornton plan was favored by George Washington. Thornton won. The prize was $500 and a plot of land in the city. Thornton went on to become an amateur painter, inventor, and the architect of the Octagon House in Washington, now home to the American Institute of Architects.

Thornton was thus widely known as the first architect of the Capitol at the time of Washington's death.

Thornton offered a truly shocking proposition to those assembled around Washington's corpse. He said the body could be thawed and "reanimated." His plan was to immerse the body in cold water, then surround it with blankets and "by friction, to give him warmth." Thornton, who was confident that he could have successfully performed a tracheotomy on the living Washington, suggested this procedure so as to allow air to be pushed into his lungs. Finally, he said that Washington could be transfused with the "blood of a lamb" in order to restore the volume of blood that had been lost. (This has an eerie second connotation as the Blood of the Lamb—the sacrifice of Jesus for the sins of the world.)

Martha Washington had common sense, as we all know. She vetoed Thornton's plan, and that was the end of it. Washington was interred a few days later in the vault at Mount Vernon, in accordance with his will—well, sort of. He had specifically asked for burial rites "in a private manner without parade or funeral oration," but this was completely ignored. There was a military honor guard, a Masonic procession, a cannon salute from a schooner docked in the Potomac nearby, and a considerable number of mourners.

At the vault on the Mount Vernon estate, four clergymen were in attendance—three of them also being members of Washington's Masonic lodge. But, insisting on it as their right, the Masons presided over the final part of the ceremony. Among them was the lodge's Worshipful Master, Dr. Dick, the physician who had attended him at his death. Washington's Masonic lambskin apron, plus a sprig of the acacia tree (a symbol of immortality or resurrection) were the last things placed in his casket.

Thornton saw to it that Washington's mahogany coffin was lined with lead (a way of preventing moisture from reaching the corpse), in anticipation of a later reburial. According to Thornton's later account, he wrote John Marshall (then a member of Congress but soon to be the first Supreme Court chief justice) and asked that provision be made for a crypt in the Capitol for Washington, "for when I composed the plan and elevation of the Capitol of the U.S., I designed the dome for his [Washington's] mausoleum."

According to Thornton, Martha Washington agreed to this plan, provided that she could be interred there next to her husband. Thornton claimed that a secret vote of Congress approving the plan was pushed through by Marshall. All of these plans were abandoned, however, when subsequent generations of the Washington heirs refused to set aside the explicit provisions of Washington's will.

A SUGGESTED READING LIST

Revolutionary Brotherhood, Freemasonry and the Transformation of the American Social Order, 1730—1840, by Steven C. Bullock, 1996, University of North Carolina Press.

Benjamin Franklin, An American Life, by Walter Isaacson, 2003, Simon & Schuster, New York.

Washington: The Indispensable Man, by James Thomas Flexner, 1969, Little, Brown and Company, Boston, Massachusetts.

Founding Brothers, The Revolutionary Generation, by Joseph J. Ellis, 2001, Alfred A. Knopf, New York.

His Excellency, George Washington, by Joseph J. Ellis, 2004, Alfred A. Knopf, New York.

A Life of Albert Pike, by Walter Lee Brown, 1997, University of Arkansas Press.

The Refiner's Fire: The Making of Mormon Cosmology,

1644–1844, by John L. Brooke, 1994, Cambridge University Press, Cambridge, England.

Early Mormonism and the Magic World View, by D. Michael Quinn, 1998, Signature Books, Salt Lake City, Utah.

The Origins of Freemasonry, Scotland's Century 1590–1710, by David Stevenson, 1988, Cambridge University Press, Cambridge, England.

Mysteries of the Kabbalah, by Marc-Alain Oauknin, translated from the French by Josephine Bacon, 2000, Abbeville Press, New York.

Sefer Yetzirah, The Book of Creation, In Theory and Practice, by Aryeh Kaplan, 1990, Weiser Books, Boston, Massachusetts.

Jesus Christ, Sun of God: Ancient Cosmology and Early Christian Symbolism, by David Fideler, 1993, Quest Books, Wheaton, Illinois.

The Rosicrucian Enlightenment, by Frances A. Yates, 1972, Routledge Classics, London and New York.

The Secret Architecture of Our Nation's Capital: The Masons and the Building of Washington, DC, by David Ovason, 1999, Perennial, an imprint of HarperCollins Publishers, New York.

The Hiram Key, Pharaohs, Freemasons and the Discovery of the Secret Scrolls of Jesus, by Christopher Knight and Robert Lomas, 1996, Fair Winds Press, Gloucester, Massachusetts.

The Second Messiah, Templars, the Turin Shroud and the Great Secret of Freemasonry, by Christopher Knight and

Robert Lomas, 1997, Fair Winds Press, Gloucester, Massachusetts.

The Templar Revelation, by Lynn Picknett and Clive Prince, 1997, Simon & Schuster, New York.

The Temple and the Lodge, by Michael Baigent and Richard Leigh, 1989, Arcade Publishing, New York.

Shadow of the Sentinel (retitled *Rebel Gold*), *One Man's Quest to Find the Hidden Treasure of the Confederacy*, by Warren Getler and Bob Brewer, 2003, Simon & Schuster, New York.

Now that you've read

Secrets of the Widow's Son

turn the page to read David A. Shugarts's exclusive
mini-biography of worldwide bestselling author

DAN BROWN

Discover how Dan Brown, an unknown musician
and writer, transformed himself from an ambitious
but somewhat failing novelist into a writer whose
success is to date unparalleled in the history of
book publishing.

Find out why and how Dan Brown came to write
The Da Vinci Code, first inspired by a single reading of
Sidney Sheldon's novel *Doomsday Conspiracy*, and
what led investigative journalist David A. Shugarts to
embark on the trail of the now-reclusive author,
whose forthcoming novel *The Solomon Key*
Shugarts's own book *Secrets of the Widow's Son* keenly
anticipates ...

IN SEARCH OF
DAN BROWN ...

David A. Shugarts

S INCE THE FIRST PUBLICATION of Secrets of the Code in April 2004, the Secrets editorial team has been inundated with questions about The Da Vinci Code and its underlying issues of antiquity, history, theology, art, architecture, cryptography, and so on. Among all the debates and controversies about what really happened at the Council of Nicea 1700 years ago, or what the real meaning of Jesus "kissing Mary frequently on the M ..." may be, or what Leonardo was really trying to communicate in the Last Supper painting, one set of questions asked at almost every forum where the Secrets editors have spoken is: Who is Dan Brown, really? Where did he get his ideas? How did he burst so suddenly on the scene as the author of the world's bestselling novel? Is he anti-Christian? Does he have a religious agenda or is he just trying to sell books?

To try to develop answers to those questions, investigative reporter David A. Shugarts spared no effort to look into the intriguing person that is Dan Brown. Shugarts will be known to Secrets readers as Dan Brown's "fact-checker" and "code-breaker." In Secrets of the Code as well as

Secrets of Angels & Demons, Shugarts analyzed the contents of Dan Brown's novels and uncovered dozens of mistakes and plot flaws in the text. He also cracked the code embedded on The Da Vinci Code dust jacket, which led to our 2005 book-length volume by Shugarts, Secrets of the Widow's Son, *addressing the themes and mysteries from history that will likely be found in Dan Brown's sequel to* The Da Vinci Code *(The Solomon Key), long before Brown even publishes it.*

Now we invite you to go on a fascinating tour with Shugarts as he walks the streets of Exeter, New Hampshire and explores other chapters of Dan Brown's life story. To Shugarts, certain things about Brown just don't add up—and he is still at work on teasing out the answers to some of his questions. As Shugarts points out, this exclusive tour of Dan Brown's past is still very much a work in progress, awaiting, among other things, an opportunity for an interview with the novelist himself. At the time we went to press, Brown remained enigmatically aloof from the normal media circus of interviews and publicity, refusing to give interviews and to allow the media to cover his small handful of public appearances ...

For about a year now, I have tried to get a handle on how Dan Brown developed as a writer, based on the biographical facts that can be collected.

What emerges is an enigmatic transformation, from an unknown musician and writer who had experienced precious little success and a lot of failure, to a novelist whose success is beyond all reckoning in the history of publishing. Perhaps the most salient point is that Dan Brown the man still clings to the same home stomping grounds, and to an attempt at quiet anonymity, even though his name is now a household word in more than forty countries where *The Da Vinci Code* has been published. His hero, Robert Langdon, roams the world's great cities and themes of religion and history, while Dan Brown sits and writes in solitude in a loft in his home town, going only on occasional research trips abroad.

Whereas the record suggests that Brown once craved fame and recognition, now he has an excess of it. At his only pre-announced public appearance in 2005—a speech at a benefit dinner in Manchester, New Hampshire—he had to be escorted by an armed guard and he left immediately after his talk.

Dan Brown hasn't sat for an interview since sales of *The Da Vinci Code* ascended like a rocket in 2003. So it's not easy to know the inner Dan Brown, although I have tried to come up with some reasonable guesses based on the facts. I have gone to Exeter, his home town. I have visited the schools he attended. I have sat in seats he occupied, looked at sights he saw as a young person—some of which he continues to gaze at today.

I have also chased his thoughts down through the canyons and over the mountains of history and philosophy. It has been wonderfully exhilarating. In writing *Secrets of the Widow's Son*, an attempt to anticipate Dan Brown's next novel, I zoomed through time and space like a video-game sprite, always searching for a glimpse of the same thematic vistas that Dan Brown must be seeing.

At the outset, I must give sincere thanks to Dan Brown for two things: His book led me into a journey that itself is certainly the most fulfilling intellectual work I have done and, if I ever finish my own novel, it will be because he gives hope to an ordinary guy sitting at a blank screen. (Indeed, I believe we are beginning to witness the torrential flow of creative works generated by the Dan Brown Effect in the current crop of novels, television series and movies.)

But journalists covering Dan Brown have caught on that he is not exactly a reliable source for his own biographical information. Among other things, he tends to slip about dates. For instance:

Daniel Gerhard Brown was born June 22, 1964 in Exeter, New Hampshire. When he gave his talk in October of 2005 in nearby Manchester, he was introduced as a lifelong New Hampshire boy, and he largely agreed with that introduction, but said, "I have lived a couple of years in Spain and a couple in California and the rest in New Hampshire. I'm 40 years old, so you do the math." Then, doing the math himself, he admitted, "Well, actually I'm 41."

This isn't the only booboo of its kind, as we will see, and it leads some to wonder why Dan Brown is keeping himself hidden from view. Is it mere shyness? Is it because parts of his career are fairly embarrassing? Or is it because his success with *The Da Vinci Code* is somehow bound up with a few personal myths about himself, which his editors, agents, and spinmeisters now don't want to see questioned?

Here is a fundamental question that has kept me on this hunt for many months: How did an otherwise undistinguished writer suddenly deliver *The Da Vinci Code*, the world's bestselling book? Was it luck or skill? Was it his lifelong destiny, or a sudden serendipity?

What I have found so far is that there is little or

IN SEARCH OF DAN BROWN

no evidence to indicate from Dan Brown's first thirty or so years of life, that his late thirties would be even modestly successful as a creative person in either of his two chosen pursuits—music or books. In fact, well into his early thirties, Brown lacked success and seemed to lack clear direction in life as well. What he made of himself after that is truly amazing. Hindsight allows for looking back and seeing little hints of what was to come, but they seem to be few and far between.

In 1998, with the publication of *Digital Fortress*, his first novel, Dan Brown at 34 made his first blip-like appearance on the radar screen of American action-adventure novels. What was the event that caused his transformation from a guy who wanted to write books to actual novelist? Dan Brown's own description is found in answer to one of the frequently asked questions (FAQs) on his website:

> In 1994, while vacationing in Tahiti, I found an old copy of Sydney Sheldon's *Doomsday Conspiracy* on the beach. I read the first page ... and then the next ... and then the next. Several hours later, I finished the book and thought, "Hey, I can do that." Upon my return, I began work on my first novel—*Digital Fortress*—which was published in 1996.

This may seem like a huge digression, but we need to fact-check Dan Brown here, and I'm not talking about the typo that remains on his high-visibility website where he misspells the *Doomsday* author's first name, which is correctly spelled *Sidney*. Another small point caught my notice here. Brown's mention of the date makes it seem like a neatly packaged, two-year effort to produce his first novel. That's partly because he fails to remember that the year of his vacation in Tahiti was 1993. And it is because he remembers the publication date as 1996.

We can be reasonably certain he's wrong about the Tahiti date because I spoke with one of the other eight people who were loosely associated with Dan and his future wife, Blythe Newlon, as the only Americans at the Tahitian resort. In her scrapbook that she keeps, Kay Borden, of Marietta, Georgia, has the plane ticket for her flight on April 9, 1993. On a website page, Mrs. Borden displays snapshots of a young-looking Dan and Blythe.

But, according to Brown's own statements in a different interview, *Digital Fortress* was actually triggered by an event that occurred on the Exeter Academy campus in the spring of 1995. As he relates it, some Secret Service agents showed up on campus to arrest a student for an allegedly threatening email message. He had opined that President Clinton "ought to be shot." I have searched, but so far not found any press account of this event.

Also, Dan Brown did not copyright *Digital Fortress* in 1996, but in 1998, the year of its first publication by Thomas Dunne Books, an imprint of the St. Martin's Press. (To be fair, publication of a book often takes a year or more from delivery of the completed manuscript to actual publication.)

One of Dan Brown's favorite sayings is that history is "written by the victors," or in other words, history gets rewritten by whomever gets control of the pen or the word processor. It's ironic, but it appears that, with little errors and other inaccuracies, Brown seems to rewrite his own history rather regularly.

The Local Boy

In order to understand Dan Brown as a writer, it is absolutely essential to visit Exeter, New Hampshire.

Exeter is a truly charming New England town situated not far from Boston and Portsmouth. It's considered part of the "Seacoast" area, even though it is about ten miles inland. Several different roads out of Exeter will lead you easily to the resort towns on the Atlantic beaches, such as Seabrook, Hampton and Rye.

Exeter is one of those old New England mill towns that lost a lot of jobs as factories closed over the years. Undoubtedly, some of the suffering was eased by the presence of the renowned Phillips Exeter Academy, which owns a large part of the central town, and provides a significant number of jobs, in addition to the intellectual and cultural benefits it brings to the town.

Exeter is compact. Practically everything is within walking distance of everything else. The main streets come down to Walter Street, whose eighteenth-century shops line the Squamscott River. Dan Brown said of it in 1996: "I've returned to this small town of Exeter. I'm learning to appreciate the silence of the woods, the clarity of the air and the bareness of winter."

It's also the kind of town where they say, "ayup" and "nope" as their long answers to a question. As I wandered around the town of Exeter and the

Academy on several visits, I was treated politely by everyone. But, whether it was because they know Dan Brown personally, or just think of any outsider as potential trouble, the townspeople button their lips if you ask about Brown. They often ask, "Did Dan Brown authorize you to write about him?" When I told them my work was independent and unauthorized, they tended to become the stereotype of laconic New Englanders. Eventually, though, I did find a few who would talk, even in Exeter.

It was here, in the early 1960s, that a young couple, Richard and Connie Brown, settled and started a family. Richard had been hired as an Academy math teacher, and Connie would make the quintessential faculty wife. But more than that, she had skills as an organist, and the pair also found a home as co-choir directors at Christ Church, Exeter's Episcopalian church. Connie would remain as the church's organist for many years. Was it nature or nurture? Math—more specifically Richard Brown's specialty, geometry—church, and music would become several of the biggest influences on Dan Brown.

Initially, the Browns lived in the Academy dorms, as was the custom—new faculty are expected to superintend the dorms for their first ten years at the school. This is where Dan Brown spent his earliest years. Two years after he was born, Valerie Jo Brown was born (1966). The third and last of the Brown children, Gregory, was born in 1974.

An interesting ballet began around 1963 involving not people, but houses. A couple named John and Miriam LeBaron lived on Pine Street, within a couple of blocks of the Academy campus. They had many

acres of land behind their house, stretching all the way
to the Little River. They decided to move the house to
an area in the rear of their property, spinning it around
in the process to afford a view of the river. The
rearrangement made it possible to sell off the rest of
their land, and the buyer was Christ Episcopal
Church, which was looking for a place to build a new
house of worship, having worn out the former
structure on Elliot Street.

This not only gave the Church a site for a Pine
Street address, but also a parking lot in the rear, and
land left over. It allowed for creation of a new road,
Nelson Drive, which would eventually yield building
lots for several more houses beyond the LeBarons. One
of these lots, which had originally been designated for a
rectory, was sold to Connie and Dick Brown and they
also chose to have an existing house moved onto the
lot, rather than build anew (this according to the recollection of Mrs. LeBaron). Around 1975 (based on a
deed of that year), they settled in at 7 Nelson Drive, on
the rim of a cul-de-sac.

(It was almost a mystical experience for me to
find the Browns' church. Within a small sector of
town, there are about six or seven churches and they
are all cozy and welcoming. For some inexplicable
reason, the Cross of St. George attracted my eye,
and I drove into the Pine Street entrance of Christ
Church to inquire. Yes, out of the multiple churches
I could have tried, I had found the right one on the
first try. As I drove out the back lot, I was again
surprised to find myself on the Browns' little road,
Nelson Drive.)

The Brown homestead's location is important for

quite a number of reasons. It is within easy walking distance of the Academy campus, as well as all the public schools, and downtown Exeter. Moreover, if Connie and Dick, or the children, wanted to be a part of a church event, they could be there in about a minute. At Christ Church, Dan Brown went to Sunday school, to church camp, and sang in the choir. To say that Dan Brown grew up in the shadow of the Church would not be an overstatement.

Over the years, Dick Brown became a stalwart of the Exeter faculty and eventually was named head of the mathematics department. Dick Brown also became a very accomplished author of math textbooks. For the space of about thirty years, he was constantly writing or editing or contributing to various textbooks, some of which remain in use today.

Dick Brown enjoyed appearing in local musical productions. In fact, when Dan was a junior at the Academy, his father starred in the Exeter Players production of *The Pirates of Penzance*. As the classic Major-General in the Gilbert and Sullivan operetta, math teacher Brown sang, "I'm very well acquainted too with matters mathematical. I understand equations, both the simple and quadratical ... I am the very model of a modern Major-General."

Dan Brown, on the other hand, was not a stand-out musician at Exeter, although he had an excellent voice and could be a part of any choir he wished to join. According to his former principal, Dr. Stephen Kurtz, Dan Brown and his classmate, William "Chip" Beckett, did put together a play that was performed to some success. But in an interview, Dr. Kurtz could not recall details of the production.

The Browns took full advantage of the great side-benefit for faculty, the opportunity to send their children through the prep school at greatly reduced fees. All three Brown children went through the Academy when their turns came. Dan graduated in 1982, Valerie in 1985 and Greg in 1993.

Dan Brown sometimes mentions to Exeter students that he once lived in the dorms, which is a true statement, because he was a child when his parents were living in and supervising the dorm. But, by the time he was actually a student at Exeter, he was living at Nelson Drive and his status was "day student." The gulf at any prep school between "day students" who live in town and "residential" students who live in the dorms while their parents are far away in Boston or New York is substantial. It usually reflects class and status issues that are often reflected, however subtly, in student attitudes about themselves and toward others. Dan Brown was apparently somewhat on the edge of student society. He was a friendly, somewhat ordinary fellow who got along well with his schoolmates, and never particularly excelled beyond the achievements of the expected standards of excellence at a place like Exeter, which was known for its bright, talented young people then—and now.

Although I searched the student publications looking for it, I could find no instance of Dan Brown stepping out as a writer. He did play squash for the varsity team, and he was among twelve students selected to be proctors at the library, assigned to patrol and enforce the rules.

In sum, Dan Brown did not appear to be headed for a career as a writer nor even a "creative type." He was simply a guy who went through the Academy. However, this raises a good question: Is it possible to get through the Academy and not be marked for future distinction? How much of an effect can the school have on an "average" student there?

Now, that's one mighty good question! In my search for the answer, I found a lot of information and food for thought. One former school official said to me, "I hope Dan remembers that he really owes it all to Exeter Academy."

Changes

By the time Dan Brown had slipped the bonds of the Town of Exeter's elementary school system and entered the hallowed halls of the Academy in 1978, the prep school had put in place a number of systematic changes that were almost certain to leave an impression on him.

Although it may appear slow to act sometimes, Exeter Academy has shown the ability to morph itself in changing times. All of the social problems of the wider society in the past fifty years have had some expression in the changes that have occurred at the Academy, from dealing with racism and civil rights, to gender equality, to environmental issues.

Three Latin text elements of the Academy seal translate into English as: "The end depends upon the beginning," "by the grace of God," and "not for oneself." The latter (*non sibi*) is taken to mean that knowledge is to be gained not only for the improvement of the individual, but also to be useful for the wider society.

Exeter Academy was founded as a boys' school in 1781, and it would remain a male bastion for 189 years. By the way, Paul Revere fashioned the first seal for the Academy in 1782. The list of illustrious graduates is too long to cite, but it includes Arthur Schlesinger Jr., David Eisenhower, Pierre DuPont III, Adolph Coors III, Sen. Jay Rockefeller of West Virginia and the late Sen. H. John Heinz of Pennsylvania. The current Director of National Intelligence, John Negroponte, is a graduate. U.S. President Franklin Pierce was an Exeter graduate. President Abraham Lincoln sent his son to Exeter (Robert Todd Lincoln), as did President Ulysses S. Grant. So in an American culture that is generally uninterested in history, Dan Brown didn't have to look too far to be surrounded by it and to develop a certain appreciation of it.

The first female faculty member was hired in 1968. The school's student body remained all-male until 1970 when a transitional period began, starting with admission of a handful of female students and culminating in full inclusion a few years later. Strides were later made in adding female teachers, and elevating them to management positions. By the time Dan Brown arrived, Exeter, a one-time bastion of the male power elite, was fully co-ed.

Dan Brown's time at the Academy came in the late 1970s and early 1980s, as Exeter made a serious effort to be sensitive to women's issues and to be more inclusive of sexual preferences and points of view. Surely, living through this time of change, some of this rubbed off on Dan Brown and may have been part of his interest in entertaining themes of feminism in his novels.

Religion in School

The Academy's founder, John Phillips, had set down a religious aspect of the school's foundation, and chapel services were a part of the school's regimen. But in the early 1960s (just a few years after the Brown family had settled in at Christ Church), a change took place at the Academy that would have reverberations much later. The principal, Richard W. Day, met an Episcopalian priest, Rev. Edward S. Gleason (at the actual dedication of the new Christ Church building on Pine Street), and soon hired him as the school's minister. As such, he was to oversee services that were Congregational, rather than Episcopalian, but this was not the big change. Principal Day charged Rev. Gleason with transforming the school's church attendance policy from compulsory to voluntary.

Gleason innovated. He started by enlisting the students themselves. He made certain students "deacons" of the Phillips Church, and with them he created special worship services, crafted to be relevant to the student congregation. It largely worked, and students continued to attend services at Phillips Church, even though not required. To this day, they keep coming to services. They are there because they want to be.

The tone was set, and over the years, Phillips Church began to be even more open to diverse kinds of worship. By the time Dan Brown was an Academy student, the structure was the place of worship for Quakers, Jews and Buddhists, as well as Congregationalists and other Christian denominations.

What had been set in motion continued after Dan

Brown left the Academy. In 2003, after a renovation, the Phillips Church reopened with an evening of prayer and celebration led by the peace activist Rev. William Sloan Coffin, to the sounds of chamber music and African drums. The evening's readings included a traditional Zulu prayer, a Shanti mantra read in Sanskrit, a meditation on world peace by a Buddhist monk, the Lord's Prayer read in Aramaic by an Exeter senior, and selections from the Quran and the Old Testament read by Exeter students in Arabic, English and Hebrew. It might have been a religious service designed for its cross-cultural symbolism by Robert Langdon himself.

It seems to me the inevitable conclusion to be drawn here is that Dan Brown was steeped in principles of religious tolerance. The contrast between his early experiences of diversity and tolerance at Exeter and the world beginning to swing toward all sorts of religious fundamentalism right around the time he graduated, may have prompted his selection of religious themes to include in *Angels & Demons* and *The Da Vinci Code*, and may also explain how deeply he was shocked by the religious furore that these novels sparked.

A Temple of Knowledge

After a long and legendary search for an architect, in 1965 the Academy hired the famed Louis I. Kahn to design the school's new library. It took six more years to complete it, but in November of 1971 the faculty and students physically carried some 60,000 books into their new library. It now holds more than 140,000

books. It eclipses anyone's expectations of a high-
school library; it is a library worthy of a very good
small college.

There is no way to overestimate the presence that
this structure has on campus, even though it is
"hidden in plain sight." It is a truly magnificent
building and thoroughly modern, but it tends to blend
into the campus without a murmur. The brick outer
construction colors it the same as the many brick
campus buildings of neo-Georgian style. The library
was given a 25 Year Award by the American Institute
of Architects in 1997, and in 2005, it was among 12
buildings selected for a series of U.S. Postal Service
commemorative stamps called "Masterworks of
American Architecture."

The library is a hub of the Academy community,
and a true temple of knowledge. Outwardly, it looks
like a cube. One of its main characteristics is the trans-
mission of natural light into the structure, made
possible by a kind of open lattice of outer walls and an
inner sanctum admitting light through giant circular
holes and a giant skylight.

Before I saw this building, I had been sensitized to a
number of strong symbols relating to Freemasonry, a
study I had taken up to be able to understand and
explain many themes in Dan Brown's works.
Freemason history and symbolism make multiple
appearances in both *Angels & Demons* and *The Da
Vinci Code*, and are expected to form the context for
Dan Brown's much-awaited next novel, *The Solomon
Key*. I had learned to notice two of the shapes revered
by the Masons, the circle and the square. In addition,
The Da Vinci Code begins with the dead Louvre

curator laid out like the Vitruvian Man, the image made famous by Leonardo showing an attempt to fit the human proportions to both a circle and a square.

I have now visited this building several times, roaming the same stacks and floors that Dan Brown himself once patrolled as a proctor, sitting in chairs that he probably sat in, looking at the same views and angles. Perhaps I am overly sensitized, but I do not see how a person could look around and *not* see unmistakable symbolic references to the Vitruvian Man, and the ancient symbols of circle and square. In addition, the view upward from the central atrium reveals an equal-armed cross. All of this is by design.

The architect Louis Kahn could, himself, have been an influence in the formation of a Dan Brown character. Although Jewish by birth and culture, Kahn is seen in architectural history as something of a pantheistic mystic. He actively sought to work into his buildings elements of sacred geometry, Kabbalistic traditions, classical Greek and Roman allusions, archetypal forms and shapes, and the spiritual essence of religions as various as Buddhism and Islam. Dan Brown's Robert Langdon often sees the male and female symbols of chalice and blade appearing in surprising places in art and architecture. These symbols are in obvious evidence in the work of Louis Kahn as well.

I do not think the young Dan Brown, Exeter student, conceived much of the detail of his novels in his high-school library. But years later, when the character of Robert Langdon begins to speak about symbolism "hidden in plain sight," it surely must have occurred to Brown that he had been immersed in a system of ancient symbolism, right at the Academy library. (Brown still maintains an office in Exeter where he does some of his writing and he often strolls over to the library, so he gets a regular dose of the symbolism.)

Famous Writers' School?

Exeter Academy has a long list of distinguished alumni, and a tradition of celebrating those alums that have become authors. Other eras featured Daniel Webster, Booth Tarkington and John Agee, but some of the famous and relatively recent ones are Gore Vidal '43, George Plimpton '44, John Knowles '45, Peter Benchley '57, John Irving '61, Joyce Maynard '71—and, of course, Dan Brown '82.

The living writers are often brought back to the campus for various celebrations and awards, or to give inspiring mentoring-type talks to the students. Thus, in Dan Brown's days as a student, he was offered the opportunity to sit in for lectures by Vidal, Plimpton and Irving. In fact, all three visited Exeter in the spring semester of his junior year, and good accounts of most of these sessions were published in the school's paper, the *Exonian* or the local newspaper, *The Exeter News-Letter*.

Irving, author of *The World According to Garp* and *The Cider House Rules*, was (like Dan Brown) the son of an Exeter faculty member, or what in Exeter slang is called a "fac-brat." Irving admitted that it took him five years to get through the Academy, since he failed math and Latin. He told the students he didn't mind staying around for an extra year, since he was "happy here," having friends both in the school and in the town. He later went to the University of Pittsburgh, but became disillusioned with the English program there and left to join the Writer's Workshop in Iowa. In 1989, Irving wrote the acclaimed *A Prayer for Owen Meany*. The book takes place in "Gravesend, New Hampshire," which is instantly recognizable as Exeter.

Plimpton was hailed as a returning Exeter alumnus even though he admitted that his many pranks got him expelled from the Academy with three months remaining in his senior year. (In fact, there was at least one faculty member who had to be kept in the shadows to avoid a violent confrontation when Plimpton came to visit.) Plimpton, in various essays, described some of his misdeeds, such as stealing a rhinoceros head from one of the lounges. Plimpton admitted he was a disappointment to his family, which had been graduating from the Academy for three generations. Indeed, the name Plimpton was attached to various Exeter playing fields and land that had been donated by his grandfather.

When Plimpton spoke at Exeter during the Academy's 200th-year festivities in 1981, he related some of the adventures of his early days as a "participatory journalist." Plimpton was known in literary circles as one of the founding editors of the *Paris Review*. But he was probably best known by the public for the book *Paper Lion*, describing how he played out the average fan's fantasy by training for and eventually suiting up for a Detroit Lions game as a quarterback.

But for the students, Plimpton related the story of how he accidentally got started in "participatory journalism." He said when he was at Harvard and trying to get a writing position on that school's famous *Lampoon*, he offered to cover the Boston Marathon. The editor told him the only way he would be given the post was if he actually ran in the Marathon, to get a first-person story. Plimpton took public transportation to a spot a few blocks from the finish line, burst out of the crowd and sprinted alongside the race leader—who nonetheless beat Plimpton to the line. (Later in 1981, the famous Rosie Ruiz attempted a repeat of Plimpton's stunt at the New York Marathon, and was promptly discovered.)

In Plimpton's amusing tales of his participatory journalistic adventures, it is not hard to see the general idea of "Everyman" thrust into extraordinary circumstances that runs through all four of Dan Brown's novels. It is also not that much of a stretch from George Plimpton as the Lions quarterback to Dan Brown playing academic iconographer and symbologist through his Robert Langdon character. Just as Plimpton inserted himself into the real-life mauling of NFL football, Brown has inserted himself into the real-life debates about Church history, religion versus science, and so on.

Gore Vidal, a precocious writer who penned his first novel at age 19, is famous for many books challenging American sexual mores, and he developed a series of "historical novels," such as *Burr*, *1876*, and *Lincoln*. According to the *Exonian*, he told students that his methods of weaving fact and fiction were absolutely legitimate, a form of moral instruction that had ancient traditions.

"Literature began as a record, real or imagined, of

gods and heroes," Vidal said, stressing that "fiction and fact" were mingled in most of the ancients' accounts. Answering questions from students, Vidal argued that "we ought to make history the basis of education." He said the Big Bang Theory and the story of the Garden of Eden should be taught to six-year-olds. Asked about Christianity, he said, "It's not one of my all-time favorites." He called it "hard to defend" and "primitive." But he said the chief fault of Christianity is its "proselytizing" in asserting that "all other religions are false."

We don't know what Dan Brown thought at the time Gore Vidal gave that talk at Exeter. But we can see echoes of most of the ideas quoted above in Brown's novels.

The open atmosphere that could entertain these ideas is just one aspect of Exeter. An important part of the teaching environment is a concept called the Harkness Table, wherein just 12 students and one teacher come together around an oval table. This promotes a collegial approach, where students often seize the discussion and direct their own learning.

In addition to the regular appearance on the campus of famous literary alumni, an aspect of the Exeter curriculum seemed tailored to preparing Academy grads to be writers. This was an assignment for juniors ("Uppers") called "Reporter At Large." The students were asked to write an English term paper depicting a character in a career setting based on an interview. Thus, for example, the student might create an interview with "a Saudi Arabian National Executioner, a Hare Krishna follower or a hog farmer," according to the *Exonian*. Students considered this a very challenging assignment, but at least one English teacher said it was the opportunity for students to "start to believe in themselves as writers."

Dan Brown himself has high praise for a ninth-grade English teacher at Exeter, Jack Heath. In response to a *Boston Globe* call for memories of great teachers, Brown recalled, "I wrote my first essay about the Grand Canyon (describing with inexhaustible prolixity the subtle hues and fissures of the limestone). Mr. Heath returned the essay doused in red pen. He had deleted 90 percent of my adjectives and given me a C-.

"At the top of the page were three words: 'Simpler is better.'

"By the end of the semester, I was barely making a C+. On the last day, I asked Mr. Heath if he had any parting advice.

"He nodded: 'Simpler is better.'"

I recently contacted Jack Heath and asked him about this. He acknowledged that the story is "probably true" and he is grateful for the compliment, but said he doesn't feel he had much to do with Dan Brown's development as a writer. Nevertheless, those who have attempted to dissect Dan Brown's writing style to discern the reasons his books are so widely read almost all point out the simplicity of the actual prose, the short, active sentences, and the sparse description. His ability to tackle as many big ideas as he does in such simple, active prose passages, suggests he did indeed learn the lesson Jack Heath tried to teach.

The Piper's Price

Outstanding as the education at Exeter is, and diverse as its student population has become today, there can be no doubt about the main reason families spend $33,000 for a year of this experience today—or spent a similarly hefty $7,000 a year in Dan Brown's day. Indeed, the biggest secret hiding in plain sight at Exeter is the real Purpose for being there. The Purpose becomes stark and graphic every spring, when the *Exonian* publishes a small table of data headed, "Where The Class Of 1982 Will Go To College." The table fairly shouts to the student: "Your Purpose is to get into an Ivy League college!"

Exeter students are so focused on the college quest that they have a special slang term, "college suck." This is defined as "the cynical term for those clubs, activities, and leadership positions that one acquires, not because of genuine interest, but in order to pad one's resume for college applications."

There are eight Ivy League schools (Harvard, Yale, Princeton, Dartmouth, University of Pennsylvania, Columbia, Cornell and Brown.) There is also a gaggle of schools known as the "Little Ivy League" (such as Amherst or Wesleyan) and some others known as the "Seven Sisters" (Bryn Mawr, Smith, Vassar). Together, these schools represent arguably the pinnacle of prestige in American colleges (or, at least, eastern U.S. prestige). Across America, any high school would be proud to have one or two graduates accepted to Harvard or Yale, one or two more at the Little Ivies or the Seven Sisters.

In Dan Brown's class of about 312 Exies, fully 100

made it in to Ivy League, and 68 more to Little Ivy or
Seven Sister colleges. In other words, half the Exeter
class made it into the top one percent of the country's
colleges. There were 20 going to Harvard, 23 to Yale, 16
to Dartmouth and 11 to Princeton. (If you want the
proper reaction to these statistics, just show them to
any high-school guidance counselor. But before you
do, refresh yourself on first-aid procedures for people
who have fainted.)

Dan Brown didn't get into Harvard, but he did
achieve something almost as good: He got into
Amherst College, one of 10 Exies that year to do so.

Amherst

Situated only a couple of hours' drive away from
Exeter, Amherst College was surely a comfortable fit
for the freshman Dan Brown. Almost identically to
the physical situation at Exeter, the college owns a big
parcel of the town, and is an enclave within the town.
And it is a compact campus, so that again, everything
is a short walk from everything else. Its enrollment is
about the same as Exeter. Like Exeter, Amherst is an
outstanding institution. Unlike Exeter, however, it is
not quite at the absolute tippy-top of reputation and
prestige.

In a 2004 report on the Amherst admissions
procedure, the Jim Lehrer Newshour gave a detailed
look at how Amherst selects its incoming freshmen,
winnowing some 5,400 applications down to 1,034
acceptances. Those candidates then decide whether
Amherst will be their choice, or perhaps another mar-
ginally more outstanding, more prestigious school

where they may also have been accepted. In 2004, this process netted about four hundred freshmen—meaning that some six hundred very bright students went to other schools. What schools? "Harvard, Yale, Princeton, Stanford, Swarthmore, Williams, Dartmouth, Duke, Columbia," an admissions officer rattled off without hesitation. "Those are the schools that we compete with."

As all fans of Dan Brown's novels know, the hero Robert Langdon is a graduate of Exeter Academy who went on to become a Harvard professor. Dan Brown has also admitted that Langdon is an expression of who he would like to be (except that "Langdon is cooler than I am."). It seems to me that all the facts align: As fans have suspected, I think Dan Brown is a Harvard wannabe, even though Amherst is, of course, one of the finest schools in the country, and nothing to be ashamed of, either.

In making Langdon's pedigree from Harvard, rather than Amherst or another smaller, more intriguing academic center, Brown reveals another technique he uses frequently. He takes something obscure and makes it as name-recognition as possible. Arguably, the key historical character he describes in *Angels & Demons* has more in common with Giordano Bruno than with Galileo. But he makes Galileo the centerpiece of the novel, since Bruno is so much less well known. Similarly, if you were looking for a fifteenth-century master painter who placed symbolic coded messages in his paintings and belonged to a secret occult society that may have worshipped the sacred feminine, you would be looking more at Hieronymus Bosch than Leonardo da Vinci. But if you called a book *The Bosch Code*, readers might think it was about the well-known fictional L.A. detective, Harry Bosch. Despite the similarities between Langdon and Brown, Langdon could not be from Amherst ... He needed to be from Harvard.

I visited Amherst and made a search of the various student publications in the archives from Dan Brown's years there. Similar to my experience at Exeter, I could find no evidence that Dan Brown stepped out in public with his writing. He pursued a combined major of English and Spanish, and it's my unconfirmed guess that he spent his junior year abroad in Spain. (*Digital Fortress* is set partly in Seville, Spain and relies in a few places on certain architectural details and place descriptions that Brown could have experienced as a student there.)

After he became a published author with his first few novels, Dan Brown was interviewed by an *Amherst Student* reporter for an article in October, 2001. As he looked back on his Amherst education, he recalled his freshman course called "Introduction to Liberal Arts," which also was dubbed "Music and Words." According to the *Student*, "In that class he learned to incorporate his two seemingly disparate talents and create one unique sound. This introductory course set the stage for his successful Hollywood musical career." (As we will explore shortly, although he had talent, Dan Brown did not have what most people would call a "successful Hollywood music career.")

The *Student* article went on to say: "Brown didn't always have a natural passion for writing. It wasn't until he attended a writing class taught by Alan Lelchunk, a visiting professor and novelist, that he felt comfortable writing. The class helped him to improve his compositional skills, which gave him the confidence to eventually write novels.

"This class, he claims, was the one that sparked his passion for writing. Only at Amherst could he have had the opportunity to study alongside a writer who, in Brown's words, was 'actually doing it.' He felt empowered by the class and his new mentor. Unique interactions like this are what captivated Brown and why he feels eternally grateful toward his alma mater."

Of course, I went looking for "Alan Lelchunk" and I found Alan Lelchuk (the correct spelling), now an adjunct professor at Dartmouth College, where he teaches Jewish Studies as well as creative writing. Dr. Lelchuk in 2003 was awarded a Fulbright Scholarship to study in Russia. He is the author of some six novels, starting with *American Mischief* in 1973. Lelchuk himself was friends with, and encouraged in writing by, the famed novelist Philip Roth (author of such classics of modern literature as *Goodbye, Columbus* and *Portnoy's Complaint*.)

Dr. Lelchuk told me that his Amherst class was very "literary in content, and at a high level," so that it would have taken a committed student to get through the course. He had "some very fine writers" that were in it around the same time as Dan Brown, including the critically acclaimed David Foster Wallace, author of *Infinite Jest* (1996) and *Brief Interviews with Hideous Men* (1999). Thus, there were writers who were "good talkers in class." In such a context, Dan Brown was not particularly memorable. Lelchuk said Brown was "a nice guy, pleasant and quiet. He was not one of the talkers."

I discussed with Lelchuk the content of the course Dan Brown took with him at Amherst. Apparently, it included short stories by classic writers, including Anton Chekhov, Isaak Babel, John Updike, Guy de Maupassant, Flannery O'Connor, Grace Paley, Milan Kundera, Yukio Mishima. When I asked whether this seemed to have any portents for the kind of pop fiction that Dan Brown would later write, he couldn't think of any. It was never part of Lelchuk's purpose to try to prepare a student for commercial success, he said. Lelchuk wasn't even aware of Dan Brown's success until he got a surprise copy of *The Da Vinci Code* in the mail with a thank-you note from Brown. (Until I told him about it, he also wasn't aware of just how much credit Dan Brown had given him in the *Amherst Student* interview.)

Part of the course involved individual conferences about the student's work and it was during these sessions that Lelchuk would offer some criticism, as well as lots of encouragement. He always hoped that this was beneficial to the student, he said, but it wasn't always possible to see an effect. Lelchuk said, in sum: "You never can tell when a quiet student is absorbing a great deal."

The reference to David Foster Wallace being one of the active talkers in the class, while Dan Brown was in the camp of the quiet, may be highly instructive. Some postmodern critics believe Wallace is the most brilliant literary figure on the contemporary scene; some have compared his role in late twentieth-century literature to James Joyce's in the early twentieth century. Whether one buys the comparison to Joyce or not, Wallace's novels, like Joyce's, are masterly synthetic

mixtures of many ideas from many different intellectual disciplines and from low culture as well as high
culture. One can imagine a smart, hard-working, well-
intentioned, perfectly decent Dan Brown feeling
utterly intimidated by the brilliance of a David Foster
Wallace. But like the fable of the tortoise and the hare,
Dan Brown watches and learns what these searing
intellects are doing in the literary world, and then
mass-produces it for the readership of the masses.
Thus, the ordinary well-educated person trying to read
Wallace may experience déjà vu of their challenging
experiences trying to read Joyce. Dan Brown, on the
other hand, mixes the same range of ideas from similar
sources, but without (or as some critics would say, with
the opposite of) the literary flair of a Wallace or a Joyce.
By the same token, of course, Brown's novelistic
mélanges are gripping page-turners, easy to read and
highly accessible to understand.

Fraternal Experiences

On the Dan Brown website (www.danbrown.com),
one of the frequently asked questions (FAQs) pages
eventually came to include this Q and A with Dan
Brown:

Q: You seem to have a fascination with secret societies.
   Can you comment?
A: My interest in secret societies is the product of
   many experiences, some I can discuss, others I
   cannot. Certainly my research of organizations like
   NSA, the Vatican, NRO, and Opus Dei continues
   to fuel my intrigue. At a more fundamental level,

though, my interest sparks from growing up in New England, surrounded by the clandestine clubs of Ivy League universities, the Masonic lodges of our Founding Fathers, and the hidden hallways of early government power. New England has a long tradition of elite private clubs, fraternities, and secrecy. On that theme, the next Robert Langdon novel (already in progress) is set deep within the oldest fraternity in history ... the enigmatic brotherhood of the Masons.

This seems to be a hint by Dan Brown that he has some first-hand knowledge, based on secret societies he encountered in his upbringing and schooling. I have made contact with Freemasons at various levels and have not found any evidence that Dan or his father were members of the Freemasons. But I did find that he was a member of a fraternity, if perhaps only briefly.

Dan Brown was initiated into the Psi Upsilon fraternity at Amherst on October 1, 1983 (as was confirmed to me by a national spokesman). This would have been at the start of his sophomore year. Unfortunately for new fraternity members, it was the year that Amherst abolished the sanctioned fraternity system, a year of turmoil.

At Amherst, the fraternity system once ruled supreme and you were not really a success at the all-male college unless you belonged to a fraternity. Boy, did that change!

Throughout the 1970s, the Ivy and Little Ivy schools transformed from all-male or all-female, to co-ed (just like Exeter Academy). Amherst made the switch in 1976 after 156 years of being male-only.

Newly admitted women at Amherst began to demand the same privileges as any student. Since fraternity housing was a form of privilege, they demanded entrance into the fraternities. Some of these brotherhoods dug in their heels, partly because they had been chartered from their very origins as men-only. But other fraternities accepted women. Psi Upsilon, for instance, found nothing in its charter to prohibit women, so it began to admit them.

However, as Amherst entered the 1980s, the trend was definitely toward taking over the fraternity housing—ostensibly for such reasons as safety and health standards—and the die was cast. In 1983, the college banned fraternity activities on campus. Again, there was a split in behaviour. Some fraternities went underground and tried to continue as they were, while others (such as Psi Upsilon) adhered to the rules and moved their activities off-campus. Today, Psi Upsilon is an active, co-ed society with a chapter house off-campus.

But, during that special year 1983–4 and for a few years beyond, "some members stuck it out and abided by the new and difficult rules, while others simply walked away," said a spokesman for Psi Upsilon. It is not possible in the fraternity's records to determine which choice Dan Brown made, he said.

It is interesting that the "Greek" fraternity system in America grew up around two basic kinds of social affiliations. On the one hand, some of the oldest fraternities were begun as literary societies, where the members sought secrecy so that they could share their poetry or stories (some of which may be assumed to have been risqué or taboo). On the other hand, there were the many brotherhoods who fashioned themselves in imitation of the Freemasons, right down to the symbolism, rituals and regalia.

Psi Upsilon is one of the earliest fraternities, stemming from a group of writers, not Freemason imitators. This cuts two ways for Dan Brown. It has a kind of auspiciousness to it, for a fellow who would later become a world-famous writer. But for a writer who would later name Freemasonry as his field of deep research, it doesn't give him much of a leg-up. Not only was his contact with fraternities minimal, he had no first-hand opportunity to absorb the rituals and symbolism of Freemasonry, not even through a derivative version of it.

Extracurriculars

In addition to his Psi Upsilon membership, some of Brown's other activities at Amherst included playing on the varsity squash team and being a member of the famed Amherst College Glee Club.

Dan Brown tends to like individual, non-contact sports. He has played some soccer, but his stated games of choice are squash and tennis. His love of squash comes out in at least a couple of his novels, although he makes the signature hero, Robert Langdon, out to be an ardent swimmer and water-polo player.

Singing and music were deep pursuits for Dan Brown in college. One of the biggest events of his college life was a two-month world tour in the summer of 1983 with the glee club. This would introduce Brown, however fleetingly, to the great capitals and buildings of Europe and elsewhere.

The then Amherst choirmaster, a legend to all his singers wherever he went, Bruce G. McInnes, recently retired after a 40-year career devoted to singing groups at Yale, Amherst, and at churches in Wisconsin and New York City. It was his policy to take his singing groups on tours and he worked out the spectacular 1983 tour, taking the glee club to about thirteen stops around the world.

Web sleuths in the blogosphere have unearthed some of the promotional statements about Dan Brown that surfaced later during his attempt to get attention for his musical work. One of these says:

> Dan's live performance experience includes a world tour with the renown [sic] ACGC and appearances in such venues as Notre Dame Cathedral (Paris), St. Marco's Cathedral (Venice), St. Stephen's (Vienna), the Acropolis (Athens), and the American Embassies in Delhi, Tokyo, Taipei, Hong Kong and Seoul. He's also performed as a solo piano/vocalist at The Rojo y Negro in Spain and in Hollywood at the National Academy of Songwriters Acoustic Underground.

The "ACGC" acronym would seem to be a way to conceal the fact that his live performance experience in these world historic settings came as a member of the Amherst College Glee Club. By not spelling it out, the acronym sounds like ACGC might be a musical group you should have heard of.

Dr. McInnes told me that he recalls Dan Brown very clearly, as a "pleasant fellow with a big smile" who faithfully showed up for the glee club during his entire college career. "I don't recall him ever auditioning for a solo, though," McInnes said. He said that when Brown arrived at Amherst, the quality of the Exeter choir program was already known to McInnes. He knew he could expect good preparation from its singers who went on to Amherst, so Brown easily made it into the glee club. Because so many singers arrive with baritone voices and a group needs tenors and basses, he said, it is common practice to assign some singers to these other sections. Thus, Dan Brown was in the bass section in the ACGC.

The former members of McInnes's choirs simply revere him: Some years ago they put together a group, the Mastersingers USA, whose sole function each year is to meet and sing during an intense three-day weekend. "These are all guys who were bitten by the [singing] bug," McInnes said. "It gives them a chance to step outside their normal lives and do something that they love." Additionally, they then go on a tour abroad every two or three years. In recent years, the Mastersingers won top honors at a large international singing competition in Wales.

As with lots of people who helped him along the way, Dan Brown takes time to keep in touch with Dr. McInnes. During the most recent tour in summer 2005, Dr. McInnes said, he heard from Brown, who was expressing hopes of meeting the choir (and, no doubt, singing with them) in Barcelona, Spain, but the dates didn't work out. However, Brown may show up at the next Mastersingers gathering, McInnes said.

Confessions of This Writer

I should confess a number of odd coincidences about myself that apply to Amherst. In early 1966, as a college student, I visited Amherst to see an old high-school buddy, and to check in with a couple of girls we knew at Smith and Mount Holyoke. While at Amherst, I was treated very well by the members of Psi Upsilon, what would later be Dan Brown's fraternity, in the old and grand chapter house just at the edge of campus. The brothers there loaned me an ideal make-out room with a crackling fire, in which to entertain my date. (I never got past first base, but I never forgot the experience.)

Moreover, my buddy (or his roommate, perhaps) was a member of the glee club and he told me that, since I had been part of the high-school chorus, I could just step up into the back risers at a rehearsal. So I did, singing merrily along with the ACGC in my clunky baritone. My only saving grace was that I could sight-read the music. But it was very memorable because the practice hall was a special building at Amherst called the Octagon House. The choirmaster, the very same Bruce McInnes that led Dan Brown years later, stopped the rehearsal at one point because the room was getting too stuffy, and commanded that we all run once around the outside of the building in the crisp winter air.

Also, like Dan Brown, I spent part of my college career playing piano in practice rooms (and as the background noise at fraternity cocktail parties). I am not trying to compare myself musically to Dan Brown, since he was a very competent keyboard artist and I was a ham-handed klutz. But I can say for sure that I know what it is to pursue music for its own sake, to commune with it in solitude.

Bottom line: I can say that I socialized with Dan

Brown's fraternity brothers, and sang in a "live performance" with his glee club!

Post-Graduation

Dan Brown wound up a college graduate in 1986 and didn't really have a career to embark on. He certainly did not declare himself a fiction writer. Music was most attractive to him. It appears that he reacted by not choosing a career, playing music locally for about a year, and going off to Spain again in the summer of 1987. Later that year, he moved to California, which he viewed as a land of promise for a musician.

Luckily for people who want to keep track, Dan Brown made regular contributions to the Class of 1986 section of *Amherst Magazine*, the alumni publication, checking in at least every couple of years. It gives an almost running record of what he considered his triumphs at any given time.

In the spring of 1988, this is the entry: "Dan Brown is still living in California working his way into the music world dodging strange people and ideas. He supports himself by working as a counselor for 'The Millionaires Club,' a well-to-do private club for singles. He sends his phone number to anyone wishing to vacation in Southern California . . ."

But later that year, an entry said: "Dan Brown has come back East after a few years in Los Angeles and is working on a record we'll get to hear in September."

Two years passed, and in summer 1991, the *Amherst Magazine* entry read: "Dan Brown was featured in an article in the *Portsmouth Herald*, detailing his singing musical career. Dan is back in Hollywood, where he has gained the support of the National Academy of Songwriters, a non-profit organization dedicated to promoting talented songwriters. NAS has promoted such notables as Billy Joel, Prince, Phil Collins, Carole King and Neil Diamond. Dan's tape, *Perspective*, has been distributed to New England record stores, and another tape of children's music, *SynthAnimals*, is selling briskly."

Then, in the spring of 1993, came this entry: "Dan Brown's debut album was recently released on DGB Records. Dan was discovered by Hollywood producer Barry Fasman, who is now backing Dan with his own resources. The *Portsmouth Press* ran a feature article on Dan in November [1992], chronicling a visit to his hometown. Dan is currently teaching English literature at the Beverly Hills (90210) Preparatory School."

To recap these events, Dan Brown had been attempting to break into the Hollywood music scene for upwards of four years, in at least two separate sojourns in California. It was on the second attempt in around 1991 that he hooked up with the National Academy of Songwriters (NAS).

This means that his earlier attempts at music productions, both audio cassettes, *Perspective*, copyrighted in 1990, and *SynthAnimals*, in 1989, were self-produced, although undoubtedly with help from friends. One such friend was Chip Beckett, who had been a day student at Exeter and graduated from Harvard in 1986. Chip Beckett collaborated with Dan Brown on a number of music projects, including an earlier pair of cassettes called *Piropo Collected Works*, in 1986-7. Dan Brown had also been collaborating with an Amherst classmate, Jas Paley, during his early post-graduate years. *SynthAnimals* was remarkable because it was a series of electronic music sounds that imitated animals, intended for children. But, although Brown probably got some local shops to hawk his wares, it is safe to say that Brown remained the prototypically struggling musician. The tapes never got any real distribution and are nearly impossible to find today.

But the benefit of the early tapes is that in 1991, he could parlay them into an introduction with the NAS, and this eventually led him to Barry Fasman, a skilled music director, arranger, engineer and musician, who could help Dan Brown get all the way to a professional-sounding production.

Also, at the NAS Dan Brown met a woman named Blythe Newlon, at the time serving as "Director of Artist Development." She would eventually become his wife. He was 27, she 39.

The outcome of all this was the audio production *Dan Brown*, created in 1992 and copyrighted in early 1993. Setting aside everything he had done before, it was his "debut" album, and it contained ten songs. At the time, the record label that bore Brown's initials, "DGB Records," had a Hollywood address, but this would soon change to Exeter.

Let's Check the Charts

Through the miracle of eBay, I was able to obtain a copy of the *Dan Brown* album on tape and CD, and I will always treasure my CD copy of it with its unbroken shrink-wrap and a little sticker showing it was probably bought in a benefit sale shop to help a local Exeter charity. (Even at that time, it appears, Dan Brown was doing his part for local causes.)

Here is what I can tell you about the album: Dan Brown has a great voice, great diction, sings on key, with great breathing and good expression. His keyboard musicianship is competent (and he had very skilled studio musicians accompanying him.)

But ... most of his songs are just not memorable. Of the first eight songs, if you heard them and then closed your eyes, you probably would not remember any of the lines nor any of the tunes. The genre has been described as "accessible New Age," and I guess that's true, but I would say more like "pseudo-Barry Manilow."

I think there are two clear problems. One is that Dan Brown's voice is excellent, but doesn't have anything to make it unique. The other problem is, the lyrics are too general. In fact, in all ten songs, I only counted two capitalized words (both in the last song: Kuhlstihl and Kampuchea). Otherwise, the rest of the songs can be characterized by grand-sounding titles but flat, disappointing lyrics, as in this snatch from "Birth of a King":

> He stands alone
> Outside your castle window
> He's traveled far
> From distant shores
> And from your throne
> You watch him kneel in silence
> And lay a flower at your door

The only real signs of departure from mundane lyrics are two songs, "976-LOVE," which is about phone sex using 900-numbers, and "Sweet Pleasure in Pain," which is open to interpretation, but probably relates to sadomasochism. As far as I can tell, "976-LOVE" is in *praise* of phone sex, by the way.

In the liner notes, Dan Brown gives special thanks "to Blythe Newlon and The National Academy of Songwriters for their belief and support." He then adds: "This album is dedicated to my parents for their unending generosity and love. Thank you both." This is among many examples of heartfelt thank-yous to his parents and family.

Sometime in 1993, Dan Brown moved back to Exeter permanently. An *Amherst* entry in early 1994 says so, but does not mention Blythe. However, a couple of activities were in motion. One was that Dan Brown and NAS did their best to promote his debut album, and Blythe was quoted in the materials in high praise of his work:

> When the National Academy of Songwriters first heard Dan Brown's music, we paired him imme-diately with one of the most respected producers in pop music today, British Record Producer of the Year, Barry Fasman. No expense was spared in the recording of this album. The tracks were cut in some of the nation's finest studios with some of the most accomplished musicians living today. When the lights came up on tracking day, the all-star cast standing ready to play was awesome. The band included Michael Jackson's sax player, Madonna's bass player, and the Doobie Brothers' drummer, just to name a few. When the dust settled, they had recorded an album we believe will be remembered as one of the strongest independently released

projects in quite some time. All of the synthesizer programming and arranging was done by Barry Fasman, whose arranging credits include Billy Joel, Diana Ross, Fame, and Air Supply. We believe Dan Brown is an artist destined to become a major talent and that this original pressing of his debut album could very well become a collector's item. Treat yourself.—Director of Artist Development, The National Academy of Songwriters.

Notably, though, Dan Brown would look back on this time and, in at least one interview, refer to Blythe as his *music agent*, not merely a staff member at NAS.

The second activity, begun in about 1993 and carrying into 1994, was the production of Dan Brown's other CD, with a title that was now a definite harbinger of things to come: *Angels & Demons*. Yes, the CD bore the same title that would become the title of Brown's *Angels & Demons*, the novel he published in 2000 that bears a close structural and intellectual resemblance to *The Da Vinci Code*, which he published three years later. What's more, Dan Brown had found the artist who is now famous for creating ambigrams, John Langdon, who brilliantly created an ambigram of the words "Angels & Demons" for the CD liner. Brown thanked "the ingenious John Langdon for attempting and accomplishing the impossible."

According to a recent article in the Philadelphia *City Paper*, the real-life John Langdon had released a book of ambigrams in 1992 called *WordPlay* and it was Dick Brown who first corresponded with him, then called him one day and asked whether Langdon could help his son with a project—which turned out to be the CD liner artwork. Years later, Brown would work

John Langdon's ambigrams into a pivotal role in the novel *Angels & Demons*.

Mention is made of some West Coast studio work on the *Angels & Demons* music CD in 1994, but the production is mainly East Coast, with local musicians, including Brown's old buddy from Exeter, Chip Beckett. (If you ever listen to this album, you will also hear the voice of Blythe as a back-up singer in some cuts.)

The *Angels & Demons* album is a vast improvement over the eponymous *Dan Brown* album, but it suffers from the same two basic problems: the unmemorable voice and the lowercase lyrics.

However, there are touches and hints of things that will eventually seem like they foretold Brown's novels. The general themes are grand ideas like chivalry, honoring one's forefathers, or asking, "Where are the heroes?"

There is a song, "All I Believe," which will no doubt fuel the fires of all the people that have accused Dan Brown of being anti-religious. It is actually clearly intended to be a love song, with a chorus "I don't need a preacher to save me / from demons who deceive / Just you / You're all I believe." However, it does contain these lines as the opening:

> There's no god above
> There's no fire below
> There's no perfect truth
> No place we all go
> There are no angels in heaven
> And no guarantees
> There's just you
> You're all I believe

Among the songs there is, again, one special cut that contains practically all the proper nouns of the whole album. It is called "Dover Beach," and I would say it is the pained lament of a bare-naked heart for a lost love. This paints a view from a lonely beach within sight of the Isles of Shoals, but also of "the lights of Kensington Green."

It was easy enough to visit the real-life place on the New Hampshire coast where I could see the Isles of Shoals. It has been frequented over the years by poets and artists (the American impressionist, Childe Hassam, painted one of his most famous works here). The Isles of Shoals area is bound up with numerous romantic legends about shipwrecks, treasure, and pirates.

Since the description was specific enough, I went looking for the Dover Beach in question. Using a combination of town maps and nautical charts, it was easy enough to find the Town of Dover, as well as Dover Point. If you left Dan Brown's house and went south a few miles, you would arrive at the little village of Kensington. Both of these are within about eight miles of the Atlantic beach, but you cannot see all of these landmarks from one spot.

Thus I am convinced a "Dover Beach" does not actually exist by that name, but is an amalgamation of several spots that Dan Brown knew. I consider this a good thing. As I see it, here is a case where artistic license was used by Dan Brown in a very appropriate way.

The *Angels & Demons* album now had DGB Records sited in Exeter, at what would be Dan Brown's digs for about ten years, an apartment on Chestnut Avenue in a converted brick mill along the

Squamscott River—again, within easy walking distance of practically everything in Exeter. According to at least one account, Brown did a lot of his local commuting by bicycle.

The album liner thanks a string of unusual entities, such as "Macintosh Computers." It contains a special note of thanks to "Blythe Newlon . . . tireless co-writer, co-producer, second engineer, significant other, and therapist."

Teaching Days

At times in his life, Dan Brown has been a teacher. From the evidence, I would say it is something he turned to in order to make ends meet, not for a true vocation. Sometimes he taught English, and other times, Spanish. During the early to mid-1990s, he taught in Exeter and at nearby Stratham.

Later on, history would be rewritten a bit to make it seem logical that Dan Brown would teach English and later write novels. For instance, many of the publicity materials issued about Dan Brown feature this statement:

> He is a graduate of Amherst College and Phillips Exeter Academy, where he spent time as an English teacher before turning his efforts fully to writing.

Strictly speaking, this is a true statement, but I think it is crafted to lead the reader to believe that Dan Brown was on the faculty of Phillips Exeter Academy. In fact, however, he was a part-time teacher there, occasionally, and never was elevated to a faculty position.

To put it more bluntly, I don't find any evidence that Dan Brown held a full-time job for any

IN SEARCH OF DAN BROWN   307

continuous period of more than a couple of years,
from the time he graduated from college in 1986, to
about 1996, when he could certainly say he was
engaged in the trade of novel-writing. Many writers
have worn their poverty-stricken hungry days as a
badge of honor, but it doesn't appear that Dan Brown
would see it that way. My hunch is that this is because
he had certain appearances to maintain. Neither the
Protestant ethic of Exeter nor the ambitions of its
bright, talented, elite students tend to favor drifting
from coast to coast, trying one's hand at music and
writing, and never demonstrating tangible success.

A Hint of a Book

In the spring of 1994, the *Amherst* entry says: "Dan
Brown is living in Exeter writing a book about the
difference between men. For example, those who wear
boxer shorts versus those who wear briefs ..."

This was certainly a signal of something significant,
since it was the first time that Dan Brown publicly told
his classmates about any aspirations to write books.
The book that would eventually emerge in 1995 was
187 Men to Avoid, written by Dan, but under the
pseudonym Danielle Brown. It is a small paperback of
humor, with a one-liner on each page. Those to avoid
include "Men who stir-fry" or "Men who own
hamsters." A friend of mine argues that this gimmicky
book, which at the time was Brown's entry-level effort
to get his foot in the publishing door, is actually
important to Dan Brown's development: Out of the
negative space of men to avoid, Robert Langdon was
sculpted, possessing exactly zero of the unfortunate

187 characteristics. I'm not so sure, but there may be something to this idea.

But what about "Men who join Mensa"?

Mensa

In some of Dan Brown's pieces intended to promote his music, there is a mention that he was a member of Mensa, a society for people with high intelligence. Mensa International's headquarters in the U.S. confirms that Dan Brown was once a member. Other materials make it clear that he did not continue his membership for very long.

Mensa membership is open to people who can demonstrate that their IQ is within the top two percent of a given population. According to the organization, "Mensa was founded in England in 1946 by Roland Berrill, a barrister, and Dr. Lance Ware, a scientist and lawyer. They had the idea of forming a society for bright people, the only qualification for membership of which was a high IQ. The original aims were, as they are today, to create a society that is non-political and free from all racial or religious distinctions. Mensa has three stated purposes: to identify and foster human intelligence for the benefit of humanity, to encourage research in the nature, characteristics and uses of intelligence, and to promote stimulating intellectual and social opportunities for its members."

The organization explains the word "mensa" as follows: "The word 'table' in Latin. The name stands for a round-table society, where race, color, creed, national origin, age, politics, educational or social background are irrelevant."

I don't think that it would be any stretch to suppose that Dan Brown would find this music to his ears, echoing the aims of the traditional Harkness Table at Exeter, where small groups of students were encouraged to lead the discussion in directions that would most benefit their self-education. It also vaguely suggests Exeter's atmosphere of religious tolerance (plus overtones of Freemasonry). Most of all, it demonstrates his strivings to be among intelligent people discussing big ideas—not exactly what he was on track to accomplish with 187 Men to Avoid. Nonetheless, he did not remain a Mensa member.

Receding Hairlines

Unchastened by a lack of public acclaim for 187 Men, Brown in 1998 released The Bald Book, another bit of silliness, intended to cheer up men who are losing their hair. This was put out with Blythe Brown's name on the cover, but the copyright is registered to Dan Brown as the author.

Dan Brown did not brag about either humor book in his newsletter entries intended to keep his former classmates posted on his activities. The main news they had of him in this period was in the fall of 1996, when the entry read: "Among other engagements in the news are Dan Brown and Blythe Newlon. The two are living happily in Exeter, NH, where Dan is writing music and books and Blythe is a dental hygienist." Would it be too much of a leap to assume that with Dan Brown maxing out his credit cards to get his CDs recorded and pressed and with his books generating only small sales at best, that Blythe—the older woman who would turn him on to art, Europe, and the spirit of the sacred feminine—was supporting his effort to find himself creatively by working in a dental office?

Several cynical bloggers have questioned the claim that appears in Dan Brown publicity materials that one of his songs, "Peace in Our Time," was played at the 1996 Olympics in Atlanta, Georgia. Blog sleuths expressed doubts that Dan Brown ever wrote such a song, noting it wasn't on the official CD released after the Olympics.

Well, the blogosphere was wrong. The *Angels & Demons* CD does contain the song "Peace in Our Time." It is exactly the kind of general anthem about peace that you might imagine. And, I have found an explanation that fits it into the Olympics. It turns out that Wei Wei, a very famous female singer in China, sang it during one of the Olympic events, according to Dan Brown. Now, I wasn't able to confirm whether it was the women's archery or the men's three-meter diving, so the only way to research it further would be to listen to all sixteen days (and nights) of 1996 Olympic tapes for some 271 events.

The Butterfly Emerges

Well, there you have it. An Exeter education, followed by an Amherst education, and about ten years of trying, and both the music and the writing careers of Dan Brown looked like scripts for the movie *Titanic*.

In fact, at long last, Dan Brown himself admitted the music thing wasn't working. Having his song played at the Olympics "was a real thrill, and quite honestly about all I have to show for my grueling four-year music stint in Hollywood is the fact that my three CDs received plenty of critical success but turned out to be bona fide commercial duds," Brown wrote to his classmates.

But it was now the fall of 1997, and without even mentioning his humor books, he could point to something big and successful. "After my last CD, I decided to take a year off and try my hand at writing a novel (a logical change of gears, I know). I wrote the novel, sent it out, and damn if the first publisher who read it didn't buy it."

The book was *Digital Fortress*. Like the boom of a cannon, it announced a new writer was launching his assault on the publishing world.

And Now, Back to Sidney

But to return (at last) to Sidney Sheldon's novel and its effect on Dan Brown: I do believe that he is telling the truth when he says that it gave him the chutzpah to write a novel (after a suitable gestation period). I think Sheldon's *Doomsday* is so important that Dan Brown should mark his life in two divisions: BS (before Sheldon) and AS (after Sheldon).

What you should also know (and please, confirm it for yourself) is that *Doomsday Conspiracy* is in the running for one of the worst novels of its type ever foisted on the public. It was written half a century after Sheldon had established a name for himself in a career that would see him on bestseller lists with numerous trashy novels and on multiple movie and TV credits as screenwriter.

Doomsday, released in 1991, was Sheldon's eleventh

novel. His tenth, *Memories of Midnight* (1990), was a sequel to a 1974 novel, *The Other Side of Midnight*, which had held the record of that era for longevity on the *New York Times* Best Seller List (52 weeks). Of course, *The Da Vinci Code* blew away that record, and anything remotely close (it had been on the list for 137 weeks at press time).

Doomsday's plot is embarrassingly predictable. A U.S. Navy intelligence officer is dispatched on a beyond-top-secret mission to identify the witnesses to a "balloon crash" in the Swiss Alps. As he pursues the mission, he realizes that the puppet-masters who dispatched him are killing the witnesses as quickly as he identifies them. Also, the "balloon" was really a UFO and the conspiracy is an international effort to cover up the fact that aliens have arrived. Early in the novel, we learn that there are some ten witnesses. We are then forced to endure ten iterations of the hero, Robert Bellamy, locating a witness, followed by a nefarious sanctioned assassin cleaning up behind. To do this, Bellamy hops around Europe and America using an unlimited government credit card. It becomes a running gag, where the only question is whether the next victim will be strangled, shot or burned to death.

But (in perfect hindsight, of course), there were things that Dan Brown could learn from *Doomsday*. Primarily, that a plot can be driven forward with a combination of keeping the chapters short, and always looking for some way to leave an impending development hanging—commonly known as the *cliffhanger*.

Anyone who looks at Dan Brown's works can see

that he learned Sheldon's lesson very well. In fact, *The Da Vinci Code* is one of the best examples anywhere of these techniques and it puts Sheldon to shame. Dan Brown was already good at it with *Digital Fortress*, though, and has been improving on it with each successive novel. All of his novels have at least a hundred chapters, and one has 137 (*Angels & Demons*). The brevity of the chapters keeps giving contemporary readers the positive reinforcement of having completed a chapter of a book—an experience most of us have all too rarely these days. Meanwhile, the cliffhangers at the end of the chapters and the intercutting of the action taking place in several different story lines keep the reader pushing on to attain the next short chapter and the next ...

Sheldon put a twist in the end of *Doomsday* to reveal that the hero's superior officer and mentor throughout most of the book, was actually the spooky figure known as Janus (the two-faced Roman god) who had been one of the evil puppet-masters. Dan Brown paid attention to this, and essentially all of his plots so far have come up to some kind of very similar revelation that the chief bad guy, portrayed throughout the book as evil incarnate, turns out not to be the source of the evil conspiracy, while another character, groomed carefully so as not to arouse much suspicion, is unmasked in the end as the evil and nefarious villain. Sir Leigh Teabing has this part in *The Da Vinci Code*, and the Camerlengo has it in *Angels & Demons*. In *Angels & Demons*, the head honcho of the evil Illuminati conspiracy is even named Janus, just like in the Sheldon novel. Moreover, *Angels & Demons*—and *The Da Vinci Code* to a degree—features a variety of murders performed in different homicidal styles, just like *Doomsday*.

But while Brown may have learned a lot about plotting and structure from Sheldon, he put a lot more work into the "research" part of his novels than Sheldon ever did. The legend of *Digital Fortress* has it that when he was writing the book, Dan Brown put out feelers through Internet newsgroups and got responses from two anonymous former National Security Agency cryptographers, giving him inside information about the world of codes and computers that crack them. He thanks the two as part of his acknowledgments.

Quite courageously for a first novelist writing in the action-adventure genre, Brown created a female heroine to carry the load. Susan Fletcher has the super-intelligence of a top cryptographer, the mental toughness to keep cool and process information under extreme pressure, and even some action-hero physical skills. In a nice twist, her boyfriend gets sent to Seville, Spain to pursue some of the clues of the mystery, and they only reunite after the main drama has been resolved. Like *The Da Vinci Code* and *Angels & Demons*, most of the action of *Digital Fortress* takes place in a 24-hour day. It is set in a reasonably exotic, cultured European setting, and features a ticking time bomb of a plot-driver on which the future of Western civilization depends. All three books pair up a brainy, beautiful math/science female heroine with a professorial humanist hero. Together, the two have to somehow crack codes and figure out the mind of the evil genius threatening the world. As indicated before, in each case the evil villain turns out to be secretly controlled by a kindly figure presented earlier in the story as a well-loved positive character who the reader is fooled into believing is on the side of the angels.

Dan Brown pioneered all of this in *Digital Fortress*, all the while using Sidney Sheldon's short chapter technique, including one with only four paragraphs, occupying less than half a page of text! Within the plot of the novel, he introduced the code method known as the "Caesar's box," using it to good effect, and also gave his readers a good indoctrination into basic cryptography techniques. He then cleverly fashioned a string of numbers printed without explanation on the last page of the book, which could be used with the first letters of each chapter to spell out a message, again using a Caesar's box: "We are watching you." This coding became a "Dan Brown thing," used in several of his novels.

Some of the codes are relatively difficult, but when it matters within a plot, Dan Brown makes a good adjustment that rewards the average reader with the illusion that he or she is participating in codebreaking. In *Digital Fortress*, there is a moment when the entire action of the plot necessitates the decrypting of a five-letter code, which turns out to be the name of the heroine, Susan. In *The Da Vinci Code*, of course, much of the plot hangs on decrypting the cryptex, which ultimately turns out to have been programmed with five-letter codes—one that is a play on the Greek word for wisdom (Sophia) and the heroine's name, Sophie; the other making reference to Newton's apple.

While Brown did far more research than Sidney Sheldon would have ever thought necessary to support a potboiler, *Digital Fortress* also commenced

Brown's troubling mix of realism gleaned from serious research, plot flaws based on insufficient or sloppy research, and outright fiction out of his imagination masquerading as factual, researched information. Some of the computer equipment and procedures in *Digital Fortress* didn't match reality and were somewhat stylized, leaving little hints that the author didn't really visit an NSA cryptography center. Also, his scenes in Seville were probably done from time-dimmed recollection. (According to one account, the Mayor of Seville said he wanted to invite Brown to come visit the city for the first time!)

One very significant difference between Sidney Sheldon and Dan Brown is how they deal with sex. Sheldon is completely explicit about sex acts, which are frequent and utterly gratuitous in his novels. Brown, on the other hand, despite the relationships of love that develop between his characters, almost never depicts an actual sex act, but merely hints that one will take place, off-camera, so to speak. But *Digital Fortress* does have at least one scene that is explicit, and it is also the only one of Brown's novels to feature a good slathering of swear words, including the F-word.

Pouring on the Coals

Although there were surely rounds of revisions, by 1997 Dan Brown had proved in *Digital Fortress* that he could write a novel, and it was time to set his sights on his next projects. It was also a time of change for him in Exeter, since his father retired from the math department after some thirty-five years. Dick and Connie Brown had a picture-perfect retirement house, on the shore of a lake in upstate New Hampshire, so they sold the Nelson Drive homestead.

It was time for Dan and Blythe to get married, and they did it with great panache and romance.

According to a college classmate who attended, the August 1997 afternoon found the guests on Connie and Dick's lawn, assembled in chairs facing the lake, with no wedding party in view. A small chamber-music ensemble stopped playing. Then they heard the faint sounds of a bagpipe and from the lake there arrived a Boston Whaler (drive by younger brother Greg Brown), towing a barge. On the barge, which was adorned with boughs, were Dan, Blythe, a minister and the bagpiper in full Scottish regalia. They alighted onshore and the ceremony began. "There was not a dry eye in the house, least of all Dan's!" said the Amherst alumni reporter. The newlyweds spent their honeymoon in Quebec City, one of the oldest and most romantic cities in North America and one of the only places on the continent that approximates the architectural beauty or historic intrigue of a place Brown would set a novel, such as Seville, Paris, or Rome.

By early 1998, *Digital Fortress* could be called a hit, going into its third printing. Dan Brown also hinted to his classmates that a movie of it might be in the works (so far, it hasn't happened, but it is probably coming after *The Da Vinci Code* movie and the *Angels & Demons* movie).

By mid-1998, Brown was justifiably crowing: "On the book front, *Digital Fortress* has sold through four printings, and Simon & Schuster just bought the rights to my next two novels. Off we go! And I always

thought I was going to be a rock star. At least now I
don't have to wear spandex."

The next book was *Angels & Demons*. In it, he would
take the character prototype he had developed in
Digital Fortress and build upon it to invent Robert
Langdon. Brown would eventually speak about a
trilogy of Robert Langdon stories (including *The Da
Vinci Code*, and the anticipated *The Solomon Key*). In
many, many respects, *Angels & Demons* reads like a
rough draft for *The Da Vinci Code*, incorporating
major secrets from history that powerful people want
to keep quiet, big issues of science versus religion,
secret societies (including Templars, Illuminati, and
Freemasons), lost manuscripts, famous characters
from history, coded messages, art and architectural
symbolism, improbable chases through the touristic
centers of major European cities, and many other
shared allusions and literary devices.

In due course, Brown announced to his classmates
in the summer of 1999 that he had finished *Angels &
Demons* and that it would be released the following
February. With a wink to his classmates, Dan Brown
talked about having had to do a "research trip/tax
write-off" to Rome for the book.

In a winter 2000 report, Dan talked of continued
success for *Digital Fortress*, the arrival of *Angels &
Demons*, and "Blythe is doing great ... very into her
Renaissance painting and sculpture (our place smells
like oil paint and marble dust) and she continues to
amaze me every day with some new artistic talent." In
the spring of 2000, he checked in again and it was clear
he was working hard on something new: "I'd really
love to tell you that Blythe and I are doing cool things

like bungee-jumping in Thailand, but lately life has been one long blur of typing, editing, and black coffee." By fall 2000, *Angels & Demons* had shot to bestseller position.

Angels & Demons opens with a statement very similar to the one that opens *The Da Vinci Code*, suggesting that all the major elements of the story are factual. It is not clear when this brainstorm for how to start a novel that is a mishmash of fact and fiction occurred to Dan Brown, but the power of suggestion has worked wonders for creating reader credibility (or perhaps I should say gullibility). *Angels & Demons* introduced the Langdon character, and, in doing so, signaled two key things about Brown's future as a novelist: a new kind of attractive action hero had been born, who is no action hero at all, but a Harvard symbology professor, and a putative genre of "fact-based fiction," richly layered with references to art, architecture, and alternative history, had been created as context.

It is ironic that Dan Brown in *Angels & Demons* played fast and loose with the Vatican's procedures for papal succession and many other matters of Vatican history. He suggested that an Illuminati conspiracy could seize control of the Catholic Church, and dredged up the 20-year-old conspiracy theory that Pope John Paul I had been murdered by a poison. Yet apparently, this was all so "over the top"—especially in a plot involving an antimatter bomb set on the burial remains of St. Peter, poised to blow up the entire Vatican—that the Catholic Church came out with no particular reaction to *Angels & Demons*. When huge acclaim followed *The Da Vinci Code*, though, the

Church denounced it through an Italian cardinal, who called it "a pack of lies."

In the spring of 2001, a classmate reported that Dan and Blythe had visited him during the winter. "Dan is feverishly researching and writing his next book. He gave the lie to the notion that writers set their own schedules and don't have bosses. Dan and Blythe spend hours every day researching and Dan writes into the night and has some very hard deadlines set by unsympathetic editors at Simon & Schuster. No extensions allowed unless you are Stephen King or John Grisham."

It seems apparent that all this intense activity was to produce *Deception Point*, released in 2001. The novel has a Sidney Brown/Dan Sheldon plot, in the sense that an evil puppet-master, disguised as a good guy, lurks and manipulates things until the big revelation scene at the end. There is a he—she pair of central characters, the heroine doing the bulk of the thinking and some of the brawling, and the hero generally in the role of physical and moral support. The novel is also populated by a rather rich cast of characters who dance around a central conspiracy. Because the secret has to do with an asteroid of mysterious composition, government agencies like NASA and the National Reconnaissance Office are involved, along with helicopters, hi-tech ultrasonic airplanes, a black-ops Delta Force with their own specialized war toys. Although it is an action tale, it does have secrets and codes and requires some brain work by the protagonists. But it is quite different from a Langdon tale, as in *Angels & Demons* or *The Da Vinci Code*. Some of the action is set in the frozen north, and some in government corridors in Washington, DC. Naturally, the White House is also implicated.

For a novel that followed *Angels & Demons*, there is a puzzling aspect of *Deception Point*, in that it involves lots of military equipment, mercenaries and the like, with plenty of shooting and very James Bond-like predicaments for the hero and heroine. Langdon novels tend to be more cerebral.

Deception Point has no dedication page. Why? Maybe this doesn't seem significant, but it will keep me wondering until I arrive at an answer. And, despite now frequent updates for his college classmates in *Amherst*, Brown never even mentioned this novel's title to them. He merely jumped from talk of his second novel (*Angels & Demons*) to his fourth novel (*The Da Vinci Code*) without explanation.

In the summer of 2001 (I think indicating that his delivery of *Deception Point* had satisfied his contract), *Amherst* reported, "Dan has recently switched from publisher Simon & Schuster to Doubleday," following the path of his editor, Jason Kaufman.

Frankly, even if Brown whacked out *Deception Point* merely in order to get clear of an option clause for his next book in a Simon & Schuster contract, it actually has a pretty clever plot, lots of action, and a fairly nifty conspiracy/sci-fi mystery involving an extraterrestrial artefact (again putting to shame Sheldon's *Doomsday*).

I think it is very noticeable that in *Angels & Demons* and *The Da Vinci Code*, Brown retained the male-female pairing of main characters, but both women (Vittoria in *Angels & Demons* and Sophie in *The Da Vinci Code*) were made far less imposing than either heroine in *Digital Fortress* and *Deception Point*.

Brown held a two-edged sword when he picked Arctic Circle scenes for a lot of the action in *Deception Point*. On the one hand, it meant that he was hardly likely to do any first-person "research" so he could not speak with any authority about life in the far north. But on the other hand, no one in his readership could, either. When he brought the action down to Washington, DC, he kept events generally within the bounds of the major tourist areas (thus keeping his on-location research to a minimum).

Although there are indications that Dan Brown was already beginning to hear from fans and critics telling him about technical errors and plot flaws, he didn't see a need to do more accurate research, even as he began to write "fact-based" novels.

"Real" Novels

In *Deception Point* Brown put an author's note that proclaimed the Delta Force, National Reconnaissance Office and Space Frontier Foundation all exist and "all technologies described in this novel exist." In a foreshadowing of the debates over his future books, the truth is that his depictions of certain technological elements in *Deception Point* were riddled with errors, despite the opening statement.

Not only were Brown's two Langdon novels based on history and conspiracy legends, but they each had a page in the front pronouncing as "FACT" certain parts having to do with art, architecture, the Illuminati, the Priory of Sion, and so on.

Moreover, in those final days when Brown still

found it necessary to sit for interviews to promote *The Da Vinci Code*, he continued to insist that the book was based on fact. He once famously said that if he were to rewrite *The Da Vinci Code* as non-fiction, he wouldn't change a thing. On other occasions, he implied that all of *The Da Vinci Code*'s content about Jesus, Mary Magdalene, the Holy Grail, and so on, was factual, because the only relevant story that he could not pin down was that Jesus did not die on the cross, but took a potion to endure the pain and was revived three days later. Since he could not confirm this story—told in books like *The Passover Plot* and alluded to in *Holy Blood, Holy Grail*, he did not use it. He made this point in several interviews and talks, as if to emphasize that everything else he had been able to document was factual. Since he was now also toying with some fundamental tenets of Christianity, it caused an uproar.

Why did Dan Brown bring on himself the burden of having to defend his assertions as true? It is actually part of a recognizable tradition almost as old as literature. But in recent times, there has been a propensity for certain bestselling novelists to support their ideas with facts.

During the heyday of the Hellenistic era when the Library of Alexandria served as the center of a great literary community spanning numerous cultures, there was a legendary debate between two camps. The older tradition held that a writer should employ poetry and prose to convey factual knowledge to the next generation. Thus, the writer of an epic tale of adventure would stop to catalog the flowers along the way, or explain how to harvest grapes. The newer writers felt that it was okay for literature merely to entertain, in the moment, and you could skip the task of educating the readers. You could just drink the wine, stupid.

Although thoroughly American, a classic adhering to the older tradition was *Moby Dick* by Herman Melville. Imitating ancient Greek writers, Melville gave the reader a complete indoctrination into the whaling trade, detailing everything that goes into hunting, killing and processing whales. *Moby Dick* tends to drive modern students to tears as they plow through hundreds of boring pages, trying to get to the action scene where Ahab, the Pequod and the white whale finally duke it out.

In 1922, T. S. Eliot published *The Waste Land*, a poem that students find inscrutable, but critics and scholars love. Like a Dan Brown novel, it contained a large collection of one-line references from a vast number of historic periods, countries, religions, cultures and languages. There are snatches of German, Italian and Hindi, as well as allusions to Greek and Indian myths, all mixed up together. Unique among great poems, it was published with numerous footnotes. It is fair to say that appreciating the poem fully requires the help of the footnotes. Eliot (though really just intending to enhance the experience of the poem) had set a standard for a kind of "fact-based poetry" that others would find impossible to imitate.

But in Brown's era, some of the biggies are Tom Clancy and Michael Crichton. Clancy came out with a series of non-fiction books in the 1980s giving insider-styled details of tanks, planes and submarines, so that the readership can assume he knows a lot about

IN SEARCH OF DAN BROWN

the war toys in, say, *The Hunt for Red October*. Clancy even became a public figure in the Reagan years commenting on defense policy and military preparedness as a result of his acclaim as a detail-oriented Cold War novelist.

Michael Crichton on several occasions went so far as to cite detailed technical references in his novels, explaining aspects of biotechnology and cloning in *Jurassic Park* and nanotechnology in *Prey*. Crichton was among the early pioneers in the use of non-fiction bibliographies in the back of his books. As early as *Rising Sun*, he included a long bibliography of scholarly and public policy books having to do with the Japanese economy and Japanese investment in the United States—the issues that formed the backdrop and context for his otherwise pedestrian action-adventure novel. When Dan Brown sought to bolster the perception of a factual basis for *The Da Vinci Code*, he put a bibliography on his website. Brown did this in 2003 and in an interview made it clear that he considered it innovative, even though Michael Crichton's bibliographies were more than a decade earlier.

Dan Brown went to Paris to be able to write about the city with some authority, but in *The Da Vinci Code* he failed to depict simple elements like routes to the Louvre and the American Embassy correctly. He got the direction of one-way streets wrong, timetables and train stations were in error, Château Villette's location was misplaced. The Louvre's now famous bathroom, where Robert and Sophie spend so many pages of *The Da Vinci Code*, has no window and only liquid soap. The tracking dot, so key to *The Da Vinci*

Code's plot, could not have been embedded in a non-existent bar of soap, nor could it have been hurled out the non-existent window. *Angels & Demons* is littered with similar errors about Rome. In fact, it seems as though the in-depth, meticulous research, claimed by Brown and praised so highly by some of the initial rave reviewers of his books, is rather deeply flawed.

Both *Angels & Demons* and *The Da Vinci Code* are dedicated to Blythe, whom Brown has given a great deal of credit, stressing her invaluable help as a coresearcher. By implication, Blythe may be the one who came up with certain references, especially in the areas of her interest: Art, architecture, and perhaps the occult. In one published account, the suggestion has been made that it was possibly Blythe Brown who first became interested in Rosslyn Chapel and then brought her novelist husband, Dan, back there the following year to see what she had seen. In various promotional materials or press accounts, you will sometimes see Blythe referred to as an "art historian," although in more recent references, Dan Brown tends to call her simply an "art history buff."

Brown's plot flaws, technical howlers, and generalized fast-and-loose approach to calling anything that comes out of research—even from dubious sources—a "fact," raises a series of interesting questions. Obviously, no novelist writing fiction has any obligation to be factual. This includes novelists who have the temerity to publish an opening note suggesting everything in their book is based on fact. Indeed, even those who proclaim in television interviews and with straight faces that they wouldn't have changed a thing if they had written non-fiction, are fully protected under the fundamental right of a fiction writer to make stuff up.

But why all this pretense of fact and research without the more common authorial notes—for example: Fact, fiction, and speculation have been uniquely combined in the imagination of the novelist? What about the disclaimer, "Any resemblance to real people, places, and historical incidents is purely coincidental"?

Did he not know, when he was writing *Angels & Demons* and *The Da Vinci Code* what kind of a fishbowl he would later be in, and therefore thought there would be no problem mixing established fact with speculation and imagination?

Is it just a marketing ploy to create more interest and credibility for the books? Is it a deliberately Machiavellian manipulation that plays on reader gullibility about conspiracy theory and how far powerful people in our society would go to cover up important secrets?

Did he ever believe that the story told in *Holy Blood, Holy Grail* and other occult and New Age tales about the Priory of Sion, its history of Grand Masters, and the secret about the royal bloodline of Jesus and Mary they kept was based on anything more than myth, legend, archetype—and the hoax of Pierre Plantard?

Of course it isn't the technical details that have been the biggest source of questions about how Dan Brown sees the bright line between fact and fiction. The overwhelming majority of his critics are people of religious faith and belief who have attacked his version of religious history and theology. For many of us, however, there is no obvious winner in the question of who is more factual in their rendering of the life of Jesus—those who believe that the Bible is entirely factual, or Dan Brown who says he believes his rendering is entirely factual.

Dan Brown has big and important things to say. He urges us to consider very interesting and important speculations about religious history and what might have really happened millennia ago—between Jesus and Mary, among the Gnostics, among the alchemists, or with the Knights Templar. He introduces extremely significant philosophical debates about the source material for Christian belief and whether modern followers of Jesus know or understand that their Bible was edited by Roman emperors, most of whom were probably more interested in developing a state religion than what Jesus may actually have said. He urges us to understand the signs and symbols, the artworks and classic texts that have come down to us from the ancients. He comes at us over and over again with provocative thoughts about the sacred feminine, gods and goddesses, the place of sexuality in the human experience, the origins of spiritual thinking and the arguments between science and religion.

In his handful of public appearances he gives a powerful, if now standardized stump speech, on how he sees fusing the common interests of religion and science and the need to oppose religious extremism and the anti-scientific bent our culture is taking. He is about to raise the same kind of provocative questions he did about early Christianity in *The Da Vinci Code* as he takes us into a new world of early American history with his next book. And as he moves on from Jesus to George Washington, he will undoubtedly have many new thought provocations for us.

The reality is that Dan Brown, whether he was ever a full-time faculty member of Exeter or not; whether history judges him as a great novelist or a "pop schlockmeister" or something in between, is an important teacher to millions of readers, posing critical questions of our time and encouraging people to go questing for their own answers.

Now that he has had such success, now that no one can question his influence as a cultural force in our society, will he be able to come down off his clever marketing and positioning of his past novels, and acknowledge that he is serving up his own home-cooked stew of fact and fiction? A dead giveaway will be what, if anything, he puts on the "FACT" page of the as yet unpublished sequel to *The Da Vinci Code*, *The Solomon Key*. He could just skip that page, or, better yet, point out he has created his own version of history—interesting, speculative, plausible, but not necessarily FACT.

Publishing-company accountants are now processing royalty checks. Not only *The Da Vinci Code*, but all Brown's prior novels have been republished and have ended up on bestseller lists in the United States and all over the world. Brown's agent recently up-negotiated the contract for his next books. Soon, *The Da Vinci Code* movie will be generating a torrent of cash flow, complete with licensed videogames and other products, not to mention all the other books being turned into movies over the next few years. Even *187 Men to Avoid* trades at a huge premium on eBay. Dan Brown's ship currently has waves of money pouring in over the gunwales. He can afford any car, house, or vacation he likes. There is no research trip he can't afford, nor any "research vacation" he could take that would have any appreciable effect as a tax write-off.

Nonetheless, he has chosen to remain in the Exeter vicinity and cling to a relatively simple, quiet life. He maintains a writing loft in Exeter. He makes the claim that he hasn't had a good start to a writing day unless he has arisen by 4 a.m. He stays fit with sports, such as tennis, and he takes frequent breaks from his desk, sometimes to hang upside down in "gravity boots" to get the stimulation of blood flowing to the brain.

The Browns have purchased two properties not far from Exeter. I have visited the addresses, and it appears to me that they are living in one home, a comfortable-looking house of quiet grandeur, while they are razing the house on their other parcel to make way for something nice—and secluded in the trees. What I find very obvious, in the context of the town that they chose, is that they avoided any temptation to snap up an ostentatious, highly visible address, even though there are prime candidates available.

Dan and Blythe—and even Dan's parents—took some time off in summer 2005 to be movie-groupies and watch Tom Hanks and Ron Howard on location as they hammered out *The Da Vinci Code* movie. In obvious response to rumors that some of the most provoking references to Opus Dei and religious matters have been sanitized in order to keep potential Catholic audiences on board, Brown told his dinner audience the movie will reflect the book. "It will be as though you have seen the book itself," Brown promised.

In honor of his father, Dan recently joined with siblings Valerie and Greg to endow a $2.2 million fund at Exeter, earmarked for computers and other high-tech equipment for students. In announcing the gift, Dan Brown said:

> My dad's contribution to education through teaching and textbooks is a powerful legacy. My sister, brother and I want to honor our father's contribution to the Academy, and his lasting impact on the thousands of students whom he taught.

Brown has also "given back" in the form of time that he spends at the Academy, meeting with current students as well as prospective students and their parents. He occasionally turns up unannounced at Town of Exeter benefit events as well.

Dan Brown is fond of mentioning how his love of codes began when his own father and mother used to hide the holiday presents and then give coded clues to the kids. In *The Da Vinci Code*, this is exactly what Sophie Neveu does as a child, decoding messages from her grandfather.

A recent local story in the Exeter papers tells how Dan is living the simple life and maintaining his relationship in the Big Brother program. For more than three years, while his fame went through the roof and his free time dwindled, Dan Brown has made a point of fulfilling his pledge to be a Big Brother. He has been taking a 12-year-old local boy, "Colby," to the Exeter Academy library, to baseball and football games, "boogie-boarding" at the beach, and even to a paintball session. Brown uses his language fluency to help tutor Colby in Spanish.

And he passes a torch:

"Dan even sends Colby coded messages in the mail. His mother, Cheryl, even wondered jokingly if they were supposed to go to the library to figure them out," said the *Portsmouth Herald*.

INDEX